# Terror in the Countryside

This series of publications on Africa, Latin America, Southeast Asia, and Global Studies is designed to present significant research, translation, and opinion to area specialists and to a wide community of persons interested in world affairs. The editor seeks manuscripts of quality on any subject and can generally make a decision regarding publication within three months of receipt of the original work. Production methods generally permit a work to appear within one year of acceptance. The editor works closely with authors to produce a high quality book. The series appears in a paperback format and is distributed worldwide. For more information, contact the executive editor at Ohio University Press, Scott Quadrangle, University Terrace, Athens, Ohio 45701.

Executive editor: Gillian Berchowitz
AREA CONSULTANTS
Africa: Diane Ciekawy
Latin America: Thomas Walker
Southeast Asia: William H. Frederick

The Ohio University Research in International Studies series is published for the Center for International Studies by the Ohio University Press. The views expressed in individual volumes are those of the authors and should not be considered to represent the policies or beliefs of the Center for International Studies, the Ohio University Press, or Ohio University.

# Terror in the Countryside

*Campesino Responses to Political Violence in
Guatemala, 1954–1985*

Rachel A. May

Ohio University Center for International Studies
*Research in International Studies*
*Latin America Series No. 35*
*Athens*

10 09 08 07 06 05 04 03 02 01   5 4 3 2 1

The books in the Ohio University Research in International Studies Series
are printed on acid-free paper ⊗ ™


*Library of Congress Cataloging-in-Publication Data*

May, Rachel A.
Terror in the countryside : campesino responses to political violence in
Guatemala, 1954–1985 / Rachel A. May.
        p. cm. — (Research in international studies. Latin America series ; no. 35)
Includes bibliographical references and index.
ISBN 0-89680-217-5 (pbk. : alk. paper)
        1. Political violence—Guatemala. 2. Peasantry—Guatemala—Societies, etc.  I.
Title. II. Series.

HN150.Z9 V543 2001
303.6'097281—dc21
                                                                2001016307

For Nicolás

# Contents

# Tables

ix

# Acknowledgments

I have an enormous debt of gratitude to countless people, both in Guatemala and the United States. Returning to Guatemala in 1999 for the first time in several years, I was struck once again by the generosity of Guatemalans. Guatemala must be the most wonderful place in the world for scholars. And it is a complicated, compelling, and magical place to love—"the beauty that hurts," as George Lovell writes. María Antonieta Barrios de Mencos ("Doña Toni") and her children have been unbelievably wonderful. I am humbled by their kindness and generosity always, and grateful for that fateful day when I walked into Doña Toni's archive at ASIES. Oscar Pelaez has likewise been a great friend and help to me. My understanding of this subject was shaped by our many conversations outside the library and in Pocket Park at Tulane. I am also very thankful for his logistical help and the assistance of CEUR during my 1999 trip to Guatemala. Miguel Angel Albizures struck me as one of the most generous men I have ever met. I wish there were something I could do to repay him. He represents everything that is courageous and creative and hopeful about the popular struggle in Guatemala. Otto Rivera, Raul Molina, Arnoldo Noriega, and countless others were remarkably generous with their valuable time and resources. I am truly indebted to so many Guatemalans who helped me in big and small ways. I can never hope to do justice to their stories.

Roland Ebel first piqued my interest in Guatemala. He is a gifted teacher, and a warm and open-minded intellect. Andy Morrison, my friend and mentor, has always been supportive and helpful. Rod Camp generously helped me out despite his own unbelievably busy life. My friends, especially Darien Davis, Ken Johnson, Karen Racine, and Alvis Dunn made all the difference in the world.

I am most grateful to my friends and colleagues at the University of Washington, Tacoma, especially Beth Kalikoff, Michael Forman, and Kathie Friedman. Many people have read and commented on this manuscript in whole or in part over the last few years. Bruce Kochis thoughtfully and carefully read the entire manuscript in the spring of 1998. I would never have been able to find the resources to see it through without his help at that crucial juncture. Michael Forman generously read a big section of the manuscript quickly and made very constructive suggestions during the fall of 1999. His help was and always is invaluable. Hank Frundt, who started out as my anonymous reviewer, invested an enormous amount of time and energy in this manuscript. He went above and beyond in every way. I am deeply indebted to him.

I am very grateful to Tom Walker, Gillian Berchowitz, and Nancy Basmajian of Ohio University Press for their patience and understanding.

I would like to thank my family, especially my father, Ron May. And, of course, I am most grateful to Marco, Nicolás, and Gwendolyn Lizarazo for reasons I could never adequately express.

# Acronyms

| | |
|---|---|
| AC | Asociación Civil (Mexico) |
| ASC | Asamblea de la Sociedad Civil |
| AEU | Asociación Estudiantil Universitaria (San Carlos) |
| AFL | American Federation of Labor (U.S.) |
| AGA | Asociación General de Agricultores |
| AIFLD | American Institute for Free Labor Development (U.S.) |
| BANDESA | Banco Nacional de Desarollo Agrícola |
| CCDA | Comité Campesino del Altiplano |
| CEB | Comunidad Eclesiastica de Base |
| CEH | Comisión para Esclarecimiento Histórico |
| CELAM | Conferencia Episcopal Latinoamericana |
| CERJ | Consejo de Comunidades Etnicas "Runujel Junam" |
| CEUR | Centro de Estudios Urbanos y Regionales |
| CGTG | Confederación General de Trabajadores de Guatemala |
| CIDASA | Compañía Industrial del Atlántico, Sociedad Anónima |
| CIO | Congress of Industrial Organizations (U.S.) |
| CLAT | Confederación Latinoamericano de Trabajadores |
| CNC | Confederación Nacional Campesina |
| CNCG | Confederación Nacional Campesina de Guatemala |
| CNCS | Consejo Nacional de Consultación Sindical |
| CNR | Comité Nacional para la Reconstrucción |
| CNRS | Comité Nacional de Reorganización Sindical |
| CNT | Confederación Nacional de Trabajadores |
| CNUS | Comité Nacional de Unidad Sindical |

| | |
|---|---|
| **COMG** | Consejo de Organizaciones Mayas de Guatemala |
| **CONAVIGUA** | Comité Nacional de Viudas de Guatemala |
| **CONDEG** | Comité Nacional de los Desplazados de Guatemala |
| **CONIC** | Coordinadora Nacional Indígena y Campesina |
| **CONSIGUA** | Confederación Sindical de Guatemala |
| **CONTRAGUA** | Confederación de Trabajadores de Guatemala |
| **CONUS** | Coordinadora Nacional de Unidad Sindical |
| **COPMAGUA** | Coordinación de Organizaciones del Pueblo Maya de Guatemala |
| **CSG** | Consejo Sindical de Guatemala |
| **CTC** | Confederación de Trabajadores Cubanos |
| **CTF** | Central de Trabajadores Federados |
| **CUCO** | Comité de Unidad Campesina y Obrero |
| **CUSG** | Confederación de Unidad Sindical de Guatemala |
| **DAT** | Departamento Administrativo de Trabajo |
| **DC** | Democracia Cristiana |
| **DGAA** | Departamento General de Asuntos Agrarios |
| **EGP** | Ejercito Guerrillero de los Pobres |
| **EPL** | Ejercito Popular de Liberación (Colombia) |
| **EXMIBAL** | Exploraciones y Explotaciones Mineras de Izábal |
| **EZLN** | Ejercito Zapatista de Liberación Nacional (Mexico) |
| **FAMDEGUA** | Familiares de Detenidos-Desaparecidos de Guatemala |
| **FAR** | Fuerzas Armadas Rebeldes |
| **FARC** | Fuerzas Armadas Revolucionarias de Colombia (Colombia) |
| **FAS** | Federación Autónoma Sindical |
| **FASGUA** | Federación Autónoma Sindical de Guatemala (formerly FAS) |
| **FCG** | Federación Campesina de Guatemala |
| **FCL** | Federación Campesina Latinoamericana |
| **FECETRAG** | Federación Central de Trabajadores de Guatemala |
| **FECOAR** | Federación de Cooperativas Agrícolas Regionales |

*Acronyms*

| | |
|---|---|
| FEGUA | Ferrocarriles de Guatemala |
| FENACOAC | Federación Nacional de Cooperativas de Ahorro y Credito de Guatemala |
| FENCAIG | Federación Nacional de Comunidades Agricolas e Indígenas |
| FENOCAM | Federación Nacional de Organizaciones Campesinas |
| FENOT | Federación Nacional de Obreros de Transporte |
| FESC | Frente Estudiantil Social Cristiana |
| FESEB | Federación Sindical de Empleados de Bancos |
| FGEI | Frente Guerrillero Edgar Ibarra |
| FNO | Frente Nacional de Oposición |
| FP-31 | Frente Popular, 31 de Enero |
| FSG | Federación Sindical de Guatemala |
| FSM | Federación Sindical Mundial |
| FTG | Federación de Trabajadores de Guatemala |
| FUR | Frente Unida de la Resistencia |
| GAM | Grupo de Apoyo Mutuo |
| IDESAC | Instituto para el Desarollo Economico y Social de America Central |
| IGEFOS | Instituto Guatemalteco de Educación y Formación Social |
| IGSS | Instituto Guatemalteco de Seguridad Social |
| INACOP | Instituto Nacional para Cooperativas |
| INTA | Instituto Nacional de Transformación Agraria |
| JOC | Juventud Obrera Cristiana |
| MCI | Movimiento de Campesinos Independientes |
| MDN | Movimiento de Democracia Nacional |
| MINUGUA | Misión de Verificación de las Naciones Unidas en Guatemala |
| MLN | Movimiento de Liberación Nacional |
| M-19 | Movimiento 19 de Abril (Colombia) |
| MONAP | Movimiento Nacional de Pobladores |
| MR-13 | Movimiento Revolucionario, "13 de Noviembre" |

| | |
|---|---|
| ONG | Organización No Gubernamental |
| ORIT | Organización Regional Inter-Americana de Trabajadores |
| ORPA | Organización Revolucionaria del Pueblo en Armas |
| PAR | Partido Acción Revolucionario |
| PCG | Partido Comunista de Guatemala |
| PDC | Partido de la Democracia Cristiana |
| PGT | Partido Guatemalteco del Trabajo (formerly PCG) |
| PID | Partido Institucional Democrático |
| PIN | Partido de Integridad Nacional |
| PMA | Policía Militar Ambulante |
| PR | Partido Revolucionario |
| PRG | Partido de la Revolución Guatemalteca |
| PRN | Partido de Renovación Nacional |
| RDN | Reconciliación Democrática Nacional—Redención |
| REMHI | Proyecto Interdiocesano de Recuperación de la Memoria Histórica |
| SAMF | Sindicato de Acción y Mejoramiento de los Ferrocarriles |
| SETUFCO | Sindicato de Empresa de Trabajadores de la United Fruit Company |
| STEG | Sindicato de Trabajadores de Educación de Guatemala |
| STET | Sindicato de Trabajadores de Empresa de Tiquisate |
| STIGSS | Sindicato de Trabajadores del Instituto Guatemalteco de Seguridad Social |
| UASP | Unión de Acción Sindical y Popular |
| UFCO | United Fruit Company |
| UNAGRO | Unión Nacional de Agricultores |
| UNSITRAGUA | Unión de Sindicatos de Trabajadores de Guatemala |
| URNG | Unidad Revolucionaria Nacional de Guatemala |
| USAID | United States Agency for International Development |

# Chronology

1954  Carlos Castillo Armas comes to power

Decree 48 outlaws all preexisting labor and popular organizations

Decree 59 (preventive penal law against communism) provides legal justification for roundups, detentions, and murder of suspected "communists"

Decree 900 (agrarian reform law) repealed

CNRS (labor reorganization committee) created

FAS (national labor federation) created

1956  New Constitution

1957  Castillo Armas assassinated

Miguel Ortiz Passerelli elected fraudulently

Followers of Miguel Ydígoras Fuentes stage protest demonstrations demanding a new election

FAS changes name to FASGUA

1958  Miguel Ydígoras Fuentes elected

1960  Marco Antonio Yon Sosa and Luís Turcios Lima stage failed military coup, then escape to Izábal and form MR-13

PGT Congress resolves to use "all means of struggle"

1961  Central Committee of PGT decides to initiate armed struggle

1962  Student-led protest demonstrations (against Ydígoras administration) and violent street confrontations between police and students

INTA (agrarian "transformation" institute) created

First campesino "leagues" established

FCG (campesino federation) created

PGT organizes October 20th Front

MR-13 launches first attack

1962–65   Vatican II

1963   Some public violence surrounding scheduled elections

Col. Enríque Peralta Azurdia takes power through military coup

MR-13 initiates operations

MR-13 and PGT combine to form FAR

FAR initiates operations

FENACOAC (savings and credit cooperative federation) established

IDESAC (rural development organization) established

1963–66   Military greatly increases spending, political dominance, and control over countryside

1964–69   145 rural cooperatives established

1965   FAR separates from MR-13

New constitution

1966   Julio César Méndez Montenegro elected

At least twenty-eight prominent intellectuals and union leaders assassinated

Mano Blanco begins terrorist operations

MONAP (squatters' movement) established

1966–68   Nineteen right-wing "death squads" formed and begin terrorist operations

1966–69   174 campesino labor organizations established

1966–70   At least 8,000 civilians murdered by armed forces in the name of counterinsurgency

1968   MCI (campesino labor movement) established

PGT separates from FAR

1970   Col. Carlos Arana Osorio elected

FENOCAM (campesino federation) established

1972   EGP carries out first public acts

FAR/Western Regional reinitiates clandestine organizing in Western highlands, and changes name to ORPA

FECOAR (agricultural cooperative federation) established

1972–73   Several labor and land disputes

1973   CNC (campesino confederation) established

CNCS (labor unity advisory board) attempted

1974   Gen. Kjell Laugerud García elected

1975   Coca Cola workers' union conflict

1975–77   Marked increase in industrial labor disputes

1976   Major earthquake devastates much of Guatemala

CNUS (national labor unity committee) established

1977   Ixtahuacán miners' strike

Mario López Larrave assassinated

1978   Gen. Roméo Lucas García elected

Panzós massacre

CUC (campesino unity committee) established

1979   ORPA carries out first public act

1980   Spanish embassy massacre

CUC sugar strike

1982   Finca San Francisco massacre

Military coup brings Gen. Efraín Ríos Montt to power

FAR, EGP, ORPA, and PGT unite to form URNG

1984   Military coup brings Gen. Oscar Mejía Victores to power

1985   Christian Democrat Vinicio Cerezo elected

UNSITRAGUA established

Terror in the Countryside

# Chapter One

## *The Effects of Violence on Popular Movements*

THE TWENTIETH-CENTURY civil conflict in Guatemala was one of the most notable in Latin America. As is typically the case in less developed countries, the rise of civil conflict in the 1950s and 1960s coincides with the emergence of popular organizations in Guatemala. The two phenomena were not unrelated. Typically the relationship between these phenomena has been explained in causal terms (i.e., violence has been a conservative reaction to the political demands of the popular sectors), or in more dialectical terms (i.e., popular movements are one aspect of an economic and political disequilibrium that typically erupts in violence). There is explanatory merit in both of these analyses, but there is also a great deal of complexity to the relationship between violence and popular movements. In fact, the two phenomena represent an evolving dynamic that is crucial to an understanding of Guatemalan politics.

A reconsideration of political violence and the relationship between violence and popular movements during the worst period of civil conflict can facilitate a better understanding of Guatemala's most consequential political and social issues. These include the spiraling crime rate, the relationship between political violence and so-called delinquent violence, the appropriate role of the army and the police, the reconstruction of Guatemala's justice system, and even the nature of democracy itself. This analysis addresses only one aspect of this complex matrix, namely the effects of political violence on popular organizations—primarily rural, campesino-based groups— in Guatemala during the period of military rule, 1954–85.

This book argues that political violence has affected the development of at least three particular aspects of popular organizations in Guatemala: their ideologies, their internal political structures, and their mobilization strategies. These developments speak to the nature of civil society in Guatemala.

## *Defining the Variables*

Ideology is broadly defined as a group's worldview. Ideology is further defined by Juan Luís Segundo as the system of prioritized goals an organization wishes to achieve, and the tactics employed in order to reach those goals.[1] Some ideologies come with ready-made names, such as Marxism, Liberalism, Maoism, or Christian Democracy. Other ideologies do not have preexisting names, but we might describe them in terms of worldview, objectives, and tactics. For example, a group that views the state as necessarily corrupt might have as its goal the desire to make all income taxes illegal and as its tactical commitment the infiltration of the representative bodies of the country through the electoral process in order to achieve this. Some might argue that tactics comprise a separate variable, but it is my contention that tactics are intrinsic to ideology. A commitment to electoral procedure or even to organized terrorism, for example, emanates from ideology and is most easily discussed in terms of its linkage to ideology.

Internal political structure is defined here, using Henry Landsberger's terminology, as the "vertical and horizontal subsystems" of the administrative system that allow a movement to function as an organization. In other words, the internal political structure consists of the vertical chain of command combined with the horizontal division of labor (the bureaucracy that carries out the day-to-day functions of the organization). These structures overlap at times, but the complexity of the vertical subsystem (the power structure or chain of command) is a revealing measure of an organization's political culture. Highly stratified vertical organizations (military organizations, for example) are less conducive to democratic "values" and often preclude participation or inclusion in decision making by the rank and file. Generally speaking, organizations that emphasize a large horizontal substructure (more bureaucracy) are more inclusive and democratic. More people have the power to influence the organization and to participate in decision making, even if there is a vertical structure that segments the participation.[2]

Mobilization strategy is the way in which an organization attracts its members and involves them in united actions. It includes decisions about where the potential membership lies, and the methods used to encourage potential members to participate. In other words it is composed of whom they target, and incentives. Mobilization strategy is often an outcome of ideology, as ideology defines a group's understanding of the organization, and is influenced by the constituency of the organization. Ideology also includes some decisions about target groups and the methods used to mobilize people.[3]

In postrevolutionary Guatemala, popular organizations evolved in their ideologies, internal structures, and mobilization strategies. I hypothesize that the changes exhibited in the organizations can be explained with reference to how violence affected these particular variables.

## The Context of the Conflict

Before we begin our consideration of the impact of violence in Guatemala, we must consider the historical context in which it arose. Between 1944 and 1954 Guatemala enjoyed a period of "revolutionary" reform, widely supported by many social sectors. Popular organizations (including labor unions and campesino organizations) thrived after suffering considerable repression during the Ubíco dictatorship of 1931–44.[4] Soon after the 1944 coup, the country elected Juan José Arévalo, who created a political structure that has been likened to the New Deal programs of Franklin Delano Roosevelt in the United States. The governments of Arévalo and his successor, Jacobo Arbenz, sought a more egalitarian participatory society via an expansive policy of organizational inclusion. Rural unions and cooperatives, for example, claimed more than 300,000 members (half the workforce).

The overthrow of Jacobo Arbenz in 1954 and the dismantling of the political institutions of the Revolution (political parties, labor unions, agrarian committees, and other popular organizations) was a process fraught with violence. Because the organized urban and rural working classes were a key support of the Revolution, Carlos Castillo Armas dismantled the labor organizations almost immediately upon his arrival into Guatemala City. Despite Castillo Armas's pledge in his Plan of Tegucigalpa to respect the workers' right to unionize,[5] the colonel decided that he could not realistically maintain power and allow the unions the same legal status they had enjoyed during the Revolution.

Within a week of the fall of the Revolution, Castillo Armas replaced the head of the Department of Labor (DAT). As his first major act, the new head canceled the registrations of all national labor organizations and local unions that were legally recognized (had juridical personality) at the time.[6] While this did not outlaw the actual organizations, it did invalidate their leadership and the orga-

4

nizational structure (i.e., their constitutions, autonomous internal procedures, and leadership). The law stated that the affected labor organizations were allowed three months to restructure themselves and to remove communists from their membership. Of the 533 labor organizations that were affected, more than 50 percent were rural unions.[7] One month later, Decree 48 did outlaw (administratively by name) all the principal national labor organizations as well as many other popular and cultural organizations.[8] This prohibited a resurgence of the former unions after the three-month "trial period."

Serafino Romualdi, the American Federation of Labor's (AFL) representative to Latin America, indicated that Decree 48 was a serious blunder which damaged the prestige of the government among noncommunist trade unionists. He and other moderate and conservative individuals involved in the "reorganization" process felt that this action was reactionary and unnecessary.[9]

Rural organizations mounted considerable resistance to the new government in the weeks following the Castillo Armas takeover. On 2 July there were reports of campesino "attacks" in Antigua, Escuintla, San Martin Jilotepéque, and San Juan Sacatepequez. In some of these uprisings, there were as many as 300 campesinos involved. On 10 July campesinos in San Marcos, apparently unaware of the fall of the Arbenz government, "armed and mobilized themselves to protect the government and agrarian reform." On 15 July campesinos in the department of Retalhuleu burned their crops before evacuating the parcels granted to them as part of an agro-experiment sponsored by the revolutionary government. Even as late as 20 August there were still reports from Escuintla of "agrarian campesinos"[10] attacking the "Liberation Army" of Castillo Armas.[11] Campesinos organized in rural unions became prime targets of official repression.

Labor "reorganization" under Castillo Armas not only took the form of legislative and judicial decree; the new government and the landed elites sought to eliminate any threat of resurgence by calculated repression, deportation, and assassination of key labor figures. Government forces murdered seven United Fruit Company labor leaders and hundreds of other leaders, mostly campesinos, within weeks of Arbenz's downfall.[12] Thousands more were held as political prisoners without due process, while countless others were forced into exile. The state encouraged massive firings of both public and private employees. Mario López Larrave claims that every union was "beheaded without exception."[13] On 2 July, *El Imparcial* reported that "*anti-comunistas*" captured and murdered seventeen workers from Tiquisate on the southern coast.[14] An early report in *Foreign Affairs* claimed that the "Liberation Forces" of Castillo Armas murdered many rural, local-level union leaders in the weeks following the overthrow. Nine young men from San Jilotepéque were killed by a firing squad in the "Liberation headquarters" in Chiquimula. After a few weeks of summary executions such as this and other forms of widespread official violence, the majority of those local leaders who were still alive and who had not yet been detained fled their communities.[15] At least 1,600 prisoners filled the two city jails and the police school (which was converted to handle the overflow).[16] Out of a sample of 267 prisoners, 75 percent admitted to membership in unions (*sindicatos*) or in agrarian committees.[17]

Decree 23 institutionalized this repression by creating the Committee for Defense against Communism in late July 1954. The committee was made up of three members, designated by the presidential junta. It obligated civil and military authorities to respond effectively and quickly as it pursued its principal target, organized labor.[18]

The committee's function became the enforcement of the Preventive Penal Law against Communism. This law designated as a crime "communism in all its forms, including activities and protests that [were] contrary to the traditional democratic institutions of Guatemala and its vital demands."[19] The law required the Committee for the Defense against Communism to draw up a "register" of the names of "all of the people who [had] in whatever form, participated in communist activities."[20] Included among those to be put in the register were "all those who contributed or participated as promoters, organizers, or propagandists of the diverse organizations which propagated communism, and those who formed part of the *directive committees* of those organizations [emphasis added]." The definition of a communist was broadly described by a list of communist "crimes," which included the spread of communist literature or leaflets, the use of communist emblems, the initiation of illegal strikes, and "terrorist acts." This was easily interpreted to mean leaders of local campesino unions and members of agrarian committees. The law allowed the government to jail for six months without charge anyone who was named in the register. Terrorism, which was punishable by death in the law, was not defined, leaving room for a very broad interpretation of this capital offense.[21] As a consequence, few workers during the Castillo Armas years were willing to take the risk of being punished under the Preventive Penal Law, and were therefore reluctant to organize or belong to unions.[22]

The overall effect of the coup and the Castillo Armas years was devastating. What had been a vibrant organized rural labor force was cowed into submission and completely disarticulated through blatant repression, violence, and legalistic maneuvering.

The repression of Castillo Armas was only the beginning. It came to a close with the assassination of the Colonel in 1957. In the elections that followed, the National Democratic Movement (MDN)[23] decided to back the interior minister of Castillo Armas's regime, Miguel Ortiz Passarelli, as its presidential candidate. The perennial presidential hopeful, General Miguel Ydígoras Fuentes, returned to Guatemala from his post as ambassador to Colombia to run against the MDN candidate. His newly founded National Democratic Reconciliation Party (RDN), or Redemption (Redención), created an appealing platform that called for national reconciliation and an end to political violence.[24] In this campaign, Ydígoras initiated a pattern of rhetoric that would persist for decades. In the

October 1957 election, the electoral tribunal, controlled by the MDN, claimed victory for Ortiz Passarelli. Ydígoras mobilized his followers to take to the streets, and threatened a coup. After a new election in January 1958,[25] Ydígoras claimed victory. By this point the violence which marked three decades of conflict in Guatemala was well underway.

In those years immediately following the overthrow of Guatemala's revolution came the violent dismantling of the nation's popular and rural organizations, especially labor unions and campesino organizations, which had been important to the revolution's achievements. The objective of this study is to understand how popular organizations responded to the violent climate in which they were forced to operate.

The violence directed at popular organizations during the time of Castillo Armas and Ydígoras Fuentes was only a prelude; nevertheless it did impact organizations dramatically—in addition to decimated membership, it affected the variables under consideration here. The particular evolution of these variables will be significant for the current project of democratization in Guatemala. The experience of popular organizations can lend understanding to the operation of democratic values within Guatemalan civil society. The evolution of these variables demonstrates a trajectory of knowledge and understanding for democratic culture within the Guatemalan popular movement.

## Hypothesis

When confronted with political violence, some segments within popular organizations radicalized their ideologies. They often shifted from pluralist explanations of state behavior to a class-based analysis of the repression. In response to the intransigence and violent behavior of government, elites, or the armed forces, some popular elements contemplated the overthrow of those elite groups, or otherwise tried to force the radical reorganization of the overall power structure. Formerly peaceful organizations were in certain cases provoked to respond violently, or to forge alliances with violent organizations; and organizations which eschewed violence were more likely to resort to more radical peaceful tactics such as hunger strikes or the occupation of buildings. On the other hand, some of the elements of popular organizations were also intimidated into submission, or appalled by the radical ideologies and violent tactics of leftist insurgencies. These advanced more limited demands out of a negative ideological opposition to communism, or in an attempt to appease authorities. In cases where ideologies became polarized, factionalism inevitably followed.

The most obvious effect of violence on internal structure was a movement toward secrecy and clandestine organization, and away from "legally recognized" organization.[26] In a semicorporatist system like Guatemala's, the government would "normally" (in the absence of conflict) serve as the ultimate authority in a vertical chain of command. The state's relationship with labor unions during the Arévalo-Arbenz period accurately reflects this traditional semicorporatist relationship.[27] But, given that the state was hostile to the interests of popular sectors, and political violence defined the state and the popular sectors as "enemies," popular organizations eventually learned to exclude the state from their vertical structures. This is precisely what occurred in Guatemala during the 1970s. The simple act of operating outside the boundaries of the state required clandestinity, but to operate without official recognition was, by virtue of legal convention, synonymous with operating extralegally. This clandestinity had a curious effect on organizational structures, which were traditionally rigid and legally bound. When confronted with violence, the traditionally vertical structures of popular organizations became less rigid, and perhaps more democratic. The climate of secrecy changed the horizontal structures of organizations as well. Where secrecy was maintained, there was a decreased tendency toward centralized direction, and therefore more of a tendency toward loosely organized, more autonomous cells of activity. In the long term this meant that more members were involved in the administrative functions of the system. And finally, an organization with a highly visible and powerful leadership cadre was particularly vulnerable to violence. As a result, the traditional preference for personalistic and powerful leaders diminished over the course of the three subsequent decades (the mid-1950s to the mid-1980s).

Violence also had an impact on mobilization strategy. Initially mobilization strategy capitalized on violence. Political violence served as a rallying point for mobilizing people to oppose state actions; however, after a certain critical level, violence also frightened members and potential members away. At this point popular movements in Guatemala adopted innovative mobilization strategies in order to avoid their complete decimation. These strategies included new approaches to self-education *(concientización)* and fresh forms of public demonstration. Popular organizations continued to employ these strategies into the late 1990s.

The responses and adaptations to ideology, organizational structure, and mobilization strategy of Guatemalan popular organizations contain important clues about the long-term effects of the violent conflict. These same organizations also have much to teach us about how Guatemalan "democracy" might eventually work. It has become increasingly evident that the achievement of peace and civility will require far more than a formalistic agreement. Just as the difficulties and failures of Argentina's, Colombia's, and El Salvador's processes of reconciliation demonstrate a complex and lengthy process, so does the Guatemalan experience show us the difficulties of moving beyond institutionalized terror.[28]

The maturation of popular movements that takes place in response to the climate of political violence is a powerful model for democracy and an enduring reminder of Guatemalans' capacity for civic responsibility. The kind of political participation that was elicited by popular movements during the darkest hours of the conflict required a kind of civic responsibility that was rare in its intensity and significance. These popular movements provide a key to understanding Guatemala's democratic potential.

# Chapter Two

## *Political Violence: What Is It?*

THE INTENSITY AND breadth of political violence in Guatemala is almost unimaginable in its proportions. The recent truth commission reports—both the Report of the UN Commission for Historical Clarification (CEH) and the report of the Guatemalan Archidiocesan Project for the Recuperation of Historical Memory (REMHI)—underscore this fact. Both in terms of numbers (200,000 dead, millions displaced in a country with only 10 million inhabitants), and in terms of the brutal nature of the violence perpetrated by the state (the widespread use of torture, disappearance, massacres that included the murders of infants and children, etc.), Guatemala is one of the world's most tragic cases of civil conflict and state-sponsored terrorism in the late twentieth century.

Other cases of long-term, widespread, and intense political violence (e.g., El Salvador, Colombia, South Africa, Israel, Northern Ireland) seem to indicate that when political conflicts become intensely violent over long periods of time, the violence itself takes on a character of its own. That is, violence cannot simply be negotiated away, and cannot be understood in simplistic or reductionist terms.

While it is true in Guatemala that the state took on the characteristics of a terrorist regime, and that the state is responsible for the
commission of genocide, this characterization of the state as repressive and terrorizing has a limited explanatory value. How is it, and
why is it that genocide occurred in Guatemala? How does violence
perpetuate itself? How does Guatemalan society move beyond such
a violent history? In order to help decipher this complicated tragedy,
I will propose a dialectical model of political violence in Guatemala.
While resisting reductionist characterizations that pit good against
evil, I do not mean to apologize for the Guatemalan state, the military, or the repressive economic elites. Guatemalan history is clear on
this point: the elites of this country have historically oppressed the
campesino majority, and they have violently suppressed any attempts
by the popular sectors to organize or demand conditions that would
allow them to live with the barest essentials necessary to maintain
basic human dignity. This suppression reached unprecedented proportions in the late twentieth century. We know who the victims are,
and we also know who the perpetrators are. We do not need to further address the question, Who started it? Political violence in
Guatemala has a much more complex identity than this question
would allow. It is important to come to terms with this complicated
phenomenon in order to understand how it might be dispelled.

Political violence has most frequently been described by scholars
and political analysts not as a discreet phenomenon, but rather as a
characteristic of some other political process or entity. The most
prodigious body of literature related to political violence is "revolution scholarship," which treats violence as a dependent characteristic of this larger process encompassing both rebellion and radical
political or social transformation.[1] More recent scholarly efforts have
begun to shift the emphasis from revolutionary movements to the
uses and abuses of state terror. But still, violence is usually treated as
a secondary characteristic of authoritarian regimes.[2]

Political theorists and philosophers have explored the relationship between power, violence, and civil society. Violence is more often than not described as an extension of power, and the ability to monopolize violence is usually thought to be an essential characteristic of the modern nation state and the Westphalian system. This is a basic assumption of theorists ranging from Hobbes to Mao. There is also the countervailing view, prominently articulated by Hannah Arendt, that where there is political violence, there is an absence of power. Arendt argues that political power is based on consensus, solidarity, and a functioning democratic citizenry. According to Arendt, violence is only useful when a real political consensus is absent, or the legitimacy of political institutions is in question. In any case, she views violence as essentially a tool, and not as a function of power.

Arendt's understanding of political violence gets directly at the heart of another classic question. What is the relationship between violence and "civil society" or democracy? This is essentially the question under consideration here. Ernest Gellner defines civil society in a way that is almost synonymous with popular movements,[3] and also claims that it is a necessary condition of liberty (democracy). John Keane astutely points out that Gellner and other contemporary theorists who have been looking at the notion of "civil society" (mostly in the wake of the collapse of the Eastern bloc) have ignored the problem of pervasive violence ("uncivility"). Keane cautions that the structure and scale of twentieth-century violence, which coincides with our increasing preoccupation with and belief in "civility," is reason for reflection and "shame." In the case of Guatemala, it is indisputable that "shame" is indeed warranted, but I would like to consider more fully the relationship between civil society (manifest in popular movements) and violence (manifest in the conflict that was formally ended in 1996).

It is precisely the relationship between violence and "civility" that might prove to be both problematic and hopeful for formally negotiated peace. There is a fundamental and undertheorized assumption that by ending violent conflict through civil discourse (generally involving a limited number of political actors), peace, reconciliation, and finally democratization will follow. Despite this assumption, it is evident that prolonged violence has a corrosive effect on civility and democracy. Although peace accords often address the need for democracy, it remains unclear how a negotiated agreement can be transformed into democratic social and political structures. Experiences of the past decade demand consideration of some of the pragmatic aspects of building a democracy from the ruins of a violent civil conflict.

Colombia, for example, was the first nation to attempt a negotiated end to the kind of Cold War/internal conflict that has plagued many developing countries over the past forty years. The first agreement (1984) between the Colombian government and the FARC, M-19, and EPL guerrillas collapsed fairly quickly under the weight of a violent right-wing opposition, escalating drug wars, and the takeover and subsequent storming of the Palace of Justice in 1985. Eventually Colombia signed another agreement with the M-19 in 1990, but the assassinations of leaders within the M-19, and the failure of the settlement to end or even mitigate the civil violence, makes this a case that few would want to emulate.[4]

Argentina made a successful transition from violent military dictatorship to civilian rule, and handled the problem of reconciliation through war trials of military personnel accused of culpability in the Dirty War. One would have imagined that this sort of efficacious and legalistic approach was evidence of Argentina's commitment to civil democracy and a strong political will to construct a meaningful peace. But this is far from the case. Police brutality is once again on the rise; the Mothers of the Disappeared, now elderly, continue to protest every Thursday afternoon, demanding "real justice." The Dirty War has not been successfully relegated to the past.[5]

The continual resurgence of political violence in Israel and Northern Ireland, and the dramatic upsurge in so-called delinquent violence in El Salvador further evidence the enduring quality of violence in those societies. And all the complexity of these examples points to the utility of reexamining the nature and movement of violence. That is, a simplistic understanding of political violence as a mere extension of power does not explain its persistence.

Edelberto Torres-Rivas has explained this need for a comprehensive analysis of political violence in Guatemala. In his work on the current transition to democracy in Guatemala, he carefully considers the nature of violence and the causes of armed insurgency in Guatemala.[6] He explains the historical and structural basis of violence as a function of economic and political injustice and racism. He explains that Guatemalan history has cultivated a hospitable environment for violence by the maintenance of a profoundly unequal and racist social structure. But he also calls on the theoretical literature of revolutionary scholarship to explain how the frustrated process of modernization in Guatemala (rife with political and economic contradictions that are not uncommon in the "underdeveloped" world, but also particular to Guatemala's post-1954 experience) contributed to the dialectic of violence that defines the 1960s, '70s, and '80s.

The coup of 1954 only reinforced the commitment of economic and political elites to maintaining the racist and violent social order that had existed for centuries. The coup, which was first and foremost a response to agrarian reform and mobilization of both indigenous and ladino campesinos, made it clear the landed elites would use their alliance with U.S. corporate interests (United Fruit) and the United States government to preserve the centuries-old system of exploitation and repression. This new alliance and the Cold War context contributed to the professionalization of a rabidly anticommunist military institution, and the consolidation of a new military elite that acted in concert with the interests of traditional landed elites. Eventually the military elites would act to protect their own ideological and economic interests.

Torres-Rivas, however, goes beyond the observation of historically rooted racism and economic exploitation. He describes the process by which violence became endemic within the culture and society. "The guerrilla and the forces of counter-insurgency created and mutually reinforced the idea of the enemy—an object to be hated. To construct 'the other' as an object that can and should be hated dehumanizes society, and it explains in general terms why wars between 'brothers' are the worst kind."[7] Torres-Rivas understands that the kind of violence which characterizes the civil conflict in Guatemala in the late twentieth century was both more brutal and more complicated than the centuries of racist and violent exploitation that preceded it. Counterinsurgent violence in Guatemala after 1960 was a new animal.

> The problem [with the strategy of counterinsurgency] was in its application of hostility to the political and social demands of the popular organizations—organizations which were not always committed to being part of a democratic political opposition. And of course this was even more true of the armed left. The objective then became the annihilation of the enemy, rather than the legitimate opposition to an opponent. In this dynamic there is a corruption of the collective order because armed confrontation (and the ability to avoid it) overshadows all other legitimate political objectives.[8]

It is simply not enough to say that the Guatemalan army was genocidal. By doing so, we oversimplify the solutions to endemic violence in societies that are attempting to make the transition away from authoritarian/terrorist rule. Torres-Rivas explains the nature of violence without absolving the state or the individual actors involved in acts of brutality. It is my intention here to similarly employ a dialectical model of violence that represents interaction between various political actors (a violence that is complex and deeply rooted in social and political structures), and that simultaneously acknowledges the brutality of the Guatemalan military and the individual actors who are guilty.

## The Terminology of Violence

The terms *violence, violent conflict,* and *force* are the most general terms employed here. These terms must be qualified by specific circumstances, actors, intensities, and results. *Political violence* is generally distinguished from the more mundane category of criminal or delinquent violence.[9]

In Guatemala, political violence has been largely committed by the state (represented by the military and the police), but it has also been perpetrated by actors outside of, or excluded from, the political regime. What defines the violence as political is that the perpetrators or the targets represent explicitly political interests.

Revolution theorists, from the early 1960s onward, shaped our contemporary understanding of political violence. These scholars produced a large and significant body of analysis on the nature of violent rebellion. Although this literature is prodigious and influential, its usefulness is limited here because it considers violence (rebellion against the state), as a "one-sided" phenomenon. My own definition of political violence is much broader. In the case of Guatemala, rebellious violence directed *toward* the state can and should be de-emphasized, given the relatively small amount of damage inflicted by "rebels" in that country.

My definition and typology—drawn from experience in Guatemala—is in contrast to the influential scholar of revolution, Ted Gurr. While Gurr defines political violence as nonauthoritative, I have created a double-sided typology of both authoritative (state-sponsored) and nonauthoritative (rebellious) violence.[10] Because both the UN's commission for historical clarification[11] and the Guatemalan Archdioceses' Recuperation of Historical Memory project (REMHI)[12] have documented that the state was the primary perpetrator of violence during the conflict in Guatemala—responsible for the overwhelming majority of civilian deaths—it is tempting to simply flip this classical definition of political violence on its head,

---

and to define political violence (in the Guatemalan case) as violence perpetrated *by* the state. While it is important to always remain cognizant of the disproportionate culpability of the Guatemalan state in perpetuating the conflict there, it is also important to move the analysis beyond arguments about moral equivalence. The dialectical model I propose here is an attempt to view Guatemalan violence in the context of a complex process, and it accurately reflects a violence that deeply permeates Guatemalan society. Again, the fact that violence cannot seem to be abated by the demilitarization of the state, in Guatemala or elsewhere, points to the utility of looking at violence

Table 2.1
## Typology of Rebellion

TURMOIL
Relatively spontaneous, unorganized political action with popular participation, which gets out of hand—including violent strikes, riots, and localized rebellions

COORDINATED ATTACK
Highly organized political violence with limited participation, including political assassinations, small-scale guerrilla wars

INTERNAL WAR
Highly organized violent political struggle with widespread popular participation, and accompanied by extensive violence, including guerrilla wars and civil wars*

*Source: Adapted from Ted Robert Gurr,* Why Men Rebel *(Princeton, N.J.: Princeton University Press, 1970), p. 11.*

*Although most nonauthoritative political violence is targeted at representatives of authority, it is possible for nonauthoritative violence to be directed at other nonauthoritative groups within any of the three categories. Examples of nonauthoritative to nonauthoritative violence are: the murder of popular leaders by Shining Path guerrillas in Peru (coordinated attack), or La Violencia in Colombia—the civil war of the 1950s in which nonauthoritative sectors of the Colombian population killed one another in the name of political ideology (internal war).

more holistically. So the definition here has been broadened to include (and even to emphasize) regime- or state-sponsored (authoritative) violence as well as nonauthoritative violence. I am, therefore, broadening Gurr's typology of nonauthoritative violence for use in this case study.[13]

Nonauthoritative political violence is political violence committed by groups who are outside the state apparatus. Rebellion is a more specific term referring to nonauthoritative violence specifically directed against an incumbent regime, its actors, or policies. Within this category, I have slightly modified Gurr's three-pronged typology (see table 2.1). These types of nonauthoritative violence can also overlap, both chronologically and within the definitions of particular acts of violence. For example, turmoil and coordinated attack often occur at the same time, and one act, such as an attack on a military installation by guerrilla insurgents, can be part of a coordinated attack, and at the same time be clearly within the context of a civil war.

Gurr's typology of nonauthoritative violence leads me to define a typology of authoritative (state-sponsored) political violence (see table 2.2). "Outwardly directed violence" refers to authoritative violence directed at nonauthoritative groups (guerrilla armies, popular sectors, etc.).[14] While authoritative violence generally escalates according to these stages, again there is overlap between the types of violence described. An act of reactionary terror can be part of an overall counterinsurgency strategy. However, unless the target of the violence is an actual combatant, an assassination or an act of generalized terror would not be part of an internal war. On the other hand, internal war is an aspect of counterinsurgency if the guerrilla attacks develop into coordinated action.

And again, it is important to remain cognizant of the fact that a grossly disproportionate share of the deaths that occurred during the conflict were the result of the last category, reactionary terror. This is the genocide that was described by the UN's Historical Clarification Commission.

Table 2.2

## Typology of Outwardly Authoritative Violence

COUNTER-INSURGENCY
Highly organized military assault on guerrilla insurgencies,
and their direct supporters

INTERNAL WAR
Generalized military response of regime to widespread, highly
organized nonauthoritative violent reactions—that is, state participation in all-out civil war

REACTIONARY TERROR
Terrorist attacks on popular sectors to halt or prevent demands
for reform (e.g., assassinations of popular leaders or violent
union busting); attacks meant to terrorize popular sectors into
socioeconomic submission; destruction directed at popular
sectors in belief that all civilians in a given geographic area, ethnic group, or socioeconomic sector are potential "enemies."
The latter example can also be referred to as politicide or genocide.

*The term terror implies a particularly intense form of violence employed to
instill a sense of fear. Timothy Wickham-Crowley defines terror in the context
of a preexisting violent conflict as "certain acts forbidden by the rules of war.
Among these are (1) beating, killing, bombing, or other assaults on a civilian
population . . . ; (2) beating, torturing, or killing combatants who have indicated a willingness to surrender; and (3) the use of weapons which do not suffi-
ciently discriminate among combatants and others." See Wickham-Crowley,
"Terror and Guerrilla Warfare in Latin America, 1956-1970," *Comparative
Studies of Society and History* 32:2 (April 1990): 202-3.

## Central American Violence and Theories of Revolution

Many scholars and activists have examined Central American violence. Histories and descriptive analyses of the crises in Nicaragua,

El Salvador, and Guatemala are numerous. And again, the prodigious literature on revolution that was produced concurrently with the conflict also provides useful insight into the nature of violence in the region.

The sociological and political theories that address the structural causes of organized rebellion appear to be the most useful in explaining the roots and structure of political violence. Jack Goldstone categorizes these studies as the "second generation" of the literature on revolution.[15] They offer a basic theoretical framework which focuses on the political economy of the region, the economic changes that have taken place in Central America since World War II, and the relationship of those economic changes to nonauthoritative political violence (rebellion). In short they argue that "societal disequilibrium" explains why conflicts have arisen in these small, agriculturally based economies where landholding elites rule in alliance with strong professional militaries. In the following sections, I will examine the phenomenon of societal disequilibrium, and how it provoked conflict in the Central American context during the past three decades. The theory will ultimately be applied to the cycle of violence model, which will be presented at the end of this chapter.

## THEORIES OF INTERNAL WAR IN CENTRAL AMERICA: THE APPLIED THEORY OF SOCIETAL DISEQUILIBRIUM

The political and economic basis of the Central American conflict is assumed in much of the literature. John Booth demonstrates how economic development policies of the 1960s and 1970s created an even more unequal distribution of income and wealth (especially land) in a region which has historically suffered from gross inequalities. This growing gap between the very rich and the very poor coincided with the massive proletarianization of both the urban and rural labor force. This "intensified the grievances" of the lower

socioeconomic sector.[16] Booth then describes how these intensified grievances led popular organizations to protest the policies of
incumbent regimes. These demands for reform were met with violent repression. This reactionary state response "helped forge revolutionary coalitions which fought for control of the state."[17]

Developmentalism or modernization has been at the root of
increasing inequalities and resulting societal disequilibrium since
the Liberal period (late nineteenth and early twentieth centuries) in
most of Latin America, including Guatemala. This development
process has gone through clearly demarcated phases throughout the
last 150 years. Beginning in the late 1950s and early 1960s the process
intensified throughout the underdeveloped world, and it produced a
drastic transformation of traditional economic relations and land
tenure patterns.[18] Robert Williams has provided one of the most dramatic and poignant examples of this transformation in his landmark
study of the Central America agro-export economy. He demonstrates
how the policies of export promotion led to the transfer of small-
holdings used for food production to large holdings used for cattle
and cotton. He argues that this transformation of the agricultural
economy (in the 1960s and '70s) led not only to increased landless-
ness, inequality, and rural poverty, but also to ecological stress.[19]

Subsistence agriculture became economically impossible to maintain due to population pressures and changing land tenure patterns unfavorable to small campesino landholders (*minifundistas*).
Consequently, many campesinos were partially or completely proletarianized.[20] Moreover, while real agricultural wages fell, landholdings became increasingly concentrated. Agrarian conflicts between
peasants and large landholders increased in number and intensity as
campesinos were forced off their lands and were increasingly unable
to maintain their traditional way of life. Both the landholders (backed
by the governments and militaries) and the campesinos became
increasingly prone to violence.

While modernization of agriculture had previously progressed during the revolutionary years, particularly between 1950 and 1954, campesinos felt more protected because of their organizational strength. However, after the 1954 coup similar land consolidation schemes offered no protection to rural smallholders. At the same time elite landholders felt much freer to summon "help" from local military officers. Campesino reactions became increasingly violent, creating what I described above as rebellious turmoil.[21]

This turmoil was channeled into new popular organizations. The growth of modern popular organizations (rural trade unions, co-operatives, Christian base communities, and guerrilla organizations) added a new level of political sophistication to this popular struggle. In a certain sense, then, authoritative violence engendered popular organization.

The relationship between turmoil and authoritative violence is analyzed by Donald Schulz in "Ten Theories in Search of the Central American Reality." In this essay Schulz outlines a dialectic theory of rebellion and counterinsurgency that is one of the more satisfactory descriptions of Central American violence.[22] According to Schulz, "revolution is a process involving an extended sequence of actions and reactions, a 'dialectic' of threat (including non-violent 'threats' to existing power structures and class relations) and retaliation."[23] In Schulz's model, popular sectors (both the middle and lower classes) pressure the regime for political and economic reform. (This can take the form of either nonauthoritative violent turmoil, or nonviolent demands and demonstrations.) This pressure is met with violent resistance by the regime. This intransigence leads to radicalization of the popular sectors, and eventually coordinated counterattacks as some popular groups make the decision to try to take control of the state. The regime reacts with counterinsurgency, which eventually evolves into a civil war. According to Schulz, "the portrait is one of self-intensifying and mutually destructive violence."[24]

Table 2.3

**The Dialectic of Revolution**

STAGE I
Increasing RD* generated by development-induced poverty, rising expectations, population pressures, and economic crises

STAGE II
Socioeconomic and political mobilization and pressure for reform [may be violent or nonviolent]

STAGE III
Conservative obstruction and violent repression

STAGE IV
Escalating RD (political as well as socioeconomic) leading to growing frustration, radicalization, and revolutionary violence

STAGE V
Heightened counterrevolutionary violence

STAGE VI
An ongoing process culminating in the eventual victory of either revolutionary or counterrevolutionary forces, or stalemate [El Salvador]

*Source: Donald E. Schulz, "Ten Theories in Search of Central American Reality," in* Revolution and Counter-revolution in Central America and the Caribbean, *ed. Donald E. Schulz and Douglas H. Graham (Boulder: Westview, 1984), 29. The chart is very slightly modified here.*

*Relative deprivation.

THEORIES OF AUTHORITATIVE VIOLENCE
(REACTIONARY TERROR)

While Schulz's concept of a dialectic captures much of the character of the Central American conflict, violence (particularly in the cases of Guatemala and El Salvador) has the ability to transform itself into something that transcends the revolutionary-counterrevolutionary dialectic. At some point in the cycle counterrevolutionary violence transcends the logic of counterinsurgency and becomes general reactionary terror against the civilian population (see table 2.2). The popular sector, both rural and urban, becomes the enemy, rather than real or imagined insurgents. There are, for example, numerous accounts which describe the brutal nature of the violence to which Central Americans (mostly Guatemalans and Salvadorans) have been subjected.[25] The intensity and scope of this violence defies the logic of the dialectic. Often this violence is aimed at the unarmed civilian population long after the actual threat of "subversion" has been removed. The targets of this reactionary violence were both urban and rural, middle- and lower-class; poor campesinos, however, were the most vulnerable to attack, and they usually suffered higher, yet less publicized, casualties.[26]

Pierre L. van den Berghe, in his anthology *State Violence and Ethnicity*, relates Central American reactionary violence to similar situations elsewhere. Van den Berghe adapts the classical liberal notion that the state exists and is able to assert authority because it monopolizes the power of destruction.[27] In the mid- to late twentieth century, Economically less developed states have turned inward to assert this destructive authority. In Central America this trend was manifested by the coming to power of military regimes. Some Guatemalan analysts saw the need by the military regime to maintain legitimacy as the cause of the prolonged civil conflict and reactionary violence. That is, the real or fabricated enemy provided the justification for the military to retain control or "order."[28] Although political justifications are often given for the massive use of terror against a civilian population, van den Berghe thinks that these political justifications are merely the result of a modern form of "mutated" nationalism. He states quite succinctly that "political murder directed at specific opponents in response to political actions, writings, or alleged intentions is qualitatively different from the massive use of terror against men, women, and children collectively accused of alleged political crimes by sheer membership in a class, occupation, religion, or ethnic or racial group."[29] This latter phenomenon clearly is what is referred to as genocide. Using this definition of genocide, the Guatemalan case clearly falls within this category.

Genocide is often assumed to be outside the logic of counter-insurgency, "irrational," or "crazy." Indeed Guatemalan military high command "explained" the widespread indiscriminate violence that characterized Guatemalan violence, particularly in the early eighties, as being excesses that they were unable to control.[30] Jennifer Schirmer has taken issue with this characterization and has analyzed exactly how the military's "logic" of counterinsurgency evolved over the period in question.

> Without a structural analysis of violence as intrinsic to the logic of counterinsurgency, a regime that violates human rights seems to occur simply because of uncontrollable, blood thirsting commanders or poorly disciplined peasant recruits who need to be given a code of conduct—a view that ironically serves as an essentialist rationale by militaries for why they cannot control their own forces.[31]

Even while acknowledging the conscious intent of the military high command to commit massacres and even genocide, this stage of counterinsurgency is categorically different from the more "tradi-tional" aim of a counterinsurgency strategy (killing guerrilla combat-ants). The "logic" of genocide, according to Schirmer, is more complex and profound than it is at other stages of counterinsurgency.[32]

The United Nations has now joined van den Berghe and the Permanent Peoples' Tribunal[33] in labeling the Guatemalan case "genocidal." The tribunal made the case for genocide already in 1983 when it heard testimony on the violent situation in Guatemala. The tribunal concluded:

> The idea that guilt and crime are transmitted biologically underlies the leveling of entire villages—to the extreme of killing small children too young to reason. It is as if they were part of an infected fabric, a

cancer or some kind of bad weed that must be eradicated. . . . to eliminate an ethnic micro group [an indigenous village] with the intention of totally destroying it, including the very small children, is an action that has not only political motives but also racist motives. It is believed that crime is biologically transmittable. We are talking about genocide in the strictest sense of the word.[34]

In 1999, the United Nations Commission for Historical Clarification in Guatemala, using the international convention on the prevention and punishment of genocide,[35] similarly concluded that the case for Guatemalan genocide was clearly established:

> After studying four selected geographical regions (Maya-Q'anjob'al and Maya-Chuj, in Barillas, Nentón and San Mateo Ixtatán in North Huehuetenango; Maya-Ixil, in Nebaj, Cotzal and Chajul, Quiché; Maya-K'iche' in Joyabaj, Zacualpa and Chiché, Quiché; and Maya-Achi in Rabinal, Baja Verapaz) the CEH [Commission for Historical Clarification] is able to confirm that between 1981 and 1983 the Army identified groups of the Mayan population as the internal enemy, considering them to be an actual or potential support base for the guerrillas, with respect to material sustenance, a source of recruits and a place to hide their members. In this way, the Army, inspired by the National Security Doctrine, defined a concept of internal enemy that went beyond guerrilla sympathizers, combatants or militants to include civilians from specific ethnic groups. Considering the series of criminal acts and human rights violations which occurred in the regions and periods indicated and which were analyzed for the purpose of determining whether they constituted the crime of genocide, the CEH concludes that the reiteration of destructive acts, directed systematically against groups of the Mayan population, within which can be mentioned the elimination of leaders and criminal acts against minors who could not possibly have been military targets, demonstrates that the only common denominator for all the victims was the fact that they belonged to a specific ethnic group and makes it evident that these acts were committed "with intent to destroy, in whole or in part" these groups.[36]

Moreover, in cases where individuals or groups were eliminated because of their socioeconomic classification or their occupation, the assumption of guilt is still a function of membership in a specific reference group (poor people, campesinos, students, etc.) That is, if the idea of genocide is broadened beyond the United Nations' legal definition, one can conclude that victims didn't need to be Mayan to have been the victims of genocide in Guatemala.

Again, genocide, while not "crazy," does not fall within the rationale of the dialectic of war which Schulz described. This kind of generalized reactionary violence which evolves out of the conflict is probably the most influential stimulus of change with regard to popular organizations—as the organizations and their members are often the targets of this violence.

This literature—the theories of revolution and rebellion, the socioeconomic explanations of contemporary Central American conflicts, and the literature on state terror and genocide—provides the analytic framework for a descriptive modeling of political violence in Guatemala.

## *The Cycle of Violence*

Violence in Central America, particularly Guatemala, followed a cyclical pattern during the past four decades. The cycle began with social and class conflict that resulted when agriculture was modernized, landholdings were further concentrated, agricultural workers were forcibly proletarianized, and basic consumption dropped for most people. These economic changes prompted violent conflicts, often played out between campesinos and large landholders. Although this conflict was truly agrarian in nature, urban violence was also common. In Guatemala, these social and economic dislocations were accompanied by an organized guerrilla response. As a consequence of these conflicts and the guerrilla threat, the armed forces initiated their own violent response. This situation evolved into a "dialectic" between popular sectors and counterinsurgency. Eventually state-sponsored violence broke out of the dialectic and became reactionary terror (which included genocide in the Guatemalan case). Over time this reactionary terror lessened in intensity and frequency. The cycle then repeated itself. The stages of violence were not mutually exclusive and there is considerable overlap between them. Nevertheless violence did usually follow this pattern in Guatemala.

This cyclical model does not serve to justify brutality. It is a description of the way political violence has evolved in Guatemala during the decades following the 1954 counterrevolution. It would be impossible to adequately address the phenomenon of violence in Guatemala without acknowledging the complexity of the phenomenon. As Jennifer Schirmer argues, demilitarization is not achieved by sending the army "back to the barracks."[37] Similarly, political violence in Guatemala cannot be eliminated by demilitarization alone.

Guatemalan political violence has evolved in this very particular way during the late twentieth century, and violence has at the same time had a specific effect on rural popular organizations. In the next chapter, we turn our attention to the nature and structure of such organizations in the Guatemalan countryside.

Table 2.4

## The Cycle of Violence

| | PARTICIPANTS | OBJECTS | GEOGRAPHICAL DENSITY | INTENSITY | LEVEL OF ORGANIZATION |
|---|---|---|---|---|---|
| 1. Turmoil | Urban and rural popular class (both lower and middle class) | Symbolic political and economic targets | Initially isolated, but growing | Low | Often disorganized, some grassroots organization |
| 2. Coordinated counter attack | Guerrillas (disaffected military, intellectuals, and remnants of previous cycle) | Elite political and economic figures, and symbolic targets | Isolated | Low to medium | Well organized |
| 3. Internal War | Guerrillas, armed forces | Guerrillas, armed forces | Can be either isolated or widespread | Medium to high | Well organized |
| 4. Reactionary terror ("genocide") | Armed forces and authoritative paramilitary groups | Urban and rural popular class (both lower and middle class) | Widespread | Very high | Well organized, although armed forces often claim there is a lack of organized control |

# Chapter Three

## *Popular Organizations: What Are They?*

THE CYCLES OF violence that erupted in postrevolutionary Guatemala had a dramatic effect on social organization at all levels—personal, familial, communitarian, and societal. The focus here is on rural-based organizations that had some kind of organization on the national level. In order to understand the dialectical interplay between violence and organizational life, I specifically consider organizations that are both national in character and are especially affected by and responsive to violent conditions engendered by the state. Thus, I do not directly address other local and community-based ethnic and religious organizations. Four types of organizations will be considered: campesino organizations, community organizations, guerrilla organizations, and labor organizations (trade unionism).[1] What is under consideration here can be characterized as the popular sector, or by the term *civil society.*

The collapse of Soviet communism has prompted an interesting and cogent political discourse about the nature of civil society. It is a discourse that began as a critique of Marxism, but has become relevant to the discussion of peace and democratization in societies that formerly suffered under the most strident anticommunist regimes (in Latin America) as well.[2] The first wave of theorists who revived this discussion certainly did not anticipate this application of the concept. It is also true that its application to Guatemalan-style regimes does change some of the assumptions of the original argument.[3] Nevertheless, the basic argument of these theorists is that civil society is a more pragmatic and meaningful description of a viable, appropriate, humane, and pluralistic political system than is procedural democracy, and that civil society consists of a set of organizations that provide a democratic space for individuals outside the realm of government. These theorists have argued that civil society consists of a space for citizens to organize themselves outside the overarching influence of the state. For this kind of civil organization to be meaningful, it has to be able to have power or influence within the state, or at least society. This is a clear and probing way of viewing the democratization process in Guatemala, and it gives a unique and important role to what have traditionally been referred to as popular movements there. This notion of civil society brings together this diverse set of organizations and gives them a deserved prominence. It also *does* have a pragmatic appeal—civil society can be more effectively operationalized than can former procedural democracy. That is, the freedom to organize, and the acknowledgment of the legitimacy of popular organizations as vehicles for participation, is politically and socially more significant than is efficient electoral machinery—which is the most typical operationalization of democracy. And clearly, both strategies are compatible and desirable.

The discourse on civil society has been adopted and at times co-opted in recent years by the United Nations, multinational lending agencies, and even multinational corporations. And in some ways it even replaces the discourse on popular or social movements. What had previously been referred to as the popular sector was officially organized and recognized as the Association of Civil Sectors (ASC) in 1993 in order to represent popular interests (which came to include the sometimes oppositional interests of the pan-Maya movement) in the peace dialogue. The period under consideration in this book (1954–85) predates the rise of civil society discourse in Guatemala. The terminology that coincides with the formation and evolution of the organizations under consideration here is found in the literature about popular or social movements (late 1970s to early 1990s). And the precursor to this literature is found in the field of peasant studies. Since I am attempting to demonstrate the relevance of the history of the popular movement between 1954 and 1985, to the current project (late 1990s) of democratization, I use both sets of terminology. That is, I am retroactively applying very contemporary discourse to a historically significant set of circumstances. But it should be noted that the organizations being considered here did not refer to themselves as civil society during the period in question.

Scholars who have studied Latin American popular movements have long understood the democratic resonance of their subject, but it has been difficult to articulate exactly how popular movements that have emerged as a response to repression can survive and contribute to the consolidation of democracies. Yet, civil society is much more than a rival of Marxism and Islam, or an argument for economic liberalism. Popular movements in Latin America, and in Guatemala in particular, demonstrate the rich potential for civil society's role in newly emerging democracies in the Americas, and perhaps elsewhere.

In Guatemala, civil society was incubated within a repressive context. Popular movements and more precisely popular organizations emerged both to express popular interests that were smothered by the political-military power structure, and also to defend the popular sector from the violent and repressive tendencies of the state. Ironically, violence has shaped these movements (civil society). This raises important questions that Guatemalans are attempting to answer. How will popular sectors evolve in a less repressive environment? If these organizations could operate freely, what should they look like?

What role can they play in checking the repressive capacity of the state? How will they influence power and decision making in the future?

In order to examine the interplay between violence and organizational life, this chapter will describe how different popular organizations behave and are organized. This analysis will focus on the following factors: (1) levels of organization, (2) the potential effects of varying state responses to popular mobilization, (3) popular organizations in the Latin American context, and (4) the traditional weaknesses of Latin American popular organizations. This is followed by a description and analysis of the case study being analyzed here—campesino organizations in Guatemala between 1954 and 1985.

## Movements versus Organizations

While it is important to understand popular movements as groups that can incorporate a broad variety of poor people who may utilize a variety of tactics, the commonly used concept of movement must be somewhat narrowed in this analysis so that it does not overlap conceptually with violence. In some of the literature the term *movement* encompasses both the entity (the organization) and the act. Henry Landsberger defines movement as "any collective reaction."[4] For the purposes of this study I will limit the focus of the analysis to include only popular *organizations*—entities with structural characteristics that can both use violence and be influenced by violence as a separate variable. If a rebellious act is committed by a popular organization, then the act of the organization will be viewed separately in this analysis from the organization itself.

Popular organizations are organizations that express the interests of "popular sectors,"[5] which according to Daniel Camacho are "sectors which suffer from domination and exploitation."[6] Thus

36

organizations that articulate and defend the interests of elite sectors would not be popular. It is important to note that organizations need not have a popular leadership to qualify as popular organizations, as long as they articulate and defend the interests of popular sectors. This will be a relevant distinction to make when discussing guerrilla organizations as popular organizations.

## The Role of Campesinos

With the changing position of the campesino (from subsistence agriculturalist to contract or wage laborer), the interpretation of the role of campesinos in politics—particularly revolutionary politics—began to change. Thus, peasant studies as a genre of literature began to challenge the traditional view of the campesino (peasant) as a conservative actor with a high aversion to political risk taking. This development in the literature corresponds to a shift in Latin American agricultural modes of production.[7]

Contemporary theorists have tied the political activization of the peasantry to the process of economic and political modernization. Whether they are considering the revolutionary potential of peasants and their ability to influence the "modernization process," or simply their political "response" to the process through their participation in modern political institutions (labor unions, political parties, etc.), the traditional view of the peasant as a conservative and basically passive figure in the process of political transformation has been modified in the past three decades.

Nevertheless, most theorists minimize the ability of peasants to *initiate* a popular response to economic change. They often assume that peasants are "taken by the hand" and led into the revolutionary arena. With the exception of Eric Wolf,[8] this "urban bias" permeates most analyses of the role of "peasants" in political change. The fact that none of these scholars discusses cases of autonomous peasant organizations may be related to the fact that a broad-based coalition (of both urban and rural, and middle and upper classes as well as lower classes) has generally been the catalyst for change in successful full-fledged social revolutions. This fact has minimized the consideration of peasants as such in scholarly evaluations since most of the literature is specifically concerned with full-fledged revolutions. Even the word *peasant* assumes a group of people with a predetermined conservative posture, and an inability to grasp sophisticated political issues—this word is more often than not an inaccurate description for rural cultivators of the underdeveloped world in the late twentieth century.[9] Although the propensity of peasants to participate in political organizations is crucial to both this study and the literature in general, the most important concern here is the popular organization itself.

## Campesino Organizations

Henry Landsberger, in the introduction to his classic 1969 anthology *Latin American Peasant Movements,* defines peasant (or campesino) organizations as "formally structured interest groups" through which campesinos "attempt to improve their lot." They organize, according to Landsberger, to "improve their individual mobility through group [socioeconomic] mobility."[10] Thus, campesino organizations can have a variety of specific goals. These goals vary according to the type of labor performed by the organized campesinos, the dominant system of land tenure, and the relationship of the organized campesinos to land and other capital inputs.

The modernization process has created a situation in which the needs and interests of campesinos are constantly changing and are not homogenous. Different individuals have different needs. As campesinos become proletarianized and land tenure patterns change rapidly, the needs of campesinos also tend to change rapidly. The ability of campesino organizations to be flexible with regard to specific goals has proven to be a key to organizational success, at least in the Guatemalan context. In order for the organizations to remain flexible in the face of divergent interests and the needs of their memberships, they must cultivate a solidarity that is based on some goal that transcends the immediate needs of any specific subgroup within the organization. Therefore campesino members must be willing to sacrifice their own immediate needs for the achievement of this transcendent goal, which is usually long-term and political in nature.

All popular organizations maintain the goal of improving individual mobility through group mobility. This is a simple definition of solidarity. Campesinos, however, are capable of acting in the interests of other members of their group or organization even when this action does not directly affect their own immediate situation. They are able to do this in some cases because they have long-term objectives and a vision of a new society which are often quite consistent. Under certain conditions a campesino organization might seek to provide safety from violence for all of its members.[11] Widespread use of state-sponsored terror clearly provides a common objective (safety) for very divergent types of campesinos.

*Campesino organization* refers to a relatively broad reference group that encompasses many types of popular organizations. Community organizations, guerrilla organizations, and labor organizations can all be campesino organizations if they represent the interests of campesinos. Because the term is so broad, it is impossible to identify a general ideological pattern, although all popular organizations have in common the popular nature of their ideology. As indicated above, this ideology can often be radical in nature because of the particular position of the twentieth-century Latin American campesino. Particular mobilization strategies cannot be specified either, except for the obvious point that campesinos are the group being mobilized. Internal organizational structures cannot be specified at all. Thus, the next sections will analyze different types of campesino organizations in order to establish a typology.

RURAL COMMUNITY ORGANIZATIONS

Different Latin American countries have different bureaucratic terms that refer to these organizations, which are recognized often within a corporatist framework. Community organizations are often subsumed under the generic category of NGO (*organizaciones no gubernamentales*—ONGs);[12] in Costa Rica, community organizations are called *asociaciones de desarollo integral,* and in Mexico there is a legal category called *asociaciones civiles* (AC), which encompasses many community organizations.[13] Every country also has its own legal definition of these organizations. Depending on the attitude of the state toward popular sectors, the definitions vary in the rigidity of their requirements for receiving legal recognition.

Community organizations may or may not be popular (depending on the community they represent), and they do not have to be recognized by the state. Activist Christian base communities (CEBs), cooperatives (which usually have their own legal category), and groups that organize for some particular goal (obtaining access to clean water, for example) are all subsets of community organization. The ideologies of community organizations have been influenced by Catholic Action, liberation theology, the rise of Protestantism in some cases, and the political climate in which they operate.

Mobilization strategy differs among organizations depending on goals. However, since community organizations tend to organize around geographically specific issues, or particular "communities," mobilization can be as simple as canvassing neighborhoods or publicizing meetings within the target community. Material incentives are also common, especially for groups with specific short-term goals. There is no common denominator for organizational structure, al-though as mentioned above, the corporatist relationship of some community organizations to the state influences organization (as well as ideology and mobilization strategy).

## RURAL GUERRILLA ORGANIZATIONS

Rural-based organizations that had as their goal the violent overthrow of the regime in power are also a subset of campesino organizations. Many scholars and other observers have rightly pointed out that the makeup of the leadership of guerrilla organizations has been disproportionately drawn from the middle and upper classes.[14] The most famous revolutionary guerrilla leaders of Latin American history—Che Guevara, Fidel Castro, and even Emiliano Zapata—were hardly representative of the "popular sectors," as defined by Daniel Camacho. Nevertheless, the fact that many guerrilla organizations claim to represent campesino interests places guerrilla organizations within the broader category of campesino organizations. More to the point, there was a trend toward increased peasant leadership of guerrilla organizations during the 1970s and 1980s, particularly in the Guatemalan case. And even during the earlier period, the majority of the guerrilla soldiers in several Latin American countries (Cuba, Guatemala, and Colombia) were campesinos. In the Colombian case, the leadership (even during the 1960s) was drawn from the *campesinado*.[15]

The Cuban experience sparked a wave of revolutionary activity within Latin America after 1959. Following the success of Fidel Castro's 26th of July Movement, young radicals all over the world (but especially in Latin America) were imbued with a sense of hope. They believed that a guerrilla *foco* of only a few men could realistically contemplate revolutionary change. This new hope, coupled with some strategic and monetary assistance from the Cuban regime,

41

sparked a wave of Marxist insurgencies all over the region. Most of the insurgencies were successfully defeated by U.S.-backed counterinsurgency operations by the late 1960s. A second cycle of guerrilla insurgencies began reappearing in the mid-1970s. Although a few countries (Peru, Colombia, and Mexico) still have some kind of guerrilla insurgency, the nature of these organizations has fundamentally changed since the end of the Cold War. The EZLN of Chiapas was the first post–Cold War guerrilla organization, and it is organizationally, tactically, and ideologically unique among Latin American guerrilla organizations.

Latin American guerrilla organizations varied widely in their ideologies, from the Maoist Shining Path (Sendero Luminoso) in Peru to the stridently anticommunist Nicaraguan Contras, but they all explicitly identified their goals with the interests of the popular sectors. Most guerrilla insurgencies embraced some form of socialism as part of their ideology, and believed in the necessary use of armed conflict (violence) to create a new social order that would be more beneficial to popular sectors. They were essentially popular *military* organizations.

Because of the success of the Cuban revolution and the revolutionary blueprint of Che Guevara, most guerrilla insurgencies waged war in the rural countryside, counted on campesinos as a base of support, and actively recruited peasants into the rank and file. They also tended to mobilize followers in universities, and less frequently, among urban labor. Organizational structure varied, but given the military nature of these organizations, a hierarchical arrangement was the norm. They were clearly always clandestine.

### RURAL LABOR ORGANIZATIONS

Rural trade unionism in the context of Latin America or any other developing region is very different from trade unionism in advanced industrial societies. Within a dependency paradigm, labor is viewed in the context of the export economy, and the relationship of labor to this export economy is the key factor in this dependency literature. Labor historian Charles Bergquist suggests that historians should focus attention on workers in the export sector.[16] Others stress the relationship of all workers to the export economy, and the labor problems that arise as a result of the expansion of the export sector. Clearly labor relations take on an added complexity when viewed within an international context.

Latin American labor organizations have spanned a wide ideological range. Although the earliest trade unions in Latin America were heavily influenced by radical European ideologies (Marxism, communism, anarcho-syndicalism, fascism, etc.), modern labor organizations vary from the extremely radical to the extremely conservative. They often exist within a corporatist framework, and are thus co-opted by the state. Within this context the organizations are often severely limited in their ability to act autonomously in the best interests of the workers. As Daniel Camacho points out, a trade union sometimes acts in favor of, and sometimes against, the interests of workers.[17]

The mobilization strategy of Latin American labor organizations is dependent on many exogenous factors, including the relationship between urban workers, rural proletarians, and other campesinos. These relationships are often conditioned by the ethnic reality of the country. The worker-campesino alliance has historically been emphasized in powerful workers' movements, because of the traditionally large percentage of the population of Latin America living in rural areas. As more and more campesinos migrate to urban areas and enter the urban informal economy, this becomes a less significant concern.

The ability of labor organizations to mobilize popular sectors is often one of the most important determinants of the strength of popular sectors in a country. As John Magill has suggested, because most members of the popular ("exploited") sectors spend a large percentage of their time working, "almost without exception working groups form a mobilizeable and potentially active sector of the population."[18] That is, popular sectors are almost by definition workers, and thus it makes sense for them to be mobilized within the context of their employment—whether or not they are physically mobilized in a single place of employment.

The organizational structure of trade unions in Latin America also is variable, but the corporatist structure of many Latin American societies often conditions their organization. That is, the state often specifies the internal organizational structure of local trade unions, and the structure of larger national units (federations, confederations, etc.). This structure tends to be rigid, hierarchical, and open to state intervention or supervision.

RURAL BROAD-FRONT ORGANIZATIONS

In Latin America it is not uncommon for popular organizations to come together under large umbrella organizations which represent the very general interests of the various member organizations, or the popular sectors in general. Broad-front organizations are a subset of campesino organizations inasmuch as they represent the interests of campesinos. These broad-front organizations can be a type of federation of smaller organizations, or a large all-encompassing (usually national) organization which simply mobilizes a large following in response to some particular problem. Broad-front organizations are often composed of a coalition of both urban and rural elements and thus are not strictly rural broad-front organizations. The Union of Trade Unions and Popular Action (UASP) of Guatemala is a broad-front organization which is not strictly rural. The Guatemalan Committee of Campesino Unity (CUC) was one of the first *rural* broad-front organizations in Central America.

There is a great deal of variance in ideology and organizational structure among broad-front organizations. Broad-front organizations often consist of little more than a top-level administration which coordinates the activities of the member group. The structural characteristics of the member groups determine the structure of the larger organization. There are often shifting memberships and objectives.

By definition a broad front will attempt to mobilize a broad cross-section of the popular sector. In some cases no mobilization strategy is needed as the broad-front organization consists of the already existing rank and file of its member organizations.

## Levels of Organization

The presence of a formal organizational structure is necessary for popular "movements" to sustain activity and to participate in the political power structure. It is not clear how levels of organization should be analyzed or measured. Landsberger notes that an "administrative system" (a bureaucracy) is the hallmark of an organization. He goes on to point out that although written documentation of such a system would prove the existence of an organization, this sort of documentation is not always evident in the case of Latin American popular organizations. According to Landsberger, it is not necessary to have written documentation to prove the existence of organization. "Much more important is the *de facto* functioning of such a system—that people act as if they were certain that it existed."[19]

Landsberger explains de facto organization in terms of two organizational "subsystems": a "vertical system" of authority (a hierarchy), and a "horizontal system" of administrative labor. That is, if there is some popular acknowledgment of local or multilevel authority (regional or national leaders) which consults with the rank and file in groups, then the vertical subsystem exists. If there are routine

methods by which membership is mobilized and by which information is communicated, the horizontal subsystem exists. Horizontal
organizational abilities are required for the existence of an organization, yet they are very difficult to acquire in rural areas.[20] In Latin
America there are many geographical, linguistic, and social barriers
that must be surmounted.

Because popular organizations are more spontaneous, more variable, and increasingly more structurally flexible than political parties, it is not possible at this stage to create an organizational typology
for popular organizations. Some organizations, particularly older
labor unions and guerrilla organizations, fit into more classic typolo-
gies that include categories such as personalistic, cell-type, cadre,
and mass organizations.[21] Nevertheless, most modern popular organizations are not modeled after any preexisting type of organization,
and so the labels that have been used in the past are no longer appropriate. A similar problem arises in any modern discussion of political ideologies. The classic "isms" no longer have dominance.

## State Response to Popular Organizations

Many exogenous variables affect the nature of popular organizations. Clearly one of the most important factors is the mode of production in which the popular sectors are engaged. As shown above,
Latin American campesinos have different incentives, needs, and
visions in the 1990s than they did in the 1890s. Education and literacy also influence the evolution of popular organizations. Similarly,
the role of the state is crucial to both the nature of violence and the
internal variables of the popular organizations that are being studied here (ideology and tactics, mobilization strategy, and internal
structure).

Jaime Malamud-Goti argues that terrorist states use "disarticulating power" because it is their only way of asserting authority—it becomes the prevailing form of political power. Disarticulating power is precisely the ability of the state to thwart popular mobilization. This is something of a circular argument, but it aptly describes the circular relationship between state terror, the citizenry, popular organization, and retaliation. The state, by employing terror (ostensibly to curb an active insurgency), eliminates the possibility of its own ability to exercise "articulating power"—power based on social cooperation. This consequently leaves the state with disarticulating power as its only option. Disarticulating power is power which fragments civil society in order to neutralize it as a threat to the state's legitimacy.[22] In Guatemala, the state's use of terror, and disarticulating power, put popular organizations in an explicitly hostile and dangerous position.

Many Latin American scholars who have analyzed popular movements and popular organizations have observed this adversarial dichotomy between the state and popular sectors.[23] That is, popular movements (and organizations) are seen as the natural representative of the popular sectors in a hostile struggle to wrest power away from the disarticulating state.

The most important popular organization of the mid-1970s in Guatemala, the National Labor Unity Committee or CNUS, was explicit in taking this posture: "The state is a repressive machine that is used against the exploited . . . it is used to oppress the entire popular sector . . . it is used against the entire people of Guatemala."[24] This adversarial role vis-à-vis the state implies a distinctly more revolutionary posture for popular organizations. As long as the state uses its power *against* the popular sectors rather than for the popular sectors, this type of response from popular organizations is logically appropriate.

47

## Popular Organizations in Latin America

Latin American popular organizations are typical of those in developing regions. Modernization and the changing roles and abilities of the campesinado are influential factors. The role of campesinos in popular movements has been crucial in Latin America, and it is the most widely studied aspect of modern popular organizations in the region.[25] In addition, Latin America has been something of a laboratory for popular organizations. It is a diverse region where the popular struggle has over time chosen many different paths.

The role of the state, on the other hand, is important to the direction of popular organizations everywhere—but perhaps it is even more crucial to the Latin American case because of the corporatist nature of the typical Latin American state. That is, in Latin America popular organizations often depend on the state for legal recognition. If this legal recognition cannot be reasonably attained, it forces popular organizations to operate outside the law, implying an adversarial position.

On the other hand, within the corporatist framework, the state has much more authority over those organizations which it officially recognizes and licenses. The state has an enormous ability to influence the success or failure of an organization when it monitors the organizations' internal variables. In some cases, such as Mexico during the Cardenas era, Peronist Argentina, and Castro's Cuba, the state has used its authority to enhance the "power capabilities" of the popular sectors.[26] In other cases, such as Colombia and Ecuador, the state has minimized the power of the popular sectors within the corporatist framework.[27]

In addition to the corporatist structure itself being a potential weakness for popular organizations, there are other "traditional" characteristics which can weaken popular organizations in Latin America. The tendency toward personalistic and patriarchal leadership—the concentration of power in the hands of a few visible leaders—can lead to a situation in which popular leaders become disconnected from the needs of the rank and file. Moreover, when the state is openly hostile toward popular organizations, powerful leaders make easy targets for violent reprisal. If the organizations are too dependent on one leader or on a few personalistic leaders, the organizations themselves are very vulnerable to violence. The movements are easily decapitated, and this decapitation often proves fatal. There are many examples in Latin American history of popular movements dependent on a singular personality for legitimacy and viability that were unable to withstand the loss of a caudillo.[28]

Latin American popular organizations also gravitate toward dogmatic or absolutist tendencies. The influence of international ideological doctrines (Marxism, Leninism, Maoism, anarcho-syndicalism, Italian fascism, and even the more moderate ideological influences of German social democracy, Christian democracy, etc.) cannot be overstated, and Latin American popular organizations have historically been quick to ally themselves with international "lines" and organizations. Resulting dogmatisms have created discord within many popular organizations in Latin America—the effect has been an amoebalike phenomenon where organizations continually split into factions, eventually creating a plethora of small individualistic organizations with very particular ideological definitions and very little solidarity. Such dogmatism prohibits unity in some cases.

Highly complicated bureaucracy is also typical of Latin American political organizations. This bureaucracy is often conditioned by legal guidelines mandated by the corporatist state. This tendency weakens the effectiveness of the organizations as both financial and human resources are concentrated on bureaucracy, rather than on the rank and file. Moreover, like powerful leaders, a large bureaucracy can distance the organization from the needs and concerns of the rank and file.

## *The Case Study: Guatemalan Campesino Organizations*

Guatemalan campesino organizations have suffered from the traditional weaknesses outlined above, but they have also changed and adapted to their situation. Howard J. Wiarda claims (in *Politics and Social Change in Latin America*) that such "traditional" characteristics of Latin American politics are deeply rooted and "enduring," yet in the case of Guatemalan campesino organizations, violence has influenced these organizations so profoundly that they *have* abandoned many of these tendencies over time. These changes are particularly evident upon an examination of ideology, mobilization strategy, and internal organizational tendencies of the major campesino organizations of the period.

Guatemalan campesino organizations between 1954 and 1985 also evolved in response to other changing variables: changing labor relations (proletarianization), changing land tenure patterns, the increased influence of women in leadership positions, the response of the state to popular demands, and the violence in which popular organizations operate. Guatemalan campesinos have confronted the state as an adversary. As a "civil society" they have faced cultural, ethnic, social, linguistic, economic, and geographical barriers to organization. In overcoming these obstacles, the popular organizations have emerged stronger and perhaps even invincible.

# Chapter Four

## *Cycles of Violence in Guatemala*

VIOLENCE HAS BEEN a persistent feature of the political landscape throughout Guatemala's history. Racial, cultural, and class conflict have motivated violence since colonial times. Historically, the state, representing a Hispanic-European economic elite, has used its repressive capability to control the Mayan and mestizo majority. A long history of peasant-indigenous uprising and resistance, exacerbated by the paranoia of Guatemalan elites, has fueled the violent atmosphere.

Economic motivation has also played a role in Guatemala's long history of political violence. The periods of greatest violence (the Conquest, the Liberal period, and the military regimes of the post-revolutionary period) can all be characterized by economic innovation and expansion. For example, attacks on the general population have often been perpetrated with the intention of forcing migration as a means of manipulating the agricultural labor force and the system of land tenure.[1] In addition, there are numerous examples of campesinos being violently forced off their lands to encourage economic development schemes.[2] Clearly the disruptions that have accompanied modernization (especially changes in land tenure that are disadvantageous to campesinos) have contributed to the violence.[3] This chapter will apply the dialectic cycles of violence model outlined in chapter 2 to postrevolutionary Guatemalan history (1958–85), a period marked by direct military rule in Guatemala.[4] It needs to be emphasized that the cycles of violence model does not pretend to locate the original source of violence, and it is assumed that violence is an ongoing phenomenon in Guatemala. Thus, the first cycle of violence outlined in this chapter emerges from a violent historical context.

## The First Cycle, 1958–1972

### TURMOIL

In the context described above, the first cycle began with the social conflict in Guatemala surrounding the election of General Miguel Ydígoras Fuentes in 1958. During the entire Ydígoras administration, public demonstrations, including mass mobilization of labor unions, were common.[5] The reorganization of a small number of campesinos into labor union organizations began to occur. After 1960 some trade union activists began to reorganize campesinos on a very small scale (see chapter 5). These early groups were particularly concerned with the unfair practices of the labor contractors, or *habilitadores*. There is no evidence, however, of violent types of protest (land invasions, etc.).

In contrast, however, urban popular sectors did engage in confrontational demonstrations. Particularly during March and April 1962, the popular sectors, led by students of the national University of San Carlos, took to the streets en masse. In the beginning they protested electoral fraud and corruption in the Ydígoras administration—but the protest grew and eventually became a protest against the system itself.[6] These disruptions were fraught with violence, with many students being killed and even more seriously injured.[7] Although the demonstrations were organized by students, organized labor and other members of the popular sectors also participated. The public demonstrations were accompanied by several strikes, most notably a strike led by the large railroad workers' union, SAMF.[8] In addition to the violent disturbances in the capital, students and professors led protests, strikes, and demonstrations in other parts of the country as well. These students and other demonstrators were treated even more violently by the armed forces than were the demonstrators in the capital.[9]

One year later, there were popular rumblings again preceding what had been scheduled as a presidential election (but became the coup of Col. Peralta Azurdia—see below). These disturbances revolved around the question of Juan José Arévalo's return to run for president. Many campesinos were mobilized by the government to oppose Arévalo's return, and to affirm their support of the military after the coup. The news coverage by the conservative daily newspaper, *El Imparcial*, implied that Arévalo's presence in and of itself was responsible for provoking the civil disturbances.[10] This conflict immediately preceding the coup has prompted some scholars to conclude that the coup was a means of preventing Arévalo's participation in the election.[11]

Students and other members of the popular sectors again protested in March and April 1963, just before and after the coup. An ongoing dispute arose between the university students and the armed forces, as reflected in the newspaper. Students decried military repression, while the armed forces denied it, saying those who were arrested, detained, and in some cases killed were outside the law.[12] One group of law students publicly protested the acquittal of military officials in the deaths of three students.[13] High school students, labor leaders, and trade unionists also publicly criticized the abuses of the armed forces.[14] The armed forces and the police detained many for "suspicious conduct," accusing them only of vague political crimes such as communism or "inciting disturbances," or both.[15] One group of these political prisoners carried out a hunger strike in Retalhuleu.[16]

COORDINATED COUNTERATTACK

Coinciding with this spontaneous unrest was the formation of the first communist revolutionary movement—the Rebel Movement of Alejandro de León, 13th of November (MR-13) and its guerrilla army, the Rebel Armed Forces (FAR)—initiating operations in 1963.

On 13 November 1960, approximately 400 Guatemalan military officers staged a coup against the Ydígoras government. The officers were opposed to the internal corruption of both the military and the Ydígoras government. There was widespread opposition among the officers to the training of Cuban exiles in Guatemala in preparation for the Bay of Pigs invasion; there was also a core of officers who still sympathized with the goals of the Guatemalan Revolution.[17] Although the coup attempt failed, several of the leaders, including Marco Antonio Yon Sosa and Luís Turcios Lima, escaped to the banana-growing region of Izábal and occupied that region in the name of their newly formed guerrilla organization. From there they initiated their guerrilla operations as the Revolutionary Movement 13th of November (MR-13) in the early months of 1961.[18]

In the meantime the Communist Party of Guatemala (The Guatemalan Workers' Party—PGT) had been outlawed after the fall of Arbenz in the summer of 1954. It continued to function as a clandestine organization—with the goal of reorganizing the popular sectors as well as the "progressive bourgeoisie." According to Gabriel

Aguilera Peralta and Jorge Romero, the PGT held a congress in 1960 at which it agreed to the use of "all means of struggle" (implying the growing acceptability of violence). The Central Committee of the PGT decided to initiate an armed struggle in 1961. In March 1962, they organized a guerrilla army in Concua, Baja Verapaz, called the 20th of October Front, in honor of the Guatemalan Revolution. This guerrilla army was almost immediately decimated by the Guatemalan army. According to Aguilera Peralta and Romero, this disastrous failure was due to "organizational errors and poor military strategy."[19]

The MR-13 eventually allied itself with the communist PGT, creating FAR, and they began to engage the Guatemala army in combat in an attempt to gain control of the government.[20] By 1963 the two principal leaders of FAR, Luís Turcios Lima and Marco Antonio Yon Sosa, had become the commanders of the guerrilla movement. Although FAR leadership was quite heterogeneous ideologically, as a guerrilla organization it did advocate the use of violence as means of taking political power. This stance toward violence became increasingly radical. Yon Sosa explained his radical stance on praxis in 1965:

> To make Revolution is *not* offering a banquet, or writing a book, or painting a picture. . . . it cannot be so elegant, so passive, so delicate. . . . It cannot be so moderate. . . . A Revolution is an insurrection. Revolution is violent action in which one class destroys another.[21]

FAR was active and destructive in the middle and late 1960s. This situation quickly evolved into a dialectic of violence played out between guerrilla and military personnel.

### INTERNAL WAR

The birth of Guatemala's guerrilla insurgency coincided with the entrenchment of the Cuban Revolution. This combination gave birth to a new level of fear and anticommunist sentiment, especially within the military officer corps, which had been trained and indoctrinated in Panama and in the United States by U.S. military advisors. Military officers accused the conservative Ydígoras of being "soft on communism." After several failed coup attempts in the early 1960s, Ydígoras's defense minister, Colonel Enrique Peralta Azurdia, deposed him in March 1963. Claiming that the entire system had been infiltrated by communists, Peralta dissolved the Constitution and the Congress and took over all the functions of government as the new head of state.[22]

The Peralta Azurdia coup signifies the beginning of a new role for the Guatemalan military. From this point forward, the military began to independently assert its own political and economic strength. Peralta founded a new right-of-center, anticommunist political party, the Institutional Democratic Party (PID), and promulgated yet another constitution in 1965. After 1963, the Guatemalan military no longer seemed to be simply at the service of the traditional landed elites—the military itself was becoming the most influential "elite" group in the country.[23]

During the three-year administration of Colonel Peralta the Guatemalan military became a much more internally cohesive institution, with a vehemently anticommunist ideology, and an ever-expanding budget. State expenditures per member of the armed forces increased faster between 1955 and 1965 than for any other country in Latin America. In 1965 military expenditures totaled 17 percent of the annual national budget.[24] The Guatemalan military spent just under half that money on U.S. hardware. Purchases of U.S. arms and other military equipment escalated during the mid-1960s, averaging more than $12 million per year, or more than 7 percent of the entire Guatemalan budget.[25]

As guerrilla activities intensified, so did the military response. During these years the military greatly expanded its control over rural areas. By 1966, it had stationed more than 9,000 rural military commissioners in various villages throughout Guatemala.[26] These commissioners were mostly former army personnel, who acted as paid informants. At the local level, politics was the function of the commander of the respective military zone. The new military—a cohesive, ideologically determined, and well-funded institution— achieved power and success. By 1970, with most of its soldiers dead or in exile, the MR-13 (the military-guerrilla wing of FAR) dissolved, which signified a military victory of the Guatemalan army over FAR.

## REACTIONARY TERROR

Guatemala held new elections in 1966 and military officials allowed the victory of Julio César Méndez Montenegro, the civilian candidate for the Revolutionary Party (PR).[27] Despite the reformist tendencies of the PR and Méndez Montenegro, the military remained in firm control during his four-year term, and in fact it was precisely during this period that the authoritative violence perpetrated by the armed forces began to break out of the revolution-counterrevolution dialectic to become authoritative reactionary assault. The use of authoritative "terrorism" directed at the popular sectors began after 1966, and according to Aguilera Peralta and Romero it was a technique learned from North American military advisors. Guatemala was one of the first countries to use government-sponsored terrorism as a means of controlling the population.[28] The use of these "tactics" within the context of civil war is one of the first signs that the military is breaking out of the dialectic.[29] Death squads were an integral part of this strategy.

The Mano Blanca, the purported death squad of the ultra right-wing National Liberation Movement or MLN (a political party) composed of "off-duty" military and police personnel, had begun to operate by 1966. Within the next two years, at least nineteen new death squads had appeared. Most of these paramilitary organizations were the product of collusion between economic elites and the military.[30] Death squad activity and authoritative reactionary assaults against the unarmed rural populace soon became commonplace.[31]

In March 1966, twenty-eight intellectuals, union leaders, and PGT leaders were murdered by the Guatemalan government. Their bodies were dropped from army transport planes into the ocean. Other popular leaders and sympathizers of popular organizations were also murdered in the late 1960s and early 1970s, including Rogelia Cruz Martínez (the former Miss Guatemala) in 1968, and the prominent lawyer and congressman Adolfo Mijangos, who was shot while confined to a wheelchair in 1971. One of the most important campesino labor leaders in the country, Tereso de Jesús Oliva (see chapter 5), was also a victim.[32]

In addition to popular leaders, state operatives murdered many citizens who had expressed leftist or "reformist" ideas, as well as the friends and families of such persons. The largest number of victims were simply anonymous workers and campesinos.[33] Between 1966 and 1970, 8,000 persons were the victims of the reactionary assault of the Guatemalan armed forces. Those who were murdered simply because of their ethnic group or social class were the victims of state-sponsored genocide.

The height of the reactionary terror came between 1966 and 1968. During this period, reactionary assault against the popular sectors grew more indiscriminate, constituting what Aguilera Peralta calls a "true system of terror."[34] In 1970 the head of the counterinsurgency campaign, Colonel Carlos Arana Osorio, was fraudulently elected president, ending the brief experiment in "civilian rule." This was clearly an assertion of military dominance. The reactionary assault continued through 1972, but after 1968 it was distinctly more targeted at popular leaders and those who were associated with them.[35]

## *The Second Cycle, 1972–1985*

### TURMOIL

As the reactionary assault of the first cycle began to abate in 1972, the rumblings of a new cycle were already reverberating. There were new labor disputes, accusations of subversion, increased "criminal" violence, conflicts involving university students and professors, and agrarian conflict.

There were several labor disputes in 1972, the most significant of which was the conflict generated by the sale of the wharf at Puerto Barrios. The once powerful railroad workers' federations, SAMF and FEGUA, protested the closing of this wharf. Workers affiliated with the CTF also opposed the closing of the wharf and petitioned the government to either stop the sale or guarantee compensation (severance pay) for the workers who would lose their jobs.[36] Also in 1972, the workers affiliated with CIDASA, the Atlantic Industrial Company, went on strike, demanding a wage increase. This strike was supported by all the major labor federations in the country, including several campesino unions who provided the striking workers with food staples as an act of solidarity.[37] There were also conflicts in 1972 involving workers in the court system and workers in the electric company.[38]

In 1973 the most significant labor dispute was the teachers' strike, which lasted over six months. This conflict led to several violent confrontations between protesting teachers and the police. Because the conflict was particularly long and intense, it provoked a response from other popular sectors, many of whom demonstrated in the streets with the teachers. According to *Inforpress,* these were the largest street demonstrations since the early 1960s.[39]

There were also numerous reports of increased "delinquency" and acts of terrorism attributed to subversives, although the guerrillas had been mostly defeated by the 1970s. *Inforpress* reported in December 1972 that there was increased "violence attributable to political motives as well as increased criminal violence."[40] Again in both June and July 1973, criminal and political violence escalated further, suggesting the reemergence of violent "turmoil."[41] As was true in the earlier cycle, conflicts involving university students were common during this phase of turmoil. These conflicts consisted of both students confronting one another, and students confronting the armed forces.[42]

There were even reports of land disputes during this period. In one instance a group of indigenous campesinos resisted government plans to relocate them.[43] One of the major confrontations of the period involved between 3,000 and 5,000 campesinos in the departments of Jalapa and El Progreso. The same piece of land had been claimed by indigenous farmer "squatters" (*pobladores*) from the hamlet of Palo Verde (municipality of Sansare, department of Jalapa) and the ladino cattle ranchers of Montepéque (department of El Progreso). In the early months of 1973, the campesinos from Palo Verde planted corn on the disputed territory, and the inhabitants of Montepéque released cattle to graze on the milpa (a field of corn which has economic and spiritual significance for Maya). The squatters poisoned the cattle and burned up the pastures. At this point the armed forces intervened, arresting several campesino leaders. Then, hundreds of campesinos surrounded a patrol of mobile military police (PMA) that had been sent to gain control of the region. The campesinos became enraged when the police tried to capture several more campesinos. Fighting broke out. Newspapers estimated that between thirty and sixty people died.[44]

As discussed in chapter 2, these rumblings intensified (not coincidentally) at the end of a decade that was marked by rapid "development" and economic growth in the agricultural sector. This development signified a further shift in the agricultural sector away from independent subsistence production to wage labor and planta-

tion agriculture—mostly cotton, cattle, sugar, and coffee.[45] As Carol
Smith observed, after the Revolution "the last formal barriers to the
free movement of labor and capital were removed."[46] By the 1970s, all
campesino households were at least partially connected to a capitalist market. Both the shift in land away from peasants and subsistence
and the changing levels of consciousness that accompanied integration and proletarianization prompted violent turmoil.

The military reasserted its dominance after Méndez Montenegro's
term was over. After General Arana was fraudulently elected in 1970,
he appointed General Efraín Ríos Montt as army chief of staff, and
like Arana during the previous administration, Ríos Montt became
deeply involved in counterinsurgency operations. Arana replaced
him in 1973 with General Kjell Laugerud García, who went on to
become the army's presidential candidate one year later. Ríos Montt
also ran for president in 1974, supported by a centrist political coalition (the National Opposition Front—FNO) led by the Christian
Democrats. Laugerud was named president in yet another fraudu-
lent election, and Arana convinced Ríos Montt to capitulate.

Despite the circumstances surrounding Laugerud's rise to power
and his association with counterinsurgency under Arana's "hard-
line" administration, Laugerud initially presided over one of the least
repressive periods in postrevolutionary Guatemala. He separated his
administration from the elitist political party (and sometimes terrorist organization) the National Liberation Movement (MLN) and
their death squad activities. He also distanced himself from his
original sponsor, General Arana, by allying his government with the
Christian Democrats and other moderate political parties and popular organizations.

## COORDINATED COUNTERATTACK AND INTERNAL WAR

The second wave of guerrilla activity began with the first public acts of the Guerrilla Army of the Poor (EGP) in 1972. The EGP was largely composed of survivors of the failed guerrilla movements of the 1960s (including members of the Edgar Ibarra Guerrilla Front (FGEI), the third wing, and the most indigenous faction of the FAR which earlier had fled Guatemala to escape the army. Upon their return to Guatemala in the early 1970s, the EGP organized into three distinct fronts: The Ho Chi Minh Front, the Augusto César Sandino Front (both operating in El Quiché), and the Ernesto Che Guevara Front (centered in Huehuetenango). The EGP's ideology was clearly influenced by Marxism; nevertheless, their indigenista focus allowed them to create a much broader rural-indigenous support base than had been established in the 1960s.[47] This also signified a shift in the scene of the war from the eastern highlands to the more densely populated western highlands. As a consequence, an internal war that involved substantially more combatants had rekindled by late 1973.

Despite Laugerud's more conciliatory stance, Arana was not easily contained and, in response to the reemergence of the guerrilla insurgency and unprecedented levels of local-level campesino organization, he instigated a new wave of terror and repression by the end of 1976. By the end of Laugerud's term, in 1978, Arana controlled much of the country. The turning point for Laugerud's administration, with respect to both violence and popular organizations, came in the form of a natural disaster.

At 3 A.M. on 4 February 1976, an earthquake ravaged Guatemala. Small towns were decimated. More than 23,000 people died, 75,000 more were seriously injured, and over a million (one out of every five) Guatemalans were left homeless.[48]

Aid poured in from international organizations, and the government set up a National Committee for Reconstruction (CNR) to coordinate the relief effort. The former president, General Arana, wanted control of the committee in order to channel funds through a major Guatemalan construction company he owned. General Laugerud chose not to indulge Arana; Laugerud appointed a moderate committee headed by the Christian Democrats. According to Jim Handy, Arana countered this decision by instigating a new wave of repression. Moreover, although Arana was not in control of the reconstruction effort, the army was able to spread its control into more rural areas in the name of earthquake relief. Laugerud appeared to be willing to confront the repressive activity as evidenced by his arrest of one of Arana's "associates" after arms and military uniforms allegedly used by death squads were found in his home. But eventually military violence again erupted in the countryside, where Laugerud was either unwilling or unable to control it.[49]

The earthquake also caused a surge in popular organization, which in turn prompted a new wave of authoritative violence. These new, nonviolent popular organizations emerged to offer a communal response to reconstruction and self-help efforts;[50] moreover, because international relief funds were available to formally organized groups there was a strong financial incentive for marginalized (popular) sectors to begin organizing at the local level (see chapter 6). The very existence of popular organizations was seen by the military as a potential political base for the insurgency, and—together with the threat of increasing class-consciousness—triggered even more repression. Thus we can see the Guatemalan armed forces breaking out of the dialectic and beginning the most horrific genocidal campaign in twentieth-century Guatemala.

## REACTIONARY TERROR

General Arana backed his protégé, General Romeo Lucas García, in the 1978 election. Despite widespread claims of election fraud, Lucas came to power in March of that year. His term (1978–82) marked the bloodiest years in modern Guatemalan history,[51] with thousands of documented cases of human rights abuses by the military.[52]

The armed forces pursued a policy of targeted assassinations of labor leaders and popular organizers during the mid-1970s. Most important among those assassinated were the prominent labor lawyer Mario López Larrave and the heads of the Social Democratic Alliance, Alberto Fuentes Mohr and Manuel Colom Argueta. Many other cases of professionals (lawyers, doctors, university professors, etc.) who were murdered have been documented by many human rights organizations.

In late 1977 popular organizations mounted a major demonstration in conjunction with the strike of the Ixtahuacán miners and sugar refinery workers from the Pantaleón plantation (see chapter 6). After a group of workers and campesinos marched 200 miles, more than 100,000 demonstrators gathered in front of the Presidential Palace, forming the largest popular demonstration since 1954. This demonstration was also a turning point in the evolution of violence. After this show of strength, government strategy changed from a policy of targeted assassination to more generalized terror.

Communiqués from popular organizations document the consequent outcome: disappearances, detentions, torture, and murders of ordinary workers and campesinos throughout the period between 1978 and 1984.[53] The most famous and widely documented was a massacre in the town of Panzós, Alta Verapaz, on 29 May 1978—only three months after Lucas assumed the presidency.

In the mid-1970s the area surrounding Panzós was undergoing rapid and drastic economic change as a result of new mineral exploitation. The most dramatic example was that of EXMIBAL, owned by International Nickel Company of Canada (80 percent) and the U.S. firm Hanna Mining (20 percent).[54] EXMIBAL promised to transfer 30 percent of the company's stock to the Guatemalan government after ten years of successful mining operations. The military (the de facto government in the late 1970s) was consequently more than willing to displace campesinos in order to free land for mining.[55]

There was also rapid growth in the cattle industry, which displaced many campesinos from land that had been minifundios.

Many of these land transfers from campesinos to cattle ranchers were sanctioned by the National Institute of Agrarian Transformation (INTA), even though the land was farmed by campesinos whose families had been in possession of the land for more than a hundred years. In response, some campesinos who were organized into local unions requested assistance from a national labor federation, the Autonomous Labor Federation of Guatemala (FASGUA), to obtain legal titles from INTA. The response of elite groups in early 1978 was to threaten, arrest, and even murder campesinos.[56]

On 29 May approximately 700 Kekchi Indians from two small villages walked to Panzós with a letter from FASGUA. The Guatemalan daily, *La Tarde,* reported that officials from FASGUA claimed that the letter was intended to inform the mayor of the legal status of the petition the campesinos had filed with INTA and to serve notice that the labor union would aid the campesinos in solving the land tenure dispute.[57] According to the survivors of the massacre, the petitioners intended to hear the letter read out loud and then present it to the mayor.[58] This was not allowed to happen; armed men inside the city hall opened fire with machine guns, killing seven campesinos immediately. The assassins then proceeded to fire indiscriminately on the crowd, killing a large number of women and children. According to one survivor, many more drowned while trying to flee by swimming across the Río Polochic. More than half of the inhabitants of the area surrounding Panzós deserted their homes during the days following the massacre.[59]

Another widely documented case was the massacre at Finca San Francisco in Nentón, Huehuetenango, on 17 July 1982. Like the situation at Panzós, the land surrounding the finca had come under dispute. In the 1960s many of the campesinos from the Ixil region had purchased public lands from the government, cleared them for agriculture, and established successful agricultural cooperatives with the help of Catholic missionaries who worked in the region. In the late 1970s the army, in collusion with the traditional landed elites, began to acquire much of this land. Many top officials of the military claimed ownership of large segments of the northern frontier zone. They converted the land to cattle ranching and undertook major highway and hydroelectric projects with international funding. This made the land considerably more valuable, and for campesinos with unclear titles to this land, this was not a positive development. To make matters worse for the campesinos who had settled there, rumors began to circulate about potential oil reserves in the area. Acquiring legal title to this strategically located land appeared very lucrative.

Competition for land was only one of the many problems faced by campesinos in this area. The EGP conducted most of its operations in northern Huehuetenango, while the army also built a military headquarters in the department, thus turning the area into a war zone. The army suspected the indigenous population of collaborating with the guerrillas. By massacring these campesinos, the army thought it would achieve a double purpose—eliminating the potential support system of the EGP, and acquiring the abandoned land.

The army entered San Francisco at about eleven o'clock on a Saturday morning. They called a meeting of all the inhabitants in the main plaza. After the campesinos had peacefully assembled, the soldiers separated them into groups, according to gender and age. The army then looted the homes of the detained inhabitants. After the looting, the military officials isolated the campesinos in smaller groups; they raped the women and systematically killed the campesinos, one by one. Soldiers slit their throats, cut off their heads and hands, and ripped out their hearts. They spared no one—not even the children. After they had mutilated and killed their victims, the soldiers set many of them ablaze in the humble dwellings of San Francisco. More than 300 persons are known to have been killed in the massacre—only a few inhabitants managed to escape, many of whom had actually been left for dead.[60]

These two cases—Panzós and San Francisco—received a great

deal of international attention, because surviving witnesses publicized their testimonies. However, hundreds, even thousands of similar stories remain to be told in detail. Corroborating information regarding the number of international and internal refugees in Guatemala, and isolated testimonies that were not picked up by the international press, as well as the recent truth commission reports commissioned by the United Nations (the Historical Clarification Committee) and the Archbishopric of Guatemala (the Recovery of Historical Memory project, REMHI), present a picture of widespread reactionary assault.[61] Dozens of clandestine mass graves have been identified, and they are being exhumed at a regular pace. Some of the graves so far exhumed have contained as many as 400 bodies.[62] Approximately 200,000 Guatemalans fell victim to the armed conflict during this period—the overwhelming majority of the victims campesinos who were murdered by the Guatemalan military. It is one of the most horrific and most documented examples of twentieth-century genocide.

By 1985 the military government in Guatemala faced a legitimacy crisis fueled by the violence and economic hardship. After a series of military coups, the army was forced to relinquish control of the presidency. By the time of the 1985 civilian elections, levels of violence were again on the decline. The end of the Cold War seems to have changed the dynamic of violence to some degree, and it is difficult to speculate about a third cycle; nevertheless, "turmoil" and the rejuvenation of guerrilla movements certainly seem to have marked the late 1980s. So-called criminal or delinquent violence has reached unprecedented levels, and clear examples of political violence, such as the brutal assassination of human rights advocate Bishop José Juan Gerardi, persist.

Table 4.1

## Cycles of Violence in Guatemala: A Historical Survey

| CYCLE | TYPE | DATES | REGIME | MAJOR EVENTS |
|---|---|---|---|---|
| 1 | Turmoil | 1958–1963 | Ydígoras Fuentes and Peralta Azurdia | Disruptions surrounding 1958 election; attempted coups (1960, 1962); popular demonstrations (March–April 1962); overthrow of Ydígoras (March 1963). |
| 1 | Coordinated counterattack | 1960–1979 | Ydígoras Fuentes, Peralta Azurdia, and Méndez Montenegro | MR-13 initiates operations (1960); PGT initiates armed struggle (1961); FAR initiates operations (1963). |
| 1 | Internal war | 1963–1970 | Peralta Azurdia and Méndez Montenegro | Military takes over government (1963); military establishes rural military commissioners (1963–66); military budget expanded (1955–70); military victory achieved (1970). |
| 1 | Reactionary terror | 1966–1972 | Méndez Montenegro and Arana Osorio | Mano Blanca initiates death squad activities (1966); 19 death squads appear (1966–68); 28 popular leaders murdered (March 1966); murder of 8,000 civilians (1966–70); murder of Adolfo Mijangos (1971). |

| | | | | |
|---|---|---|---|---|
| 2 | Turmoil | 1972–1975 | Arana Osorio | Labor disputes (1972); major land dispute (1973); election fraud and violence (1974). |
| 2 | Coordinated counterattack | 1972–1984 | Arana Osorio, Laugerud García, Lucas García, and Ríos Montt | EGP commits first public acts (1972); earthquake (1976); ORPA emerges publicly (1979); URNG formed (1979). |
| 2 | Internal war | 1973–1984 | Arana Osorio, Laugerud García, Lucas García; Ríos Montt, and Mejía Victores | Earthquake (1976); military coup (March 1982); military coup (August 1983). |
| 2 | Reactionary terror | 1978–1984 | Lucas García, Ríos Montt, and Mejía Victores | Panzós massacre (1978); Finca San Francisco massacre (1982); murder of thousands of popular leaders, members of popular organizations, and campesinos (1978–84). |

## Conclusion

This chapter outlined the phases of violence that emerged in postrevolutionary Guatemala—the phases emerged within two cycles between 1958 and 1985. Following the outline established in chapter two (table 2.4), this chapter explores each of the four phases: turmoil, coordinated counterattack, internal war, and reactionary terror. While such phases overlap, they represent an increasing escalation and spread of violence throughout Guatemalan society. The specific phases, dates, regimes in power, and key events are summarized in table 4.1. While such a framework is largely descriptive, it sets the stage for a concrete examination of the effects of violence on popular organizations. It also offers a basis for some theoretical explanation of how state-sponsored and nonauthoritative violence evolve together in a dialectic relationship, how a system of unrestrained state-sponsored terrorism can break out of such a dialectic, and how violence can become deeply entrenched in a political system and a society.

This history of violence has been the most important variable to shape the evolution of popular organizations during the postrevolutionary period. Popular organizations have been created, destroyed, and resurrected within the context of these cycles of violence. This chapter, which provides a history of Guatemalan political violence, sets the stage for the history and analysis of popular organizations presented in the chapters which follow.

# Chapter Five

## *Guatemalan Campesino Organizations, 1954–1972*

AS CARLOS CASTILLO ARMAS seized power, in late June 1954, a new phase of Guatemalan history unfolded. The period between 1954 and 1985 was one in which diverse elements of the popular sector utilized the organizational skills that had been acquired during the revolution to challenge the hegemony of the economic elites and the military-controlled governments. It was also a time in which elite groups (including the military) feared the kinds of organizations which had been loyal to the Arbenz government; most significant, they feared the campesino organizations. For landed elites, agrarian reform and organized campesinos represented the most dangerous element of the ten-year revolution. Moreover, after 1959 the Guatemalan military viewed all campesinos with suspicion in light of the Cuban revolution and the guerrilla insurgency that followed in Guatemala. This meant that campesino organizations were operating in an increasingly hostile legal and physical environment. The hostility of this environment and its interplay with campesino organizations is one of the defining features of the period from 1954 to 1985.

This chapter will provide a detailed history of campesino organizations during the first cycle of violence in the postrevolutionary period. First, I have outlined how the repressive measures of the Castillo Armas regime forced the reorganization of labor and campesino cooperatives. Then I examine how this context of violence affected the ideology, structures, and mobilization strategies of these two groups. Finally, I discuss the emergence of armed insurgency, as a third model for popular campesino organization.

The experience of popular campesino organizations is crucial to understanding postrevolutionary political history. This history also provides the framework for the analysis of the effect of violence on popular organizations, a task which is undertaken in chapter 7.

## The Reorganization Process

Because the new government had completely decimated the base of the labor movement after 1954, the labor reorganization process was extensive.[1] New organizations with new members had to be reinstituted from nothing. A group of anticommunist North American labor organizers founded the Committee for the National Reorganization of Trade Unions (CNRS) in late July 1954. The committee met in the old headquarters of the largest labor confederation of the revolutionary period, the General Confederation of Guatemalan Workers (CGTG).

The CNRS was largely controlled by U.S. labor representatives. The State Department wired the U.S. ambassador to Guatemala, John Peurifoy, near the beginning of July to ask when Serafino Romualdi, the Latin American representative of the American Federation of Labor (AFL), could begin the reorganization process in Guatemala. A week later Romualdi arrived in Guatemala.[2] He and David Benedict of the Congress of Industrial Organizations (CIO), and Raul Valdivia of the staunchly anticommunist Confederation of Cuban Workers (CTC) directed the activities of the CNRS. Romualdi claimed in an editorial in *El Imparcial* that he was not in Guatemala for the purpose of interfering, but only to "declare the solidarity of the AFL." He implied that his role in the CNRS was only that of an observer. He specifically mentioned that neither he nor the AFL would interfere in social philosophy, trade union theory, declarations of principles, technical structures, or elections of new leaders.[3] Despite his rhetoric in 1954, Romualdi conceded several years later that he and his colleagues were "put in charge" of the labor unions, and that they were to fill the void left by the removal of the "communist" leaders.[4] Despite the paternalistic intervention in the organization of the CNRS, Romualdi and his AFL colleagues indicated a genuine desire to create a strong anticommunist labor movement in Guatemala after 1954. These U.S. labor leaders eventually demonstrated their sincerity by openly criticizing the government repression of nascent unions.

Twenty-six representatives of local labor unions attended the first organizational meeting of the CNRS.[5] The committee was not intended as a new federation; it was created as an advisory committee charged with the task of salvaging labor union activity. *El Imparcial* reported that the CNRS was created because of the "dangerous situation posed by the disappearance of workers' organizations in the country." Although the Guatemalan labor force remained predominantly agricultural, none of the twenty-six unions represented at the first CNRS meeting included campesinos.[6] The state vigorously discouraged all forms of rural organization after 1954. The discouragement of rural organizations during this reorganization period was only the beginning of official hostility toward organized campesinos—this hostility increased in scope and intensity during the thirty years that followed.

Originally CNRS was expected to oversee the election of new leaders in the already existing labor unions and federations. However, after Decree 48 outlawed the majority of these organizations on 10 August, the task of CNRS became unclear. Consequently it ceased to exist after a few months.

Despite the failure of the CNRS, three new labor federations did register with the Department of Labor between 1954 and 1958: the FTG, the CSG, and FAS (which later changed its name to FAS-GUA). These federations represented forty-eight local unions, forty-four of which were urban and only four of which were rural.[7]

The first of these federations, the Federation of Guatemalan workers (FTG), organized in 1956 and disbanded within one year. FTG included some campesino organizations, but rural participation was minimal. This federation did not reorganize until 1964.[8]

In 1955, Serafino Romualdi and the Regional Inter-American Organization of Workers (ORIT) founded the Labor Union Council of Guatemala (CSG); CSG was almost entirely funded by ORIT throughout its history. This "council"—unlike the CNRS—*was* a labor federation, but its leadership and membership came out of the CNRS. The CSG gained official disfavor from both the Castillo Armas regime and the Ydígoras regime that followed.[9] During the late 1950s, it was the only national labor organization that included campesino groups. It included two campesino member unions—the Union of Workers of the "Finca El Salto" (*Sindicato de Trabajadores de la "Finca El Salto,"* with 414 members) and the Union of Campesino Workers of the "Finca El Baul" (*Sindicato de Trabajadores Campesinos de la "Finca El Baul,"* with 337 members). The workers on these two fincas—who were members of the CSG—were the only nationally organized campesinos during the aftermath of the revolution.

The Autonomous Federation of Labor Unions (FAS) was founded within a month of the Castillo Armas takeover. José García Bauer—a prominent and extremely religious labor lawyer—

announced on 19 July that a number of local unions were trying to form a national federation (FAS) with a Social Christian orientation. It would maintain the "most absolute respect for Christianity and its morals," and the right to "work freely for economic and social advancement of workers." García Bauer, when asked about the CNRS, said that although he did not oppose the other group, he did eschew the idea of a unification with them because this would produce an environment that would be favorable to the reentry of communism.[10] This idea—that large, all-encompassing federations were dangerous—was fundamental to the labor union philosophy of the Castillo Armas regime and the regimes that followed.

Two days after the announcement of the founding of FAS, García Bauer claimed that twenty-five local unions had signed up with FAS, representing over 50,000 workers; none of the twenty-five unions listed in *El Imparcial* on 21 July included campesinos.[11] Edwin Bishop correctly points out that this figure must have been grossly exaggerated and that membership claims were "potential rather than real,"[12] since the level of labor union participation in Guatemala has still not approached this level since 1954.

Jim Handy asserts that Castillo Armas and his National Democratic Movement (MDN)[13] gave preferential treatment to the FAS and, in effect, created this federation as a government-sponsored corporatist interest group.[14] In the federation's original announcement, García Bauer alluded to an alliance with Castillo Armas when he said that the federation would attempt to maintain the "social conquests" of the new regime. By mid-1955, the secretary general of FAS, Luís Felipe Balcarcel, began to complain about the political restrictions placed on unions. Some cite this as evidence that FAS had official ties to the MDN—otherwise this would have been a dangerous point of view to express.[15] There is other evidence to support a clear link between FAS and Castillo Armas. Castillo Armas spoke at one of the first meetings of FAS, and FAS members were always able to obtain regular meetings with him. For a time,

FAS was meeting with Castillo Armas on a monthly basis for a discussion of labor problems.[16] Also, Castillo Armas paid FAS leaders monthly salaries of up to $300. All this occurred despite the federation's claims of being apolitical.[17]

However, everything began to change in June 1957, when FAS changed its name to the Autonomous Federation of Guatemalan Labor Unions (FASGUA) and was finally given legal status *(personeria jurídica)*. Less than a month later, FASGUA became embroiled in controversy for electing Juan Ortiz Sastre, a suspected communist, as secretary general. Ortiz had been a labor organizer during the Arévalo-Arbenz years, and he had worked primarily with campesino unions in the Committee for Campesino/Worker Unity (CUCO). When Castillo Armas was assassinated on 26 July 1957, a temporary state of siege made all trade union activity illegal, suspending the conflict within FASGUA. Although Juan Ortiz was arrested, he was later released and went into exile in Costa Rica.[18] By 1963, however, the repression directed against FASGUA was much more extensive. In February 1963, thirteen FASGUA leaders were arrested and imprisoned after the police interrupted a meeting between the leaders and Victor Manuel Gutierrez, the ex-secretary of the largest labor federation from the revolutionary era (CGTG) and a member of the communist Guatemalan Workers' Party (PGT). The headquarters of FASGUA was ransacked and its library and office equipment were destroyed. In November and December 1963 more FASGUA leaders were arrested and detained. The Social Christian orientation of FASGUA eventually began to shift leftward and FASGUA eventually affiliated with the Marxist World Labor Federation (FSM).[19] FASGUA incorporated campesinos in the mid-1960s and subsequently strayed further from its conservative Social Christian roots. Eventually FASGUA would become one of the strongest and most radical labor federations in Guatemala, speaking out against human rights abuses toward labor activists.[20]

The ideological shift of FAS/FASGUA was reflective of the ideological shift taking place within Catholic social philosophy. The 1960s saw a dramatic repositioning of Catholic political actors in Guatemala, and elsewhere in Latin America, where the Church found itself, for the first time in its almost 500-year history in the New World, institutionally exercising its "preferential option for the poor."[21] Liberation theology is the theological manifestation of this shift in social and political philosophy and political position for the Church. Although the Catholic hierarchy remained staunchly conservative in Guatemala, many foreign missionaries did bring these ideas into Guatemala in the 1960s, and the ideology of liberation theology had an enormous impact on labor unions, as well as other popular organizations.

The last major unions that included campesinos in the 1960s were the restructured UFCO unions. Although they were not aligned with any national organizations, two major labor unions of the United Fruit Company (UFCO) had regained legal status by 1955. STET, on the Pacific coast (Tiquisate), and SETUFCO, on the Caribbean coast (Puerto Barrios), were reorganized under the close supervision of United Fruit management. Because of fear, SETUFCO remained without members and completely inactive between June 1954 and May 1958. After receiving an oral guarantee from President Ydígoras in March 1958, a group of workers decided to reorganize the union in Puerto Barrios.[22] STET, on the other hand, had more trouble and exerted tight restrictions on membership—for example, excluding any former member of one of the agrarian committees of the revolutionary period.[23] The interference of the company and the restrictions on membership rendered the Tiquisate organization powerless. In September 1958, STET workers demanded a pay raise. In response, United Fruit threatened to shut down operations. STET requested a labor court settlement, or labor court permission to strike (in accordance with the guidelines of the new constitution), but UFCO then staged a lockout. Although a lockout was permissible under the new constitutional and labor code guidelines, this was the first in Guatemalan history. The lockout lasted thirteen days, and the workers finally agreed to go back to work with no pay increase after the Fruit Company threatened to discharge 1,000 workers.[24]

The CSG (and ORIT) unsuccessfully attempted to bring the UFCO workers into their national organization. When the UFCO unions declined, the U.S.-backed CSG began to accuse the United Fruit Company of sponsoring company unions and using union-breaking tactics.[25] It was around this time that Romualdi and the AFL began to reevaluate United Fruit's role in the overthrow of Arbenz and the sincerity of the new regime's support for organized labor.[26]

CASTILLO ARMAS AND LABOR POLICY

*The 1956 Constitution.* Congress drafted a new constitution in February 1956 to replace the 1945 Constitution. The new constitution contained several articles relevant to campesinos and to labor. It retained many guarantees to labor: the minimum wage, equal pay for equal work, the freedom to quit a job, a guarantee of working conditions that would "assure the workers' dignity," an eight-hour workday and forty-eight-hour work week, one guaranteed day of rest per week, paid annual vacations, protection of women and children, and indemnification for being fired "without just cause." It guaranteed the right to remuneration for services, but unlike the 1945 Constitution (written during the reformist pro-labor administration of Juan José Arévalo) only 70 percent of wages had to be paid in legal currency. (The other 30 percent could be in basic necessities, food, housing, etc.)[27] The right to trade unionization was also guaranteed in Article 116:

> [The law guarantees] the right of free trade unionism for workers and *patrones* for ends that are exclusively for economic defense and social

betterment. The law will regulate this right attending to the conditions for and the differences between the rural and urban worker. Leadership posts are only to be held by Guatemalans . . . and neither trade unions nor trade union leaders may engage in politics.[28]

The right to strike was guaranteed, but only as a last resort after all means of conciliation had been attempted. While many of the ideas and labor policies of the revolution were left in the Constitution, the means of enforcing the Constitution were eliminated, and the right to organize, although not blatantly forbidden by the Constitution, was greatly infringed upon, especially for rural workers.[29]

*Castillo Armas and the Labor Code.* The 1947 Labor Code was not immediately repealed after 1954, but significant changes were made with regard to its content and enforceability. The first amendments came in February 1955 in Decree 217. Although this law established the duty of the state to develop unionism and that there would be no distinctions drawn between urban and rural workers with regard to this right, it deleted key amendments to the 1947 Labor Code, making it once again necessary to have 500 rural workers working for the same employer in order to unionize. It also mandated that all union leaders and at least 60 percent of the members of a given union be literate. This effectively made unions illegal in rural areas.[30]

One year later, in 1956, immediately before the promulgation of the new constitution, Decree 570 further amended the Labor Code. This decree stipulated that an employer could fire any employee who had violated the Preventive Penal Law against Communism, and that strikes of agricultural laborers were in all cases illegal during harvest, and only legal at other times after arbitration by the labor courts.[31] Many progressive guarantees such as mandatory indemnification and the labor inspector system were kept on the books after 1954, but the labor inspectors were not as active in seeking out violations as they had been during the revolution.[32] The absence of local unions, especially in rural areas, also hindered the enforceability of labor guarantees. In many cases workers, especially campesinos, were told that the Labor Code was no longer in effect, and in the absence of a labor organization to inform them of their rights, they pragmatically accepted the word of the employer as truth.[33] In one case workers in the Ixcán were being paid substandard wages and forced to work 84 hours per week. "Representatives" of the workers appealed to the director general of agrarian affairs and were told that the workers had no recourse. The director general simply said, "they must obey the instructions of their employers."[34]

By the time the Labor Code was amended in 1956, even Romualdi believed that the antilabor forces in Guatemala were dominant and the possibilities for negotiation had substantially deteriorated. "I had already learned, in the course of my previous visits to Guatemala, that employers, with the connivance of the governmental authorities, had resorted to wholesale dismissals of every active trade unionist whom they classified as agitators."[35] Romualdi returned to Guatemala representing ORIT in 1956 to petition Castillo Armas to "take some remedial steps before it was too late." According to Romualdi, Castillo Armas agreed that the Labor Code as it stood in 1956 "could actually make difficult, if not impossible, the normal development of democratic trade unionism."[36] And he agreed to have one of his advisors, Ernesto Zamora, work with FAS and the CSG to revise the code in a way that would be more favorable to labor. Castillo Armas was assassinated before he fulfilled this "promise." Romualdi recalls that although the project of revising the code was initiated, a substantial amount of time had passed with no action on the part of Castillo Armas before he was killed.[37]

The lack of organizational opportunities and the slavelike conditions of rural workers particularly concerned Romualdi. On one occasion he personally petitioned Castillo Armas to release fifty-eight campesinos who had been jailed unjustly on false charges of communism. For this, Romualdi himself was accused of being a "bad subject," and a "dangerous agitator."[38]

## POSTREVOLUTIONARY AGRARIAN POLICY

The rural working class was doubly injured—both by the dissolution of the unions and by the regressive agrarian policies of the postrevolutionary regimes. At the end of July 1954, Castillo Armas also canceled Decree 900 (the Agrarian Reform Act of 1952), and at the end of August he returned to the state public lands that had been parceled out.[39] The latter action was significant because there was little political pressure from the landholding class and the U.S. government to return the public lands. The cancellations revoked most of the titles that had been given to campesinos through Decree 900.[40] By 1956, only 400 families were still on land that had been granted through the 1952 Agrarian Reform Act. Thomas and Marjorie Melville cite this and the cancellation of the voting franchise for illiterates as evidence of Castillo Armas's recognition that he lacked support among the rural population. They speculate that he feared he would not be able to count on campesinos as a constituency, and that consequently he needed to exclude them from participation in the new "liberation government."[41] Castillo Armas was only the first of a series of military leaders who viewed campesinos with suspicion.

Castillo Armas set up his own agrarian commission in December 1954 to promulgate a new agrarian law. The commission had five members representing the following five institutions: the General Department of Agrarian Affairs (DGAA), the Guatemalan Association of Landowners (AGA),[42] the banking institutions, the University of San Carlos, and the Ministry of Agriculture. Campesinos were not represented.[43] Decree 559 was drawn up by this commission and promulgated in late February 1956. The decree had the appearance of an agrarian reform. It targeted three types of land for development: public idle lands (this referred to the northern highlands and the Petén), national farms that were not efficiently exploited, and private lands to be acquired by the state after the promulgation of the law. Eventually cooperatives were the officially preferred type of rural organization, as they were viewed by both the landed elites and the state as less threatening than labor unions.[44] These legislative acts were accompanied by progressive-sounding rhetoric as well.

In mid-1956 Castillo Armas outlined his agrarian policy in a new magazine, *Guatemala.* As was the case with his revolutionary predecessors, the stimulation of agro-export was the crux of Castillo Armas's plan, and like his predecessors, his rhetoric was progressive and anti-latifundia.

> Latifundismo in Guatemala is one of the most notorious defects that afflicts our country, and which the authorities in our country have to confront. The "thief of land" must be reprimanded for maintaining his land idle and unproductive. The punishment must be for the government to expropriate the said land and exploit it and distribute it to campesinos. Every agricultural enterprise in Guatemala, and they are numerous, is obligated to leave 25 percent of its land so that the government can create space and protection for the campesino. . . . [As] more than 900 caballerias were bought by companies and by the revolutionary plan of the liberation, they have been returned and distributed to campesinos in Tiquisate. The same procedure will be followed in regions where latifundismo operates in the manner of an octopus.[45]

Despite the progressive tone of his rhetoric, and the reality of legislation that appeared to allow for the redistribution of lands, the government proved itself unwilling to redistribute the public lands specified. Although there was some later colonization of the Petén and the northern highlands,[46] the "agrarian reform" of Castillo Armas was for all practical purposes an empty program.

During the Ydígoras administration, the Department of Agriculture was transferred into the newly created National Institute for Agrarian Transformation (INTA), created by Congressional Decree 1551, the Law of Agrarian Transformation, on 11 October 1962. The task of INTA as stated in the law was to "plan, develop, and execute the better exploitation of idle or inefficiently cultivated lands."[47]

The laws and the agrarian policies of the period were superficially progressive. Between 1954 and 1973, this strategy distributed a total of 235,000 hectares, including cooperative farms and urban lots.[48] This compared poorly to the 610,000 hectares distributed by the Arbenz government in less than two years. In many respects working conditions worsened for campesinos as they were increasingly forced off lands they had previously held, and forced into migrant farm labor at very low wages.[49] Work-related deaths among campesinos, mostly migrant workers, increased every year in the 1960s.[50] In terms of practical benefits for campesinos, the agrarian program of the 1960s and early 1970s can only be viewed as a failure.

The Castillo Armas administration created the political environment that conditioned campesino organizations after 1954. His administration encouraged divisions within the labor movement as a means of preventing "communist domination." The tendency toward government-sponsored hierarchical structure was still evident in the early part of Castillo Armas's term with his official support of FAS. Following this example, later governments would occasionally favor one of the many labor organizations (usually federations that did not include campesinos) or cooperative federations. Despite this tendency, organized labor, particularly organized campesinos, would never again be incorporated into the central government hierarchy as a fully supported corporate interest group. This was the difference between the political structure of the revolutionary labor movement and the postrevolutionary organizations. The requirement of official recognition and the highly complex bureaucratic structure of labor organizations (described below) remained intact, but after 1954 the national power structure excluded all popular organizations, and actively attacked organizations which included campesinos. Consequently labor unions did not as actively mobilize campesinos. Despite the elimination of communists within the labor movement, prepackaged ideologies continued to be present in organized labor with the emergence of new labor ideologies such as "anticommunism" and Social Christian ideology. But the most important characteristic of this political climate affecting the new organizations was violence. From the very beginning (summer and early fall of 1954) violence marked the dissolution of the revolutionary labor movement (see chapter 1, pp. 4–8). The particularly rural violence that marked this process was the first example of postrevolutionary repression of popular organizations. This repression became the most important variable to affect the character of the postrevolutionary campesino organizations.

## The Development of New National Campesino Organizations

The labor "reorganization process" came to a halt with the assassination of Castillo Armas in July 1957. Nevertheless, the context of violence and the government's attempt to control the nature of organizational life endured. The state imposed rigid restrictions on the manner in which rural workers could defend their interests, restricting the effectiveness of internal group operations. One notable effect was the disarticulation between leaders and group members. But this also meant new approaches to garnering members and creative strategies for publicizing unjust conditions. Political turbulence and a surprising amount of rural activity on the part of national labor organizations marked the next decade and a half. The agrarian policy spearheaded by the newly created INTA became the basis of a rural program that has endured for three decades. The first postrevolutionary campesino federation, the Campesino Federation of Guatemala (FCG) was founded in 1962; FASGUA and the Confederation of Guatemalan Workers (CONTRAGUA) began active organization of campesinos soon after, and several other small national organizations emerged.[51] The Catholic Action–inspired cooperative movement grew enormously during the mid-1960s, and several "professional organizations"[52] became involved in rural development, often with political ramifications. Guerrilla organizations also emerged during the 1960s—and following the example of Cuba, the new insurgents based their struggle in the countryside, among campesinos. The following sections will provide a history of the newly constituted campesino labor organizations, cooperatives, and guerrilla organizations of the 1960s.

LABOR ORGANIZATIONS

In 1962, several members of the Young Christian Workers Association (JOC; created in 1945), began to organize campesinos. Within the framework of the Central Federation of Guatemalan Workers (FECETRAG),[53] the first campesino leagues were formed among the "poorest sector"—independent campesinos, small landholders, and irregular or temporary farm laborers. The first "campesino league" was organized in San Pedro Ayampuc by a JOC activist, Tereso de Jesús Oliva, a young campesino known for his natural leadership qualities and personal charisma. This league finally gained legal recognition in September 1963, after months of legal wrangling with the Department of Labor (DAT).[54] Also in 1962, Julio Celso de León, a labor leader from the textile workers union, split from the government-supported National Trade Union Confederation (CONSIGUA) to form a new workers' central, FECETRAG. FECETRAG subsequently divided into its original urban-based federation (FECETRAG) and the Campesino Federation of Guatemala (FCG). Tereso de Jesús Oliva again played a leadership role in the FCG, along with other young activists of the JOC.[55] The FCG received its legal recognition *(personeria jurídica)* in 1967. In 1968, the FCG, along with FECETRAG and the National Federation of Transport Workers (FENOT) united to form the National Confederation of Workers (CNT).[56] The activity of the FCG prompted other existing labor federations, most importantly FAS-GUA and the Confederation of Guatemalan Workers (CON-TRAGUA; founded in 1963), to begin programs of rural labor organization.

Unions confronted a much more hostile state after the military coup of 1963; nevertheless, it was precisely during this period that campesino trade unions reemerged. Of the twenty-five trade unions that were recognized between 1963 and 1966, six were campesino organizations.[57] Between July 1966 and June 1969, 174 of the 230 new labor organizations established were campesino organizations; 120 of those were campesino leagues.[58]

*Ideology and Tactics.* The overall effect of the first cycle of violence on the ideology of labor unions was one of radicalization. The major national labor organizations struggled with ideological issues over the course of a decade. These ideological questions centered on the general issue of whether or not to pursue long-term political goals. The pursuance of long-term political objectives was a comparatively radical approach, and position the labor organizations more clearly in opposition to the state.

In 1968 there was extensive factionalism within the FCG, which resulted in the splintering of the movement into several organizations (detailed below). In response to this crisis, the FCG began to reconsider its strategy. Nelson Amaro of the Institute for the Economic and Social Development of Central America (IDESAC) distinguished two possible strategies for the FCG in 1968. The first was to concentrate support in campesino groups that were attempting to exert political pressure for long-term goals (such as agrarian reform) and major political reform. They would support local groups politically and organizationally, but they would not dole out economic resources to local groups for the satisfaction of immediate needs. This strategy would exemplify the idea that immediate economic concerns could be resolved naturally with the acquisition of political power. The second strategy, according to Amaro, would address those immediate needs. The FCG seemed to follow the first strategy, as evidenced by its attention to the more politically oriented campesino leagues (as opposed to cooperatives). The FCG avoided cooperatives because it was potentially difficult to inspire national labor solidarity in a cooperative; a cooperative was concerned primarily with making economic gains for its particular community, and therefore was not necessarily interested in collective political strength. In many ways, the cooperatives did not fit into the ideological framework of a national labor organization.[59]

In the late 1960s "growth-oriented" goals complemented the more concrete political goals of the campesino leagues and unions within the FCG (agrarian reform in the highlands and the elimination of intermediaries on the Pacific coast). These strategies involved the consolidation and integration of the organizations that were already members, the reintegration of groups that had dropped out of the FCG during the mid-1960s, and the promotion of new local organizations. In the last part of the cycle, the FCG devoted most of its resources, both monetary and human, to these large organizational problems.

Thus in 1968 the largest national campesino federation made a crucial choice. After some hesitancy, this federation, the FCG, chose the more radical of two strategies—they chose to pursue a strategy that had as its goal the acquisition of political power. In many ways this implied a willingness to engage in a power struggle with political and economic elites.

The decision to pursue a political strategy, even though it

involved sacrificing the ability to work for the satisfaction of the immediate needs of the rank and file, may have come too late. Julio Celso de León has stated that the failure of all these labor federations (FCG, FASGUA, and CONTRAGUA) in the 1960s stemmed from inadequate attention paid to political ends. Surely the hesitancy of the organizations came from the legal ban on "political activity" within trade unions. Most of these national labor organizations were officially dissolved by the end of the first cycle. Nevertheless, the trade unions which emerged during the second cycle *were* more radical in their political posture.

*Internal Structure.* The first cycle of violence caused an extraordinary amount of structural movement within national labor organizations. As organizations reorganized and tried to operate around the state-imposed restrictions on labor unions, they created new forms of local-level organization (leagues), and tried to withstand repeated assaults on their leadership and organizational integrity. Shifting alliances were commonplace. The overall structure that emerged at the end of the cycle was extremely complex and top-heavy.

All three of the big national organizations (FCG, FASGUA, and CONTRAGUA) were consistent with the legal definitions of labor federations and confederations. Because these definitions stipulated certain organizational guidelines, the internal structures of these organizations were similar. A confederation represented an alliance between various federations (national organizations), which in turn represented a cluster of *uniones* (regional organizations) and local organizations. A local organization did not need to belong to a regional organization to belong to a federation. Ordinarily local organizations have elected representatives who work on the regional and perhaps national level. In the case of rural organizations, however, the leadership was less actively involved in regional and national "organizing."

Some unions attempted intriguing responses to the imposed structure. The early leaders of the FCG wanted to fill the absence left in the area of rural organizations after the fall of Arbenz, "to recuperate what had been lost."[60] The immediate problem facing them was the lack of legal alternatives for the organization of campesinos, particularly those who were not wage laborers (*mozos colonos* and small landholders), and migrant workers who did not work consistently for the same employer. Since these groups could not be legally organized into local trade unions (*sindicatos*), Tereso de Jesús Oliva conceived the idea of "campesino leagues," a term that labor activists had used to describe local campesino organizations in South America. The horizontal structure of the campesino leagues resembled the campesino sindicatos of the revolution. When the leagues received legal status, the government called them independent sindicatos, a recognition that the leagues operated as trade unions.[61]

In addition to the campesino leagues, three other types of local organizations were mobilized into large labor federations before 1973. There were rural trade unions (sindicatos) made up mostly of *jornaleros* (wage laborers), who were the only ones who met the legal requirements for a union. There were the agricultural and production cooperatives made up primarily of small landholders, and also indigenous community organizations that held lands collectively.[62]

Regional offices manned by professional organizers handled the coordination of the activities of local leagues, sindicatos, cooperatives, and community organizations. These professional organizers carried out the administrative duties of the organization. By 1968, the FCG had set up regional offices in El Quiché, Chiquimula, and Escuintla. These offices were in turn coordinated through a central office in Guatemala City. Thus, the decision-making powers of the organization were concentrated at the regional and national levels, and it failed to incorporate the rank and file into the daily workings of the organization.

Despite some relative success in the beginning, FASGUA was the classic example of a top-heavy labor organization (as reflected in both its classical vertical hierarchy and the distance between the horizontal structures and the rank and file). According to former FASGUA organizers, the FASGUA leaders were overly concerned with their personal relationships to the leftist international organization FSM and with gaining "organizational experience." It seems likely that the lack of state facilitation and the hostile climate forced leaders to look elsewhere for support, and they found it in the FSM. According to former FASGUA members, the organizational experience which the leadership sought did not filter down to the rank and file. Divisions began to occur over whether the organization should emphasize the national or the local level. These divisions were ideological in nature as well. As these divisions began to splinter the organizations, many of the national leaders of FASGUA became the victims of the targeted reactionary terror of the late 1960s. The combined effect of the factionalism and the repression had a detrimental impact on FASGUA; the federation suffered a period of stagnation until it experienced a revival in the mid-1970s.[63]

The Confederation of Guatemalan Workers (CONTRAGUA) was formed in 1963 when the powerful railroad workers union, SAMF, left the ORIT-controlled CSG to form a new workers central with the Aviateca (Guatemalan airline) workers' union, and the unions of two large sugar plantations, "El Pantaloon" and "El Salto." With these two rural unions, CONTRAGUA began to organize campesino leagues following the example of the FCG and FAS-GUA.[64] This confederation originated as an attempt to escape domination by ORIT. But in 1970, CONTRAGUA joined with the ORIT-dominated Confederation of Guatemalan Unions (CON-SIGUA) and other unions (including rural ones) to form the Federated Workers' Central (CTF).[65] Despite their consolidation, both organizations maintained their respective juridical personalities.[66]

The administration of Méndez Montenegro offered preferential treatment to CONTRAGUA; the president's ties to SAMF (and the leadership of CONTRAGUA) were established when he served as legal council to the railroad workers' union in the 1950s. As it became clear that CONTRAGUA was indirectly linked to ORIT (through CONSIGUA and the CTF), the U.S. government also offered preferential treatment. In 1967, the U.S. Agency for International Development (USAID) gave $51,200 to the American Institute for Free Labor Development (AIFLD) in Guatemala. Almost half that amount was to go toward the training of rural labor leaders—the development of a stronger horizontal subsystem. Almost all the campesinos trained through the AID program were affiliated with either CONTRAGUA or CONSIGUA; six were affiliated with the Movement of Independent Campesinos (MCI), and none with the FCG or FASGUA.

*Mobilization Strategy.* Just as violence created changes and divisions in union ideologies and structures, so it affected union methods of outreach to potential constituencies. The effects of the first cycle of violence on mobilization strategy are actually more evident during the second cycle (see chapter 6). Nevertheless, during the 1960s the national labor organizations worked diligently to mobilize campesinos despite the considerable legal and logistical constraints placed on campesino organization.

During the early 1960s, the FCG concentrated its efforts in the organization of campesino leagues in the municipio of El Palín, in the department of El Quiché. Later it expanded its efforts into Chimaltenango. The stated objective of the federation during this time was the recuperation of lands lost to large agro-export producers. The FCG offered technical and legal assistance, and help with the acquisition of titles. While this often required that it work within the framework of the INTA, the long-term goal of the FCG was a new, effective agrarian reform.

In the late 1960s, the FCG began to extend its activities to the Pacific coastal plain, mostly among migrant workers in the department of Escuintla. For these workers the immediate goal was the elimination of intermediaries (habilitadores) who contracted with plantation owners to bring in wage laborers from the highlands. The system worked to the advantage of the intermediaries who received a major share of the wages earned by the jornaleros.[67]

Most FCG efforts were spent on the campesino leagues, and eventually those on the Pacific coast came to be the most important. The production cooperatives—mostly in indigenous communities—were of secondary importance, and the most neglected were the heavily indigenous credit and savings cooperatives where membership was actually concentrated. This neglect was probably a function of the inability and unwillingness of the national organization to provide material incentives. It could also be a function of cultural and ethnic divisions between national leadership and the indigenous rank and file of the highlands. At that time, the participation of indigenous community organizations was nominal.[68] FASGUA began organizing campesinos, mostly ladinos on the Pacific coast, in 1965. According to Julio Celso, FASGUA proved more adept at organization in this area than did the FCG.

It is clear that overall national labor organizations were not particularly successful in mobilizing campesinos during the first cycle of violence. There were enormous obstacles to such mobilization, brought on by the hostile climate. The inability of these organizations to attract members led to more creative strategies during the second cycle.

*The Breakup of the Labor Federations.* The changes in ideology, structure, and mobilization strategy brought about a continual shifting in the union federations and alliances which, of course, was expressed at both personal and political levels. According to Julio

Celso, differences would often occur due to personal and political divisions within the leadership. For example, in 1968 a group of campesino leaders left the FCG to form an independent union, the Movement of Independent Campesinos (MCI). Two indigenous former campesinos who had risen to positions of power within the FCG headed the MCI. Eventually these leaders became officials in the international organization, the Federation of Latin American Campesinos (FCL). In 1967 these two men, along with two Mexican leaders in the FCL, were accused of misappropriating $40,000 in FCL funds. The two Guatemalans then withdrew from the FCL and the FCG. Because they were indigenous and had strong local followings, their separation made many local organizations waver between the FCG and the new MCI. In particular, there were two other national leaders from within the FCG (also indigenous, and also former campesinos) who began to vacillate between the FCG and the MCI. Both of these secondary leaders commanded substantial followings. In the end, one moved his leagues to the MCI, and then back to the FCG, and the other moved his leagues into CONTRAGUA. The MCI went on to join FENOCAM in 1970.

In January 1973 the CTF (and thus CONTRAGUA) lost many of its campesino affiliates when they separated to join two other newly formed campesino labor federations, the National Federation of Campesino Organizations (FENOCAM) and the National Federation of Agricultural and Indigenous Communities (FENCAIG). FENOCAM and FENCAIG together formed the National Campesino Confederation (CNC). The CNC gained legal recognition in March 1974.[69]

The FCG became part of the CNC when FENOCAM and FENCAIG joined together in 1973.[70] The FCG—which had been a united federation in 1962—split into more than a half-dozen national organizations by 1973.

The history of these national labor organizations is complex and dynamic. Many national organizations were actively organizing in the campo throughout the 1960s and early 1970s, but they proved relatively unsuccessful at attaining their stated goals. Not one collective agreement or contract was attained by a campesino labor federation during this period. There were no gains in political power for campesinos. This failure is attributable to the conflicting visions of local groups and the national organizations; local groups were more interested in achieving immediate goals, and the national organizations wanted to stress long-term political agendas.

Although the national organizations were asking local member groups to sacrifice their immediate goals for a long-term collective good, there was very little effort expended on teaching the rank and file the meaning of participation in national organizations. A survey of local members of campesino leagues in the late 1960s revealed that in 90 percent of these organizations there was no "union education," no particular preparation for local leaders, a general lack of understanding about what the goals of their local and national organizations were, confusion over alliances with diverse national organizations, a lack of understanding of what a campesino league was, and a general sense that cooperatives (which sought to satisfy immediate needs) were better than leagues and unions. The result was that the rural rank and file had minimal loyalty to the national organizations. This, in effect, made the national organizations powerless.[71]

The violence of the late 1960s and early 1970s remedied this problem to some degree. The violence itself became a sort of education for organized campesinos. It created a sense of labor solidarity that had not existed before, and changed the focus of both individuals and organizations to issues of personal safety and structural problems within the Guatemalan socioeconomic system. Campesinos were quick to understand that their vulnerability to violence had much to do with their economic situation. The organizations that emerged during the second cycle evidence this fact.

## COOPERATIVES

The climate of violence also affected cooperatives, which were the dominant type of campesino organization during the 1960s, although they were not as organized at the national level as were the sindicatos. The first cooperatives were organized and legally recognized before 1954, but it was not until after 1964 that the cooperative movement really began in earnest. By the late 1960s, government legislation, the Catholic Church, USAID, and the Christian Democrats had all contributed to the creation of 145 cooperatives with a total membership of 27,000—most of whom were indigenous campesinos.[72] Many of these cooperatives were established in the Ixcán region of the northern highlands, the future scene of the intense program of state-sponsored terror (reactionary terror) in the late 1970s. Nevertheless, the more modified violence of the 1960s served as a rationale for nongovernmental organizations to advocate cooperatives rather than trade unions.

Cooperatives had another raison d'être—to fill the gap left by the gradual disappearance of local indigenous leaders. The power structure of cooperative movement, which was typically organized by foreign priests (particularly Maryknoll missionaries) or development workers, came to replace the traditional indigenous power structure that was represented by the *cofradía*. Traditional indigenous local political power structures were disappearing throughout this period (1950s and '60s) for a number of reasons—the work of Catholic Action (beginning in the 1940s), changing economic circumstances, and the insertion of national political parties into rural community life.[73] However, the cultural violence that this entailed was replaced by a far weightier form of state-imposed restrictions, and eventually targeted repression.

*Ideology and Tactics.* Most of the national organizations that mobilized cooperatives were committed to centrist and "socially conscious" ideologies like Christian Democracy or Social Christian ideology. In April 1963, a group of professionals (academics, lawyers, architects, etc.) allied with the Social Christian movement decided to form the Institute for the Economic and Social Development of Central America (IDESAC). IDESAC began as a professional organization providing educational, technical, and financial assistance to both urban and rural organizations—mostly to community organizations like cooperatives. The ideological base of IDESAC was fundamentally Social Christian,[74] and encompassed the idea of empowering the poor masses through organization. They allied with the Christian Democratic Party (PDC),[75] and served as the central planning organism for all of the mass organizations affiliated with the PDC. IDESAC received its legal status in March 1964. During the 1960s, IDESAC concentrated its efforts in assistance on various labor organizations, including FECETRAG and the FCG. It also provided assistance to nonaffiliated campesino leagues and cooperatives. Although its assistance was often intended to satisfy immediate goals, its educational and technical assistance programs were often directed more toward the long-term goal of political power. IDESAC was not a labor organization per se, and it officially was not a political organization, despite its ideological and party affiliations. Nevertheless, in many ways IDESAC worked toward meeting the needs of workers and campesinos that the labor organizations in theory should have been meeting.[76]

The National Movement of Pobladores[77] (MONAP) originated within IDESAC, and eventually went on to form an autonomous organization. MONAP was established when a group of squatters began organizing in the La Limonada section of Zone 5 in Guatemala City to fight government plans to turn their settlement into a baseball diamond. They appealed to the Social Christian Student Front (FESC), and the FCG for help. Both these organizations were closely tied to IDESAC. In 1966 the original pobladores and those members they had recruited from FESC and the FCG were given the name Pobladores' Movement of Zone 5. When they were given juridical personality in 1970, their work had extended beyond Zone 5, even outside the city itself, thus their name was shortened to the National Movement of Pobladores, or MONAP.[78]

The leadership of MONAP subscribed to the theory that economic needs had to be taken care of before the development of political goals. This contrasted with the "power-first" strategy of the FCG during this time. The emphasis on short-term objectives was possibly a result of the more marginalized status of the original MONAP leaders. MONAP truly grew out of the rank and file. Perhaps the fact that so many participants in campesino leagues perceived the cooperatives as "better" (in the mid-1960s) indicates that the rank and file initially did not share the "radical vision" of groups like the FCG.[79]

The questions of tactics and strategy arise out of deep-rooted ideological convictions. An organization which concentrates its efforts on the satisfaction of the immediate needs of its membership (the strategy of the cooperative movement and MONAP) is very distinct ideologically from an organization which believes that the acquisition of political power (inherently a challenge to the power structure) is the path to follow. During the first cycle of violence, conflicts between leaders often arose over this question. While the former strategy was initially chosen by the cooperative movement, this strategy (and the ideology that encompassed it) evolved during the first cycle. While the ideologies that governed the movement were inherently moderate at the beginning of the decade, fundamental changes took place within the Catholic Church that influenced the evolution of this ideology. Much of the leadership of the cooperative movement came out of the Catholic Church and Catholic Action. These Church workers were part of a radical transformation within Catholicism that had far-reaching effects beyond the cooperative movement of Guatemala. The 1960s saw Vatican II, the guerrilla priest Camilo Torres, the 1968 CELAM conference at Medellín, and the beginnings of liberation theology.[80] Many of the Church workers in rural Guatemala were deeply influenced by these changes, and their religious message became increasingly politicized. A process of rural *concientización* was taking place within base communities and cooperatives. This process made campesinos aware of their political and economic rights (in the here and now) and obligated poor campesinos to engage in a struggle for justice. By the end of the first cycle the political ideologies of these organizations were still the same in name (Christian Democracy, Social Christian ideology, etc.), but they had moved substantially leftward.

The new campesino organizations that emerged in the mid-1970s proved to be much more flexible and thus successful in achieving a balance between concern for immediate needs (often the protection of campesinos from violence) and the acquisition of political power. Again, this change in campesino organizations from this early phase to the next was related to the violent atmosphere in which these organizations were forced to operate. The political violence, particularly as it evolved into reactionary terror and became both more intense and more random, effectively conflated material and political concerns. Physical safety became increasingly contingent upon political transformation.

*Internal Structure.* Cooperatives on the local level would usually be considered community organizations, although some cooperatives were federated within national labor federations (as mentioned above), and some, particularly the agricultural cooperatives, served the same function as the campesino leagues created by the national labor organizations. Thus, on the local level leagues and cooperatives could be either labor or community organizations, or both.

Organization of cooperatives on the local level was dependent on the size and type of the cooperative, and the array of services offered. For example, a large agricultural cooperative which provided many different services in addition to a credit union would have had a more complex horizontal organization on the local level than a small credit union. The typical vertical structure included a five-member board of directors elected from the local membership. This representative body would be in charge of local decision making. The horizontal structure (the bureaucracy) comprised a manager, a treasurer, and a secretary. In addition, the horizontal structure often included committees of self-defense or health and education.[81] On the national level, cooperative organizations were vertically organized in much the same way that labor federations were, with regional and national bodies and full-time professional organizers working at the top. The cooperative movement was in fact even more "top-down"[82] than the labor movement, with U.S. Peace Corps workers, USAID officials, church officials, missionaries, and urban professionals being heavily involved on every level.

In addition to the labor federations that organized cooperatives, local cooperatives were also organized into "cooperative federations" after 1963 with the creation of the National Federation of Savings and Credit Cooperatives (FENACOAC).[83] This federation received legal status two years later in 1965. Just as with unions, the U.S. government intervened—ostensibly to prevent conflict. USAID took over operations of FENACOAC in 1966, and began actively funneling money for rural development through FENACOAC to the cooperative movement. Leadership positions were mostly filled by AID officials from 1966 to 1969.

In 1969, USAID increased its financial support of FENACOAC in order to give the federation long-term viability. While the funding was increased, American administrators and technicians were slowly replaced with Guatemalans—USAID hoped that the local leadership would make the organization more autonomous and legitimate. USAID also stopped creating new local cooperatives, deciding instead to concentrate efforts and funds on the existing ones.[84]

"Professional organizations" like IDESAC and its offshoot,

MONAP, also undertook the task of organizing cooperatives on the national level. MONAP leaders found it difficult to engender a sense of solidarity among the different local squatter settlements. According to an interview with one of its former leaders, MONAP at times had to pay local leaders in order to guarantee the participation of MONAP members at political gatherings.[85] This lack of solidarity was not addressed by IDESAC or MONAP leaders through education or concientización. The personalism of local leaders often hindered the effectiveness of MONAP's programs. By the time MONAP received its legal status in 1970, relations among the leadership of MONAP and IDESAC were strained because of MONAP's emphasis on satisfying the immediate needs of its members. There were also conflicts over IDESAC's control of international funding. By 1975, ties between IDESAC and MONAP had been broken.

The internal structures of cooperatives on both the national and local levels were prescribed by the Guatemalan government and USAID. In response to the violent atmosphere, campesino leaders did restructure agricultural cooperatives, and also disbanded agricultural cooperatives in favor of less rigidly defined organizations, but these changes are more evident during the second cycle (chapter 6).

*Mobilization Strategy.* Cooperatives are organized community by community. Organizers used the promise of financial reward in order to attract a membership. Since many of the cooperatives were affiliated with national organizations that had international funding and considerable technical expertise, the incentive to join a federated cooperative was great. USAID strongly encouraged the introduction of chemical fertilizers in highland indigenous agricultural communities through the cooperative movement. The use of fertilizers greatly increased yields, profits, and consumerism (in the short term) among indigenous campesinos. It was an important element in the integration of indigenous campesinos into the national cash economy. The noticeable (although ultimately temporary) increases in consumerism and living standards provided by international sources such as USAID became the most important incentive for mobilization in the cooperative movement.[86]

In the case of MONAP, the grassroots leadership of the organization actually sought out the national affiliations in order to have access to the material benefits provided by organizations such as IDESAC. In general, mobilization strategy for cooperatives was dependent on short-term financial rewards. Eventually (during the second cycle of violence) these benefits would seem insignificant when balanced against the physical risk of joining a politically dangerous organization.

The Christian Democratic Party and the cooperative movement became the targets of military repression due to their involvement in the politicization of indigenous campesinos. Because the Christian Democratic Party (PDC) had ties to the Catholic Action church workers—many of whom were foreign missionaries—involved in the cooperative movement, the party was associated with the political concientización that was an integral part of this missionary activity. And as the 1960s progressed, the radical shifting of Catholic ideology was increasingly apparent. The Church, which was "siding with the poor," became more and more of a political threat to the anticommunist military.

The PDC was organizationally linked to the cooperative movement and FENACOAC already by the late 1960s. In addition, many indigenous communities entered the political arena (by voting and running candidates for municipal offices) during this period under the auspices of the PDC. This political activity (both on the part of Catholic missionaries and indigenous communities) was unacceptable to the Guatemalan military, particularly after 1970—when the Christian Democrats were thought of as "communist subversives" in the minds and rhetoric of the nation's military leaders.[87]

Although this first cycle of violence was not witness to the mass destruction of cooperatives and cooperative members, cooperatives which operated in the areas where there were guerrilla fronts were dismantled in the late 1960s. Moreover, several cooperative and labor leaders were victims of the targeted reactionary terror of the late 1960s, and many of the thousands of civilian campesinos who were murdered during this period were involved in labor or cooperative organizations. This meant that by the end of the reactionary terror of the first cycle, material incentives could no longer be the basis for mobilization strategy, because the risk of involvement outweighed the potential benefits.

GUERRILLA ORGANIZATIONS

The first guerrilla organizations in Guatemala originated from the military coup attempt of 13 November 1960, as outlined in chapter 3. Lieutenants Marco Antonio Yon Sosa and Luís Augusto Turcios Lima returned from exile in March 1961, and with another officer from the failed coup attempt, Alejandro de León, they decided to continue their struggle against the Ydígoras regime. Security forces captured and assassinated Alejandro de León soon thereafter. In February 1962, the rebels launched their first attack, calling themselves the 13th of November Revolutionary Movement (MR-13). They attacked two army posts in the Bananera region and robbed the United Fruit Company office.

In March 1962 the communist party of Guatemala (PGT) established a new guerrilla front (the 20th of October Front), which was quickly destroyed by the Guatemalan army. The 20th of October Front was significant because it marks the beginning of the PGT's guerrilla activities.

Guerrilla organizations are not always or even often included under the heading of *movimiento popular* in Guatemala. "Revolutionary" organizations are very obviously distinguished from other sorts of popular organizations, and for most of the period in question, there were clear strategic reasons (for both guerrillas and noncombatants) for maintaining the conceptual distinction between revolutionary military organizations, and organizations which attempted to occupy a legal space in Guatemalan political life. In fact, in 1984 popular and guerrilla leaders cooperatively agreed that the "popular movement" (excluding the guerrillas) should maintain its autonomy from the revolutionary movement.[88] Despite the tactical political distinction between the two forms of struggle guerrilla organizations fit well within the parameters of "popular" as defined in this analysis. That is, revolutionary guerrilla organizations, from their inception, claimed to represent the interests of popular (non-elite) sectors of Guatemalan society. And indeed, during the high point of both the guerrilla struggle and the nonguerrilla popular struggle (1979-1980), there was cooperation and even a merging of tactics and ideology between the guerrilla organizations and the other popular organizations. It is important to include the guerrilla organizations in this study because they also responded in a very marked way to the dialectic of violence in Guatemala, and because they (more than any other popular group) are expected to become a force for democratization inside post-1996 Guatemala.

*Ideology and Tactics.* Perhaps more than any other variable under consideration here, the ideology of guerrilla movements was the most conditioned by the cycles of violence in Guatemala. The ideology of guerrilla movements became increasingly radical and internationalized during the 1960s in response to the dialectic of violence described in chapter 4. This radicalization (accompanied by a certain amount of dogmatism) had the effect of splintering the guerrilla movement by the end of the first cycle.

In the very early phase (1960), the MR-13 strategy was to attack military installations; it was not planning a "prolonged peoples' war," but rather a quick overthrow of the Ydígoras regime. The rebels, in these early months, were primarily nationalists in the model of an Augusto Sandino of Nicaragua.

Although its members came directly out of the PGT, the 20th of October Guerrilla Front (the PGT's first guerrilla initiative) also claimed to have modest nationalist intentions in seeking to overthrow the Ydígoras regime. They claimed to have modeled themselves after the broad-based coalition of nationalist "revolutionaries" who overthrew the dictatorship of Jorge Ubíco in the fall of 1944.

As time went by, the differences between the ideologies and tactics widened between the MR-13 and the United Resistance Front (FUR); FUR was the directorate body which represented the alliance between the MR-13 and the PGT. FUR primarily represented the views of the urban leadership of the PGT. The guerrilla experience radicalized the MR-13 fighters, while the PGT took a more conciliatory stance. The FUR leadership was increasingly withdrawing from their commitment to a radical overthrow of the Guatemalan government; they instead hoped to use the guerrillas as a bargaining chip which would eventually allow them to participate in electoral politics as they had during the revolution.

The MR-13, influenced by the dialectic of violence and the abject poverty in the countryside, saw its own relationship to the masses differently than did FUR and the PGT. Agrarian reform became its most crucial concern. The leadership of the MR-13 was increasingly drawn toward Marxism and eventually toward Trotskyism, which caused division within the MR-13 itself. The second front, based in the eastern part of the country and led by Luís Trejo, completely dispersed after a struggle broke out between communists and anticommunists within their ranks. According to Richard Gott, the Fourth International's Latin American bureau sent several Trotskyites to Guatemala to "take advantage of MR-13's abandonment by and lack of assistance from other political organizations."[89]

The Trotskyites urged the rebels to attempt a more sweeping mass struggle. That is, they wanted to incorporate organized peasants and workers into a massive revolutionary movement. Francisco Amado Granados, a Trotskyite member of the national directorate of the MR-13, said in 1965:

> We plan to organize underground committees of armed workers and also students similar to those now existing among peasants; we shall promote trade unionism, legal or underground; and we shall prepare the conditions and mentalities of the masses for a revolutionary workers' *central*. And our slogan, which is already spreading, will become a reality for important sectors of the population: "workers, peasants, students, arm yourselves." [90]

The FGEI wing of the MR-13 was decidedly anti-Trotskyite, and its tactics followed a more Guevara-ist line. It also opposed the conciliatory stance of the PGT. As outlined below, these ideological and tactical divisions eventually resulted in the Rebel Armed Forces (FAR, which came to represent the FGEI), the MR-13, and the PGT splitting apart and operating independently of one another. These divisions made all the organizations increasingly vulnerable. The ideological divisions are explicitly manifest in the structural shifting that took place within the Guatemalan guerrilla movement during the 1960s. These structural shifts are explained in the following section.

*Internal Structure.* Turcios Lima approached various urban-based political parties—including moderate bourgeois organizations—throughout 1961, in an attempt to forge political alliances. After launching their guerrilla offensive, the PGT publicly pledged a willingness to ally with the MR-13.[91] In December 1962 the MR-13 decided to ally itself themselves with the 20th of October Front and a group of students calling the 12th of April Movement[92] to form the Rebel Armed Forces (FAR). (See table 5.1.)

FAR was officially responsible for handling the military strategy of the PGT. Despite this, the power of both political decision-making and military strategy in reality remained within the ranks of the PGT leadership. The PGT remained at the top of the vertical hierarchy. The PGT organized FUR as a directorate body within FAR. It was within FUR that all military decisions were made, yet the MR-13 was not represented in FUR. According to Adolfo Gilly, who had extensive experience with the MR-13, leaders of the MR-13 began to feel pressured into a situation in which they were being guided by "outside political leadership in whose decisions they had no input."[93]

In June 1964 the MR-13, led by Yon Sosa, declared that it was splitting from FAR in its "Declaration of Sierra de las Minas" (see table 5.1). The split occurred as a result of the ideological dispute between the Trotskyites of Yon Sosa's front of the MR-13 and the more conservative revolutionaries of the PGT.[94]

Eventually Turcios tried to unify the three factions of FAR by calling a "unification meeting" in March 1965. When Yon Sosa refused to attend, Turcios separated his Edgar Ibarra Guerrilla Front (FGEI) from the MR-13. Consequently the MR-13 left FAR (see table 5.1). In response to these ruptures, the PGT agreed to more fully support the armed struggle of FAR (and thus the FGEI). The FGEI expanded its base and grew significantly between 1965 and 1966. In 1966, Turcios decided to strengthen the political base of the struggle by going to Guatemala City and personally joining the PGT. He was killed in a car accident on 2 October 1966. This was a blow to morale, and his leadership was not easy to replace.[95]

In 1968 the FGEI and FAR broke away from the PGT and allied themselves once again with the MR-13. Later that year the head of the FGEI, Camilo Sánchez (who replaced Turcios after his death), was captured and killed. Yon Sosa (and the MR-13) again withdrew from FAR. Once again personalistic divisions began to split FAR apart (see table 5.1) By 1970 the MR-13 and FAR had been neutralized by the army.

The changing alliances of these guerrilla organizations were extremely complicated—and these shifts affected the vertical structures of the distinct groups. Moreover, the ideological differences and changes had a direct impact on horizontal organizational structure. For example, the Trotskyites favored the organization of local

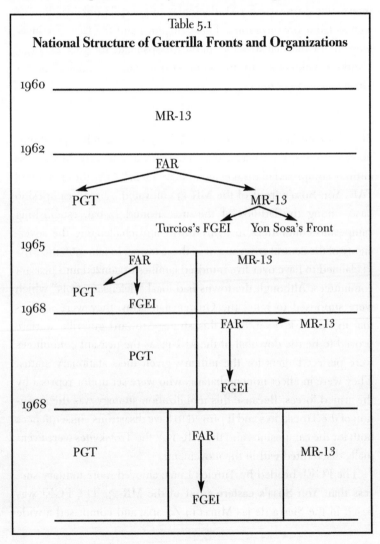

Table 5.1

**National Structure of Guerrilla Fronts and Organizations**

noncombatant peasant committees, while the "Guevara-ists" and the PGT did not. Consequently internal structures—both vertical and horizontal—were constantly changing during this period, on both the national and local levels.

Personalistic and ideological disputes were often the result of international pressures and ideologies in guerrilla organizations as well as labor organizations. These disputes and the lack of consistency in the internal structure of the groups made the guerrilla organizations vulnerable to the counterinsurgency campaign of the Guatemalan government.

*Mobilization Strategy.* When the MR-13 first began its operations, no campesinos were recruited into the rank and file; the MR-13 was entirely comprised of disaffected military men.[96] After the creation of FAR, Yon Sosa's front of the MR-13 cultivated a broad campesino base among the ladinos of the area around Izábal, establishing campesino committees in many towns and challenging the sovereignty of the central government in those towns. In late 1966 the MR-13 claimed to have over five hundred families organized into peasant committees. Although the towns had local "defense patrols" which were supposed to repel the Guatemalan army, they were ineffectual in this task. Eventually this strategy toward guerrilla warfare proved to be the downfall of the MR-13, as the peasant committees were perfect targets for the military, given their stationary status. They were in effect noncombatants who were set up for reprisal by the armed forces. Because this mobilization strategy was the invention of the Trotskyites and it proved to have disastrous consequences both for the campesinos and the MR-13,[97] the Trotskyites were eventually discredited within the movement.

The FGEI, headed by Turcios Lima, enjoyed more military success than Yon Sosa's eastern front of the MR-13. The FGEI was based in the Sierra de las Minas in Zacapa, and comprised a wide base of popular combatants—members of the communist youth organization, students, workers, and peasants. Turcios was critical of the Trotskyite tactics of Yon Sosa's front of the MR-13, and he was also critical of the PGT's conciliatory stance with regard to the political bourgeoisie. The PGT comprised urban-based intellectuals and they were somewhat removed from the mobilization process. They did virtually no recruiting of campesinos.

## Conclusion

Conditions of violence in the 1960s affected the emergence of three major types of campesino organization—trade unions, cooperatives, and guerrilla organizations. In each case these organizations were faced with repressive conditions which brought about divisions between leaders and the rank and file. The hostile environment also fueled ideological and strategic divisions between those who wanted to work toward the satisfaction of the immediate needs of the base, and those who wanted to work for a political transformation.

Although the number of campesino organizations consistently increased throughout this period, this did not represent increased participation of the rank and file,[98] but rather represented divisions and power struggles at the top. The percentage of economically active Guatemalans participating in labor organizations never reached 3 percent during this period, and among campesinos participation never reached 1 percent. More campesinos participated in the cooperative movement; however, cooperatives too failed to incorporate more than one percent of the economically active population engaged in agriculture.[99] Guerrilla organizations did not include many campesinos during the first cycle either. In many ways, the proliferation of organizations during this period was a sign of the weakness, fragmentation, and a lack of true solidarity. Clearly these weaknesses were in part due to the hostile environment in which these organizations were forced to operate.

Campesino organizations of the 1960s were attempting to employ the model of the revolutionary period. Guerrilla organizations were also influenced by the revolutionary model, particularly between 1962 and 1965, when the PGT continued to press for a role in electoral politics. Most of the popular organizations of the 1960s were trying to employ inappropriate models and strategies left over from a less hostile time, but the violence propelled them to learn to adapt. The next round of organizations would be stronger and more appropriate to contemporary Guatemala.

# Chapter Six

## *Guatemalan Campesino Organizations during the Second Cycle, 1972–1985*

POPULAR ORGANIZATIONS WHICH emerged during the second cycle of violence were distinct from the first-cycle organizations. Traditional labor federations were overshadowed by a new approach to national labor solidarity; cooperatives became increasingly politicized by violence; guerrilla organizations actively mobilized indigenous campesinos in the altiplano; and campesinos for the first time developed their own unique national grassroots organization.

For popular organization, the mid-1970s was the most active and fruitful period of the postrevolutionary epoch, due in part to a less repressive environment during the early part of the presidential administration of General Kjell Laugerud García. The earthquake of April 1976 provided an additional impetus for organization as the need for economic and technical assistance became pronounced and popular organizations had some access to international funds.

When military repression began to resurface in 1977, it temporarily served to crystallize and unify popular movements even more.

The level of rural organization and participation markedly increased during this period. In this case, both the relative peace of the beginning of the cycle and the intensification of violence in the middle of the cycle prompted growth in popular organizations. The calm of the beginning of the cycle provided the necessary political space for the initial formation of organizations, while the intensification of violence helped these organizations to focus their efforts and mobilize members. After a certain critical level, however, the cycle of violence began to decimate the organizations.

The willingness of campesino organizations to make demands on the system culminated in the founding of the Committee for Campesino Unity (CUC) in 1978. Although CUC suffered great losses from the reactionary terror of the late 1970s and early 1980s, it reemerged in 1985 as one of the strongest campesino organizations in postrevolutionary history.

This chapter will follow the evolution of campesino organizations through the second cycle of violence (1972–85). This history will highlight the structural, ideological, and tactical changes that occurred within popular organizations as a result of the violence.

## LABOR ORGANIZATIONS

During the early years of the second cycle of violence, the labor movement was still splintering and reconstituting itself. When Colonel Carlos Arana Osorio assumed power in 1971, a formal state of siege made all "political and trade union activities" explicitly illegal.[1] The organizations incorporating campesinos seemed most vulnerable to this fragmenting activity. The Independent Campesino Movement (MCI) created a larger labor federation in 1970—the National Federation of Campesino Organizations (FENOCAM), which then joined with another new federation, the National Federation of Agricultural and Indigenous Communities (FENCAIG) in 1973 to form the National Campesino Confederation

(CNC). According to Mario López Larrave, the CNC grew at the expense of the ORIT-affiliated Federated Workers Central (CTF).[2] The campesino movement that was represented by the MCI and its descendants suffered a grave loss with the assassination of Tereso de Jesús Oliva in 1971. Many trade unionists believed that the assassination of Oliva was part of the price they paid for supporting the Revolutionary Party (PR) candidate, Mario Fuentes Perussine, against the military victor, Carlos Arana, in the elections of 1970.[3]

Labor activists attempted a labor unity platform in 1973 when they formed the National Labor Advisory Board (CNCS). This group was never fully organized and it never received legal recognition. Its failure to thrive was partly due to the ideological differences among the labor union leadership at the end of the first cycle of violence.[4]

In 1975, personalistic quarrels split the CTF, the largest labor organization at the time. CONSIGUA and five smaller federations separated from the CTF in 1974 and 1975. By the time the National Committee for Labor Unity (CNUS) emerged in 1976 the labor movement was polarized ideologically, divided physically, and weak.

CNUS was born when the CNT (which included the campesino federation, FCG), FASGUA (still with campesino affiliates), and several other urban-based trade unions together formed a new committee to express labor solidarity; more than sixty-five locals directly participated in the initial organization of the new committee. On the suggestion of the prominent labor lawyer Mario López Larrave, they named the new movement for an organization that served a similar function during the revolutionary period.[5] CNUS was the third attempt at labor unity since 1954,[6] but unlike the other attempts, CNUS was not intended as a new labor central. It was a national committee that was created in the model of the mutual-aid societies of the Liberal period (late nineteenth century).

CNUS began as a "unity of political action," or political action organization in response to both the earthquake and the violent events surrounding the formation of a union at the Coca-Cola bottling plant in March 1976. The Coca-Cola workers had been denied the right of unionization and were threatened with violence by an alleged friend of Arana (the former military president) and the MLN (the ultra right political party, which operated death squads).[7] Blatant violations of the labor code and the accompanying violence only intensified the turmoil caused by the earthquake. This tension provided the atmosphere for this new type of labor organization to emerge. According to one labor leader, "what made the formation of CNUS possible were the concrete needs of the workers. . . . It was born out of the workers' own concerns."[8]

*Ideology and Tactics.* Although as a political action organization CNUS had very specific goals which responded to the particular needs of the time, the general objectives and ideology of CNUS were not defined in the beginning, and there was great ideological diversity within its leadership and its ranks. By 1979, this ideological diversity became increasingly apparent as the administrative commission of CNUS began to polarize ideologically. Popular leaders are in agreement that this was as a result of the violence, which had the effect of radicalizing some and intimidating others. Early in 1978, CNUS joined an international labor organization known as the Worldwide Labor Federation (FSM), which was associated with a Marxist line. In March of that year, in reaction to this ideological shift to the left, the Latin American Confederation of Workers (CLAT), a Social Christian international labor central, forced several of the member unions of the CNT to withdraw from CNUS. The CLAT-affiliated unions came under the leadership of José Pinzón. The original CNT withdrew from CLAT and remained in CNUS. So for a time there were two CNTs. The FCG and FECETRAG remained with the CLAT-affiliated CNT. Some of the campesino leagues from the highlands stayed in the CNT, which was affiliated with CNUS, but CNUS was effectively emasculated by the withdrawal of the FCG and FECE-TRAG.[9]

After the breakup of CNUS, the violence intensified, and the national organizations were so divided by this time that they offered little protection to the rural rank and file. As the leaders of most of the labor organizations were targeted for assassination, the movement disintegrated even further. Thus political violence contributed to the dissolution of the movement in two stages—by first polarizing the movement ideologically, and then removing the leaders who were holding the already weakened organizations together.

The CNT, FASGUA, and with them CNUS were destroyed by repression. One union leader said: "CNUS wouldn't have disappeared if the CNT and FASGUA hadn't disappeared. And CNT and FASGUA disappeared because their principal leaders disappeared. Even the rank and file of these organizations were disappeared. CNUS wouldn't have disappeared if they [the army] hadn't managed to break the local unions."[10] For pragmatic reasons CNUS began without a specified ideological agenda. As the leaders and rank and file of the labor movement became more ideologically dogmatic and differentiated as a result of repression, the role of CNUS became more and more obscure.[11]

*Internal Structure.* The organization of CNUS was distinct from the traditional hierarchical structure that defined labor federations and confederations. This structural-organizational innovation was a direct result of the violent climate in which CNUS emerged. CNUS was a political action organization whose vertical organization was directed by a collective leadership that included Mario López Larrave and the secretary general of the CNT, Miguel Angel Albizures. CNUS never had its own secretary general; they had a more democratic participatory organization that functioned through various "commissions" which were responsible for performing agreed-upon duties. These commissions constituted the horizontal structure of CNUS.[12]

CNUS utilized input from the rank and file, and incorporated workers and campesinos through the "commission of organization." This commission was described by one union leader as the place "where all the unions participated; there they discussed the particular problems of each union; it was a meeting of the leaders with the rank and file, and there was always open participation of both."[13] The commission of organization was a means of incorporating more workers into the horizontal structure of the organization.

CNUS also helped coordinate the activities of other popular movements which had traditionally been separated from trade unionism, such as the Association of University Students (AEU), various teacher organizations, MONAP, an association of families of the disappeared, and eventually CUC (see below).[14]

Throughout 1976 and 1977, CNUS coordinated almost all labor activity. The visible presence of organized labor was stronger than it had ever been in the postrevolutionary period. The success of CNUS in resolving conflicts in the workers' favor varied, but they became less successful over time, as Laugerud lost control of the government to the more repressive elements of the military.

*Mobilization Strategy.* CNUS grew in response to repression, as exemplified by its advocacy of membership solidarity with the workers of the Coca-Cola bottling plant. In this instance, repression was used as a tool for mobilization. On 8 June 1977, the noted labor lawyer Mario López Larrave was assassinated. López Larrave was an important part of the leadership of CNUS, and he was the committee's legal representative. He had been a driving force behind the labor movement for more than a decade. After his assassination, workers organized a spontaneous public demonstration which was attended by 15,000 protesters.[15] His death mobilized the masses in the same way that the repression at the Coca-Cola bottling plant had, and in this sense his assassination was a catalyst for CNUS.

The most important public demonstration of CNUS in the months following the assassination of López Larrave was the Ixtahuacán miners' strike and march of November 1977. The mining company that employed these workers threatened to shut down in an attempt to break the newly formed union, a local affiliate of the CNT. On 11 November the miners set a historic precedent when they set out on foot from Huehuetenango for a 350-kilometer march, or *caminata,* to the capital. As they marched they gained the support of many campesinos who gave the miners food and shelter and listened to the miners' story. According to CNUS leader Miguel Angel Albizures, the miners "unified campesinos and factory workers, educating [the campesinos] about the level of exploitation suffered by workers in general."[16] The caminata was an innovative mobilization strategy which proved very effective.

Because of the press attention given to the strikers and the local mobilization of campesinos in support of the miners, the dispute was settled in the miners' favor before they reached Guatemala City.[17] Nevertheless, they continued to march in support of sugar mill workers from the Pantaleón plantation on the Pacific coast who were also members of CNUS, and who were also striking. The sugar workers, in response, began their own march to the city. They too mobilized workers and campesinos on the way, many of whom joined their caminata. When they arrived in Guatemala City on 19 November 1977, they joined a demonstration of more than 100,000 workers and campesinos in front of the Presidential Palace. Workers in other parts of the country also gathered in support of the demonstrators. It was by far the largest labor demonstration since 1954. The caminata became one of the most effective tools of mobilization employed by popular movements after 1977. In addition, these experiences consolidated the tactic of "solidarity striking"—the practice of workers who participated in national strikes not because of problems or issues in their own places of employment, but rather to support the demands of other workers.[18]

The November 1977 demonstration was also a turning point for the violence. After this show of strength, the strategy of the armed forces changed from targeted attacks to a more generalized terrorism that resembled genocide.[19]

The beginning of the end for campesino organizations was marked by the massacre at Panzós in 1978 (see chapter 4). Panzós was significant for several reasons. The press coverage was extensive, both within Guatemala and internationally, and this coverage linked the army and the government to the massacre. The army was forced to make feeble and implausible explanations, which in effect delegitimized military rule. This eventually led to a series of military coups and the transition to civilian government in 1985. The second significant result of Panzós was that the labor centrals and CNUS rallied around this disaster in one final show of labor unity. The Panzós massacre (like the Coca-Cola dispute, and the assassination of López Larrave) served to further mobilize followers of CNUS.

The reaction of labor organizations to Panzós represents the high point in labor organization of the post-1954 period, especially with regard to campesinos. Within weeks after the massacre, the CNT, FASGUA, and CNUS had all published position statements in major newspapers and other publications.

The various manifestos published by the labor centrals and CNUS were all similar in content. They all published the campesinos' version of the massacre, and most of them pointed out the historical culpability of INTA.

> This institution, INTA, has been an instrument of the agrarian capitalist landowners, and it has favored their voracious exploitative appetites. At the same time INTA has benefited its own administrative staff, and their reactionary allies in government, as they are able to make themselves rich by illegally obtaining titles to lands.[20]

Without exception, every organization stressed the urgency of campesino-worker unity. In addition, CNUS organized "self-defense groups" within factories in order to provide at least the semblance of protection within the organization.[21] During this period, popular organizations were both visible and combative.

The visible sign of this feeling of unity was a demonstration which was planned for the commemoration of López Larrave's murder. After the Panzós massacre, the demonstration on 8 June 1978 was used to protest the military excesses at Panzós. *El Imparcial* reported that thousands from "the most varied of social strata" came out to protest Panzós in this CNUS-sponsored demonstration. The number of people participating surpassed the number at the miners' and sugar workers' rally of November 1977. CUC (see below) marched publicly as part of CNUS for the first time in this demonstration, thus making CNUS the most important example of post-1954 worker-campesino solidarity.[22] Although there was a feeling of optimism, the violent nature of Guatemalan political repression had only begun to reveal itself.

*The Death and Rebirth of Labor Organizations.* When Efraín Ríos Montt came to power in April 1982, he immediately declared a State of Emergency, making it illegal for more than three persons to meet. All labor organizations were for a time outlawed. The legal restrictions—enacted in a climate of general reactionary terror—brought the entire labor movement, which had already suffered hundreds of casualties in the early 1980s, to a halt.[23] No one wanted to assume a leadership position, and no one wanted to be a member. There was a brief period during the summer of 1983 when some leaders and organizers of the FASGUA, CNT, and CNUS attempted to reorganize, but many of these organizers were murdered later that same year and in early 1984.

In May 1983 the Ríos Montt coalition created the Confederation of Guatemalan Trade Union Unity (CUSG). It had close ties to the U.S.-sponsored American Institute for Free Labor Development (AIFLD).[24] Initially the CUSG included the CLAT-affiliated remnants of the CNT, which by this time had changed their name to the General Confederation of Guatemalan Workers (CGTG); the CGTG still included the FCG. But by 1985 the CGTG, still under the auspices of CLAT and the leadership of José Pinzón, had withdrawn from the CUSG. Despite its more genuine interest on the expanding urban workforce, in 1989 the CUSG estimated that 70 to 80 percent of its affiliates represented campesinos.[25] Hank Frundt acknowledges that rural membership numbers were sometimes inflated, and many rural CUSG affiliates were federations "in name only."[26]

The more radical elements of the labor movement (the remnants of CNUS) reorganized as the Workers' Labor Unity Organization of Guatemala (UNSITRAGUA) in February 1985.[27] UNSITRAGUA unofficially included the new CUC as one of its affiliates. Many of its leaders participated in the rank and file of the labor movement of the 1970s, but most had never before held leadership positions. UNSITRAGUA's leadership constituted a new more radical and more determined generation of labor organizers.[28]

## COOPERATIVES

Cooperatives continued to be important during the early 1970s as the cooperative movement became increasingly tied to colonization projects in the unsettled northern reaches of Huehuetenango and El Quiché. These regions eventually became the scene of the internal war between guerrillas and counterinsurgency forces. The presence of cooperatives in these regions provided a potential base of mobilized campesinos for the guerrilla fronts operating in the area. This fact was not lost on counterinsurgency strategists. Consequently, the primarily indigenous cooperatives were the first casualties of the generalized reactionary terror of the late 1970s and early 1980s (the second cycle). In addition to the violence, cooperative members suffered great economic losses during the second cycle as well. When fertilizer prices began to rise in 1973, indigenous farmers were unable to purchase these inputs. Both the campesinos and the soil had become dependent on chemical fertilizers—without the fertilizers, the land would not produce. Eventually many highland minifundistas lost their lands and joined the increasing numbers of campesinos migrating to the southern coastal plain.[29]

*Ideology and Tactics.* As cooperatives expanded beyond credit associations and as they grew larger, they also took on important social objectives. Most agricultural cooperatives tried (usually unsuccessfully) to obtain legal titles to land through legal assistance and INTA. They often also sponsored social projects (the building of schools, clinics, etc.).[30] In other words, the agricultural cooperatives of the 1970s, although they were community organizations, fulfilled much the same function as the campesino "leagues." Ideologically many cooperatives were still tied to the Christian Democrats, Social Democrats, Social Christians, and Catholic Action, although certain elements within these ideologies (particularly those elements tied to campesino organizations) became more "political" and more combative. Consequently, the Christian Democratic, Social Christian, and Social Democratic movements began to rupture ideologically.

A new kind of *indigenismo* also began to emerge during this second cycle. This "Maya renaissance" would later spawn "Maya nationalism" and the pan-Maya movement, which really began to flourish only after 1985 (see below). Among Mayas and in popular organizations consisting of Mayas, there was a new emphasis on Maya ideals and concerns and a rejection of Western ideologies and solutions imposed from outside. This new indigenous ideological influence was the most important development within the cooperative movement during the second cycle.

*Internal Structure.* Cooperatives during the first cycle of violence were intimately tied to USAID and the promises of developmentalism. Even cooperatives sponsored through Catholic Action were using organizational models provided by USAID and other international agencies. Some aspects of these models revealed themselves to be inappropriate by the mid-1970s. Savings and loan cooperatives (the dominant type during the early 1960s) were increasingly difficult to maintain because of the poverty of the participants. Indigenous subsistence farmers with many immediate critical needs were unable to save enough capital to keep the credit unions running, and in many instances these same campesinos were unable to repay loans.[31] Consequently, as credit cooperatives declined, consumer and agricultural cooperatives became more powerful by the end of the first cycle and the beginning of the second cycle.[32] However, even these cooperatives, especially the cooperatives organized by smaller landholders, began to go bankrupt and the Guatemalan government and USAID systematically dismantled them. USAID had an explicit agreement with the Guatemalan government to favor the creation of new, larger cooperatives over the continued support of smaller, weak cooperatives (many of which were thought to be too "political" because of their association with Catholic Action).[33] The government occasionally jailed cooperative leaders, and more often delayed their legal dealings.[34] This situation proved to be dialectical—as disillusionment of local leaders grew they became increasingly politicized.

The larger agricultural cooperatives of the 1970s had a much wider base of functions than did the smaller credit cooperatives of the first cycle. In addition to providing access to loans, agricultural cooperatives also sponsored bulk purchases of agricultural inputs (seeds, fertilizers, etc.), which reduced costs. Like the labor organizations which attempted to abolish or mitigate the labor contractor system, the agricultural cooperatives were also interested in eliminating middlemen in the sale of their surplus produce. The larger cooperatives also had direct access to international markets through USAID. Some of the cooperatives had access to technical assistance as well. Because of the broader array of functions, the larger agricultural cooperatives had larger and more complicated systems of horizontal organization on the local level than did the earlier credit unions.

As FENACOAC, largely a federation of credit cooperatives created in the 1960s, became associated with the Christian Democratic Party, USAID began sponsoring a new federation of cooperatives, the Federation of Regional Agricultural Cooperatives (FECOAR), which was founded in 1972 and received its legal status in 1973. Reflecting the general trend in the movement, FECOAR was a federation of agricultural cooperatives (whereas FENACOAC had been a federation of credit cooperatives during the 1960s).

Because so many of the cooperatives of the 1970s were tied to the government-sponsored colonization schemes, the new agricultural cooperatives were more directly tied to INTA and the National Institute for Cooperatives (INACOP). Thus the government (through INTA and INACOP) became the top rung of the vertical hierarchy during the second cycle of violence. This arrangement would prove to have disastrous consequences for the cooperative movement.

*Mobilization Strategy.* While the functions of cooperatives became increasingly complicated, many of the services they provided became increasingly political, as a result of the dialectic of violence in which they operated. The connection of the cooperatives to the fertilizer debacle and the disappearance of national and international technical support, and the violence and disillusionment associated with the colonization schemes gave cooperative leaders an increasing sense of political responsibility toward the campesinos who participated. This disillusionment and the sense of betrayal that came out of the decimation of the colonization programs was accompanied by an ideological shift precipitated by the Christian "consciousness-raising" programs (concientización) of the 1960s. One priest and cooperative leader claimed that by the mid-1970s cooperatives had really been transformed into "popular organizations through which people were beginning to take control of important aspects of their lives."[35] The result was that material incentives became irrelevant (especially in the face of violence) and political incentives took precedence. By the time of the reactionary terror, cooperatives were already adopting a mobilization strategy that involved promises of political power. Organized campesinos demanded agrarian reform for the first time since 1952.

*The Destruction of the Cooperative Movement.* Despite the ideological shifting and the similarities between cooperatives of the 1970s and the more explicitly political campesino leagues, the participation of USAID officials and Peace Corps workers made the activities of the cooperatives seem less political and more "safe" than the activities of other popular organizations.

The perception of safety proved to be erroneous. The cooperative movement was particularly targeted during the reactionary terror perpetrated by the administrations of Lucas García and Ríos Montt (1978–83). Cooperatives were often converted into instruments used by the military to spy on the highland indigenous population. Since cooperatives were required to apply for juridical recognition and INACOP kept records on all of the agricultural cooperatives in the country, the security forces were provided with ready-made access to information on organized campesinos. INACOP became the headquarters for collecting the names of community leaders so that they could be eliminated.[36] Between 1978 and 1984 security forces murdered thousands of cooperative leaders, and most cooperatives, including those under USAID supervision, and the towns in which they operated were destroyed.

### GUERRILLA ORGANIZATIONS

Between 1968 and 1972, guerrilla leaders began to reevaluate their failure to take power during the first cycle of violence. According to Suzanne Jonas, the failure of the FAR in the 1960s was not attributed to poor military strategy so much as it was deemed a political failure. FAR documents from 1973 corroborate this assessment. The FAR leadership conceded that campesino masses were never fully integrated into the struggle. The repression, in effect, only further isolated the guerrillas from the popular sectors (*la base*).[37] In addition to the personalistic divisions which split the leadership and the rank and file of the organizations, the guerrillas blamed the leadership of the PGT for their failure. They had "subordinated their decision-making" to the PGT according to Jonas, which resulted in the bourgeois political orientation of the struggle and the decision not to organize in the predominantly indigenous central and western highlands during the first cycle. The PGT had viewed Mayas paternalistically and firmly believed that because of their "backwardness" they lacked revolutionary potential during the 1960s.[38] During the second cycle of violence, the FAR remained separate from the PGT.

The remnants of Turcios Lima's Edgar Ibarra Guerrilla Front (FGEI) reentered Guatemala from Mexico in 1972 and began to reorganize in the predominantly indigenous Ixcán region of El Quiché. This guerrilla front became the Guerrilla Army of the Poor (EGP). The EGP organized into three distinct fronts: the Ho Chi Minh

Front (centered in El Quiché), the Ernesto Che Guevara Front (centered in Huehuetenango), and the Augusto César Sandino Front (also in El Quiché).[39]

Another splinter group of the FAR which was also critical of the racist and paternalistic tendencies of the guerrilla movement of the 1960s began operating clandestinely in the area around Lake Atitlán and on the southern coastal plain in 1971. This organization called itself FAR/Western Regional (Regional de Occidente) in the early 1970s. Eventually the group changed its name to the Revolutionary Organization of the People in Arms (ORPA) and in 1979 they emerged publicly.[40]

The PGT barely survived organizationally during the 1970s. Its leadership role was rejected by the most successful guerrilla groups, and the PGT continued to suffer from the personalistic divisions which defined them in the 1960s. The PGT did continue "the struggle" within small segments of the urban labor force, and among proletarianized workers on the southern coast. According to Jonas, "the transformation from a Leninist party to a [more Guatemalan] political military organization was a far greater adjustment for the PGT than for any of the younger organizations."[41]

FAR, the EGP, ORPA, and the PGT united into a national broad-front organization, the Guatemalan National Revolutionary Unity (URNG), in January 1982. This organization did not imply ideological homogeneity of the member organizations, or even a common horizontal substructure, but it did represent a new degree of flexibility and cooperation. The ability of these new organizations to put aside rigid ideological differences stands in contrast to the original FAR, which was supposed to represent the alliance between the M-13 and the PGT. The organization of the URNG was for the guerrilla movement what CNUS was for the labor movement.

*Ideology and Tactics.* In general the new guerrilla organizations of the second cycle were less dogmatically tied to European ideologies, and more responsive to the indigenous base than they had been during the first cycle. The older organizations, FAR and the PGT, were less influenced by Maya ideas and more influenced by the revolutionary experience in Vietnam, but the newer organizations, the EGP and ORPA, attempted to respond, on some level, to the ethnic reality of Guatemala. The increased attention paid to racism and Maya worldviews was, however, limited. And Maya nationalists accused the guerrillas of being "out of touch" with Maya campesinos.

FAR continued its commitment to armed struggle during the second cycle, but its guerrilla base was comparatively small and concentrated in the Petén. Like the PGT, FAR also worked within urban trade unions in Guatemala City and Chimaltenango. Its ideological tendencies were less dogmatic during the second cycle. Like both Mao and Ho Chi Minh, FAR leaders spent considerable time engaged in educating (or propagandizing) the masses.[42]

Like FAR, the EGP was also influenced by the example of prolonged peoples' struggle in Southeast Asia, particularly Vietnam. Consequently it launched its own "prolonged peoples' war." The EGP worked for three years developing a committed popular base among the campesino masses before committing its first public act in 1975—the assassination of Luís Arenas Barrera. Arenas was a large landholder in the Ixcán area who was known as the Tiger, or the Jaguar, of Ixcán for his brutality and cruelty toward campesinos.[43]

The ideological leadership of the EGP thoughtfully considered the "Indian question" throughout the 1970s in order to develop its evolving understanding of a multiethnic Guatemala toward which it was striving. And its revolutionary vision did openly seek to integrate indigenous concerns of ethnic oppression with the more general concerns of economic exploitation (or class struggle). The EGP, while clearly still influenced by Marxism, was also slowly but profoundly influenced by the indigenous perspective of its members during the 1970s.[44]

ORPA began carefully and clandestinely developing its base of support in 1971 and began to commit public acts of violence in September 1979. ORPA, like the EGP, was influenced by Marxism, but, again, it was even more influenced by its indigenous base. It officially stood for "an end to racism" and "the development of indigenous culture."[45] Further emphasizing its autonomy, ORPA officially rejected association with the Soviet line. Geographically it complemented the EGP, operating in the central western highlands and among the indigenous populations in San Marcos, Toctonicapán, Quezaltenango, and Solola (in the area surrounding Atitlán).[46]

The decision to move the revolutionary struggle to the western highlands (the altiplano) was essentially a strategic and tactical decision determined by geographical and demographic considerations. But the effect of this move was to force the revolutionary movement to address the Indian question. Ethnic consciousness, however, developed and evolved slowly within the guerrilla movement during the 1970s, '80s, and '90s.[47] Despite the real consideration of ethnic politics by the EGP and ORPA, the political and ideological distance between the guerrillas and the representatives of Maya nationalism and the pan-Maya movement were starkly evident during and since the peace process and the signing of the peace accords.

The PGT maintained its conservative posture and its links to Soviet-line communism for most of the second cycle. The organization rejected the armed struggle until 1978, when part of the leadership nucleus of the PGT broke away from the organization and took up arms. The rest of the organization joined the armed struggle in 1982.[48]

*Internal Structure.* While guerrilla organizations of the second cycle maintained their vertical military structure for the most part, the main structural development during the second cycle was the increased ability to cooperate and coordinate actions. This new-found coordinative ability culminated in the formation of the URNG in 1983.

There was also a considerable amount of cooperation at the local level between the EGP and ORPA and the nonrevolutionary popular movement. This cooperation took the form of technical assistance, self-defense programs, and similar development and defense projects. During the high point of the guerrilla resistance (1979–80), when the EGP and ORPA combined with more than 3,000 active combatants, the space for legal popular resistance was rapidly diminishing because of the evolution of political violence and the beginning of reactionary terror. The guerrilla movement was a sort of place holder for resistance during this period. ORPA in particular forged relationships with other popular movements (especially at the local, rural level), and changed its strategy from one of open visible opposition to one of invisible organization, and active resistance.[49] At the same time, the prominent labor and popular leader Miguel Angel Albizures believes that the guerrilla have failed to recognize the importance of the autonomous resurgence of the legal popular struggle, which was a separate process from the growth and resurgence of the revolutionary movement. That is, Albizures takes issue with the argument, outlined by Ricardo Falla and others, that the legal popular struggle derived its strength and motivation from the revolutionary struggle.[50]

On an immediate level, the internal structure of the various guerrilla fronts, organizations (the EGP, ORPA, the PGT, etc.), and the URNG as a whole did not diverge from its traditional vertical military hierarchy. There was no real transformation in decision making or power structure within the movement as there was for other categories of popular organizations. The URNG and all its components functioned as military organizations. Their goal was to take control of the state through military force. This reality is perhaps what prohibited a creative internal restructuring of the guerrilla organizations. This has indeed had ramifications on the democratization process in Guatemala. The URNG has had some difficulty in making the structural transition to an internally democratic participatory political party.[51]

*Mobilization Strategy.* FAR organized among elements of urban labor, and on the plantations of the southern coastal plain, and in the Petén. In contrast to their mobilization strategy in the 1960s, during the second cycle FAR concentrated on educating the popular sectors and giving the rank and file a personal stake in the struggle.[52]

Like the new FAR, the EGP rejected the PGT's evaluation and analysis of the revolutionary potential of the indigenous population. The EGP mobilized the same campesinos who had been politically influenced by changing labor relations, the Church, and education—the same campesinos who made up the nucleus of CUC.[53]

ORPA was also committed to the political organization of the indigenous campesinos. More than 90 percent of the membership of the ORPA was indigenous, as well as much of the local leadership. Nevertheless, its national leadership was still predominantly ladino.[54] And again, this was a period of evolving ethnic consciousness on the part of the organizational leadership.[55] And ORPA, more than EGP, took the question of ethnic consciousness and racism more seriously. Raul Molina claims that the EGP viewed the indigenous base as a potential and real ally of the revolutionary struggle, while ORPA increasingly came to view the indigenous campesino as the protagonist of the revolutionary struggle in Guatemala.[56]

The PGT was a "remnant organization" during the 1970s and '80s. The PGT continued to mobilize within urban trade unions, student groups, and to a lesser degree within trade unions on the southern coast and on the Atlantic coast.[57] This mobilization strategy, which ignored campesinos, proved weak as the PGT attracted a very small following during this period.[58]

*Successful Counterinsurgency.* In 1982 when Ríos Montt came to power through a military coup, the tide began to turn against the guerrilla organizations. Ríos Montt, largely through terror and genocide, managed to achieve a near military victory over the guerrilla organizations which was more or less complete by 1985.[59] Despite great casualties and military defeat, the URNG and all its member organizations managed to survive as organizations. This outcome stands in contrast to the complete dissolution of guerrilla organizations after the first cycle of violence.

A BRAND NEW BROAD-FRONT ORGANIZATION:
THE CUC

The second cycle of violence prompted trade unions, cooperatives, and guerrilla organizations to modify their ideologies, structures, and mobilization strategies in significant ways, but this violence also prompted a completely new organizational model—a broad-front organization organized by and for campesinos which included elements of the three other types of organizations, but was nevertheless innovative and distinct.

The beginnings of the Committee for Campesino Unity (CUC) lie within a cluster of Christian base communities in the municipio of Santa Cruz del Quiché in the early 1970s.[60] At the same time that religious communities and cooperatives were becoming increasingly politicized, "associations" for the promotion of ethnic awareness were also emerging in the Quiché. In 1971 the Association for Maya-Quiché Culture (Asociación pro Cultura Maya-Quiché) was founded, and in 1973 the Association of Initiators of Quiché Ideals appeared. These groups, in alliance with the religious communities, made up what would be the base of CUC. CUC members and social scientists have attributed this "stimulation of conscience" to the work of Catholic Action and the fact that for the first time a number of indigenous young people had access to secondary and even university education. These young indigenous students returned to their communities in the mid-seventies with organizational enthusiasm and new ideas.[61]

The formation of CUC was greatly influenced by three events of the mid 1970s: the earthquake, the founding of CNUS and the vision of CNUS leaders Miguel Angel Albizures and Mario López Larrave, and the Ixtahuacán miners' strike. CUC began to take the form of a national organization after the 1976 earthquake, when individual communities began to coordinate their relief efforts nationally. Groups of both Indians and ladinos traveled in brigades to neighboring communities to help with the reconstruction effort. The experience of developing reconstruction committees in small communities had multiple effects. It aided in the development of political organizational skills that could be transferred to the national level, and it stimulated the development of leaders. It also created a feeling of optimism, as campesinos saw the effectiveness of their work. Most important, the reconstruction effort fostered cooperation between indigenous peoples and ladinos. This idea of true campesino solidarity was the hallmark of CUC.[62]

With the advent of CNUS, these campesinos came into contact with more labor organizers than they had since the Revolution. It was the dream of Albizures and López Larrave to create a united labor movement of workers and campesinos in the model of the CGTG and the CNCG (the two largest labor federations of the revolutionary period). Accordingly both FASGUA and the CNT began to focus on rural organization in 1976. The number of affiliated rural leagues and unions increased tremendously, particularly after the miners' strike, which brought many campesinos into direct contact with the labor movement.

*Ideology and Tactics.* In their General Assembly of April 1979, CUC defined itself in the following manner:

> CUC is an organization of youths, children, old people, men, women, indigenous people, and ladinos. It is our hope that we

encompass the decisions, the general will, and the best interests of all rural workers. For many years we, as campesinos, have been searching for a way in which to organize ourselves to be able to fight for our basic rights.

(1) CUC should have a *clear head* in order to properly analyze the situation of the campesino, and to know who are our friends and who are our enemies. . . .

(2) CUC should have a *heart of solidarity* because our organization was born to unite all campesinos. . . . CUC is one step further toward worker-campesino solidarity. This alliance should be the motor and the heart of the struggle for liberation for all of the people of Guatemala.

(3) CUC should have a *raised fist* because we have learned that exploited workers only achieve their rights with the force of action brought about by their organizations. Workers do not gain anything by humiliating themselves in the face of promises, laws, and lies. . . . [63]

The slogan "clear head, heart of solidarity, and a raised fist for the rural worker" became the centerpiece of CUC ideology. It is significant that CUC statements and publications are free of ideological dogmatism. Its ideology of "clear-headedness" is, in a sense, a non-ideology, inasmuch as ready-made European ideologies prohibit unity ("hearts of solidarity"). Despite its rejection of dogmatic ideology, CUC—with its "raised fist"—is nonetheless radical in its posture.

It defined its goals in terms of certain basic rights to which campesinos felt entitled. These rights included: (1) the right to life, (2) the right to land, (3) the right to work for decent wages, (4) the right to fair prices for basic goods, (5) the right to just working conditions, (6) the right to organize, and (7) the right to culture (freedom from discrimination and respect for indigenous customs and language). [64]

CUC often mentioned the culpability of various government

institutions such as INTA and BANDESA (Bank of Agricultural Development) in its public manifestos and demonstrations. CUC called for a more just system of land tenure, and was even instrumental in organizing local groups to fight for their lands and titles in the Guatemalan legal system. However, given the secret nature of CUC, they did not have much success in this area. The major success of CUC involved the demands for higher wages and better working conditions for the campesino proletariat, most of whom worked on the Pacific coastal plantations, many as migrant laborers. The most important activity coordinated by CUC was a strike on several sugar and cotton plantations in February and March 1980.[65] This strike was precipitated by the tragic events at the Spanish embassy in Guatemala City earlier in the same year.

A group of twenty-nine campesinos organized by CUC came to Guatemala City in January 1980 to protest the army occupation of the department of El Quiché. The campesinos had decided that they would occupy various embassies as a means of mobilizing international support. When they occupied the Spanish embassy, they hoped to be given political asylum in Spain and thereby publicize their struggle abroad. The Guatemalan police stormed the embassy on 31 January. Twenty-eight of the campesinos were killed in the embassy when the army bombed the building and started a fire; the sole campesino survivor was later assassinated in the hospital.

This massacre had important ramifications for the campesino population, CUC, and the Lucas government. Guatemalans were outraged, and support for the campesinos became widespread after this incident. Rigoberta Menchú said that "never in all [Guatemala's] history had the people been so militant on every level."[66] CUC announced that it had initiated "an accelerated process of mass organization."[67] A meeting was held in Iximche, organized by members of CUC, in which every ethnic group in Guatemala was represented. At the meeting the CUC members vowed vengeance for the blood of the martyrs.[68]

*Internal Structure.* The formation of a new type of organization was initially considered at the end of 1976 by a group of campesinos from different communities in the Quiché. These discussions were influenced by the campesinos' prior experiences with different types of organizations. Some of these campesinos were already organized into campesino leagues and cooperatives. They wanted a national organization that included all kinds of poor campesinos—mozos colonos, jornaleros, and small landholders. They wanted to include women and children. They did not want to form a trade union–type organization that would have to make lists of members and register with the government to receive legal recognition. This, they reasoned, would only lead to a targeted violent reprisal. These campesinos wanted a new type of organization—they wanted to create their own organizational structure. "We wanted an organization that would be of *all* the campesinos, of all indigenous people, but not only the Indians, but ladinos as well, and all rural workers . . . an organization for all of us together. We wanted an organization that would be able to fight for our needs, for the rights of the campesinos."[69] What they wanted required a secret organization.[70] They completely rejected the traditional role of a corporate interest group.

CUC emerged from the grassroots at a time when there was a need for unity, and at a time when the urban working class also desired a closer bond to the rural proletariat. The importance of CUC was its new vision for rural organization as articulated by the rural, primarily indigenous rank and file.

On 14 and 15 April 1978, a group of campesino representatives from Chimaltenango, El Quiché, Suchitepéquez, and Escuintla met to prepare for the public participation of their organization in the May Day rally two weeks later. Many of these founding members were members of the campesino leagues which had remained with CNUS when the FCG withdrew (under the auspices of CLAT). It was at this meeting in mid-April that this group of campesinos decided to formally organize and name their organization the Committee for Campesino Unity, or CUC.[71] The major issues that CUC addressed at this founding meeting were the forced military conscription of campesinos,[72] the legal prohibition against cutting down trees (which hindered the highland campesinos' ability to collect firewood), the general loss of land, and their opposition to certain government agencies such as INTA and BANDESA.[73] Ten days later, on 24 April, CUC released the first statement of its new organizational status, which stated the committee's purpose:

> It is not a federation or a new labor central; it is a "committee." The only thing that it requires of its members is that they present themselves with honor, conviction, sacrifice, and constancy to our collective task—the struggle for the cause of rural workers. And they should also be ready to fight for the interests of all the exploited in Guatemala.[74]

The May Day appearance would be the first time that their organization, which had existed on an informal basis for some time,[75] publicly would acknowledge its existence. Although its membership and its structure remained "secret," the public emergence of CUC marked the beginning of a more combative stance. When CUC marched in the May Day parade, it was the first time that Guatemalans had seen indigenous campesinos march side by side with ladinos, and it was the first time that there was mass participation of women and children in an organized workers' demonstration. Pablo Ceto, an Ixil and a leader of CUC, said: "The surprise was in seeing our rural compañeros [comrades] parading in their traditional dress: Quiché, Cakchiquel, Tzutuhil, Mam, Kekchi . . . we all marched together. The indigenous people had begun to have a presence in the national political struggle."[76]

After joining CNUS in June 1978, CUC developed a formalized— although highly localized—organizational structure. The campesinos were organized into local committees, which were in turn organized into Local Coordinating Bodies. The Local Coordinating Bodies were organized into Regional Coordinating Bodies, which sent representatives to the executive branch, called the National Coordinating Body. The reasoning behind the traditional complex bureaucratic structure was that it helped the local communities overcome the *patria chica* phenomenon.[77] It also created a certain amount of vulnerability to violence, and consequently there is no uniform vertical organizational structure of the contemporary CUC. Moreover, the horizontal administrative organization of CUC varies over time and between localities. This is a means of prohibiting governmental and military authorities from gathering intelligence about the organizational structure of CUC.[78]

There were many notable leaders of CUC during the late 1970s and early 1980s. Among the most important were Emeterio Toj Medrano, the announcer of "Radio Quiché," Pablo Ceto, an Ixil from Nebaj who had studied agronomy in San Carlos, and Domingo Hernández Ixcoy and Efraín Rosales, catechists and teachers. These men were all educators in basic literacy programs that had been coordinated through Catholic Action. Also among the more famous leaders of CUC were Victor and Rigoberta Menchú. Victor Menchú was one of the founders of CUC, and he was killed during the massacre at the Spanish embassy on 31 January 1980. His daughter Rigoberta Menchú, also an active CUC leader, published a testimony of her life in 1983 that has now become a classic personal account of the indigenous struggle and Guatemalan violence.[79] Ms. Menchú was also the recipient of the 1992 Nobel Peace Prize. This award lent considerable international credibility to CUC.

*Mobilization Strategy.* The networking system of CUC was "powerful and extensive" according to José Manuel Fernández. Like Rigoberta Menchú, many organizers became multilingual in the process of coordinating the political activities of different indigenous communities. CUC also pioneered the use of migrant workers as organizers.

Permanent workers on the Pacific coast were generally more organized than migrant workers. Despite this, CUC focused its efforts on migrant workers because they migrated between farms and between the Pacific coast and the highlands and could therefore become an ethnic and geographical "link" for CUC. Since overt mobilization could not safely take place, these migrant laborers proved to be a useful way of secretly creating national links. This was another example of innovation in mobilization strategy. During the fall of 1979, CUC initiated an intense campaign to win the support of these migrant workers. The objective of this campaign was to elevate the political awareness of all campesinos, and to mobilize more local communities into CUC. The primarily indigenous migrant workers were taught to demand a wage of thirty quetzals per month, comfortable and safe transportation, decent dwellings, sufficient nutritious food including meat at least every third day, medicine in the case of illness, and a minimum wage of Q3 per ton of cane or 100 pounds of coffee or cotton. They were taught by CUC organizers to demand these conditions in advance, to organize themselves as soon as they arrived at a plantation and to try and initiate a collective dialogue, and to be ready to defend themselves forcefully if necessary.[80]

The problems that had traditionally hindered the unification of the distinct ethnic groups were overcome to some degree by CUC. It was able to penetrate the Pacific coast, not only by means of migratory workers,[81] but also through organizers sent to the coast for the specific purpose of creating new local committees. It also (somewhat less successfully) penetrated the Eastern highlands.

Campesinos had begun to mobilize in the aftermath of the earthquake and the miners' strike. CUC as a formal organization came into being after the mobilization process was well underway. This process was begun in Christian base communities (CEBs), campesino leagues (trade unions), and in informal community organizations.

The publication of *De sol a sol* was only one tool of mobilization that predated the official organization and public emergence of CUC. CUC was born on the assumption that there already existed a politicized rank-and-file base for the movement. In other words, CUC was created with an already mobilized base.

While the incentives employed by CUC were primarily political, the CUC also advocated for agrarian reform, higher wages, worker protection legislation, and even attempted to provide some measure of physical protection for its members. CUC organized a "commission of self-defense," which organized and sponsored local self-defense organizations. The function of these local groups closely paralleled the urban "self-defense groups" organized by CNUS. Physical protection is clearly both a political and a material incentive.[82] After the massacre at the Spanish embassy, CUC decided to use this obvious and public example of terrorist violence perpetrated by the state in order to stage the largest and most significant mobilization of campesinos since 1954.

*The CUC Sugar Strike.* In addition to planning the strike through propaganda and organization, CUC staged several small strikes and organized many collective demands on coffee and sugar farms from December 1979 through February 1980 in preparation for the general strike. In December CUC also completed an economic survey in Escuintla to determine the basic monetary requirements for a typical campesino family living on a plantation. They determined that a family of six needed a minimum of Q4.40 per day to cover nutritional needs, and Q8.00 to cover all basic needs. In January 1980 CUC issued a statement asking for the support of CNUS and other popular sectors in their demands for an increase in the agricultural minimum wage. The wage had been frozen at Q1.12 per 100 pounds of cotton, or per ton of sugar cane, and Q1.05 per 100 pounds of coffee. Approximately eight hours of steady work are required for one individual to harvest these amounts. CUC was demanding an overall increase to Q5. In well-reasoned and articulate arguments, CUC argued that the minimum wage had remained artificially low despite increased agricultural productivity and increased profits, and despite inflation of the prices of basic goods. Soon after this statement was issued, CUC announced its intention to hold a general strike.[83] In calling for this strike, the major theme was national unity: "We know that the only way is to face our challenge united for combat: both Indians and poor ladinos, rancheros, those who work permanently on the coastal plantations, and migrants from the highlands. We are all united by the same exploitation."[84] The strike they were planning was illegal since all agricultural strikes were prohibited during the harvest by the Labor Code.

The massacre at the Spanish embassy triggered the beginning of the strike. One of the campesinos killed in the incident was CUC leader Juan José Yos, the head of the Regional Commission of Coordination, and one of those actively participating in the organization of the strike. His death provided impetus to begin the strike immediately. On 18 February cane cutters on the Tehuantepec farm in Santa Lucía Cotzumalguapa stopped working.[85] On 19 February these workers began going to neighboring farms to urge solidarity and to set up commissions to travel to other plantations. Within a week, several other sugar plantations had joined the strike, and some mill workers were also participating. By 20 February workers from over sixty farms were striking.[86] The strike spread through three departments: Escuintla, Suchitepéquez, and Retalhuleu. Strikers instigated acts of sabotage. They slashed truck tires, stopped trucks carrying sugar and cotton, and set fire to several fields of cane. Highland campesinos sent food and staged local demonstrations in support of the strikers. By the end of February, nearly 80,000 people were on strike.[87] The strike eventually halted operations on eighty sugar plantations, fourteen cotton plantations, and eight sugar refineries.[88] CUC continued to emphasize unity: "The landlords and the repressive forces asked us to choose our representatives, our leaders to dialogue with them. We responded that we were all representatives and leaders. That's how we applied self-defense to protect our leaders and our struggle. All of us shouted out the response, so that none of us would stand out."[89]

The workers on seventy farms presented petitions to the government with the help of CNUS on 23 February. On the 25th, they began negotiations between workers' representatives, landholders, and government representatives. While this was taking place, thousands of campesinos were occupying several sugar mills. On 3 March the government raised the minimum wage to Q3.20.[90] Fernández calls this strike "the most significant [event] in the history of the campesino movement in Guatemala."[91]

In response to the fact that the minimum wage was not raised to the level originally demanded (Q5) and the fact that the new minimum wage was not enforced on the coffee farms, CUC staged another general strike on fifteen coffee farms during the fall of 1980. This strike was less successful than the sugar strike had been. The campesinos were demanding that the government enforce a law that already existed, so symbolic victory was ruled out. Moreover, the climate of repression contributed to a relatively silent response from Guatemalan journalists.[92]

*The Continued Evolution of CUC.* In January 1981 CUC joined a new mass front organization called the 31st of January's Popular Front (FP-31). The FP-31 represented CUC and five other clandestine organizations, both urban and rural. It was the founding of this organization that marked CUC's official ties to guerrilla organizations. After 1982, because of the large death toll within the rank and file, CUC went underground. It reorganized in 1986 over the issue of forced participation in the civil patrols.

The organization after 1986 has been even more flexible than it had been before. Especially on the local level, there is considerable variance in internal organization. Ideologically it has become more flexible, incorporating members of a wide variety of ideological, religious, and cultural tendencies. It does not limit itself to any particular goals or tactics, but adopts new ones as they become important or useful. Despite this flexibility, the new CUC is committed to the vision of a new society in which ladino and Maya have equal rights and equal opportunities.[93] This is a radical vision for Guatemalans.

CUC's contributions to campesino labor organization were numerous. It overcame traditional ethnic and linguistic barriers to organization that had never before been successfully surmounted, and CUC rank and file created a mass movement from the ground up. But unlike the numerous peasant or Indian rebellions that are scattered throughout Guatemalan history, CUC had an enduring political character and complex and successful organizational techniques.

## Maya Nationalism

In the early 1970s Maya nationalism began to emerge in Guatemala through organizations like the Association for Maya-Quiché Culture, and the Association of Initiators of Maya Ideas (see above). In addition to providing one of the impetuses for the formation of CUC, this new emphasis on Maya ethnic awareness also contributed to a political movement that was seen as a Maya alternative to the traditional ladino left. Maya nationalists were not active in confrontational politics during the period in question, but they did begin to reemerge as a political organization after 1985. According to Carol Smith there are two approaches to modern Maya politics. The first is the more recent indigenista approach (Maya nationalism or pan-Maya activism), which has been represented by various umbrella organizations, including the Guatemalan Council of Maya Organizations (COMG), the Coordination of Organizations of the Maya People of Guatemala (COPMAGUA), and the National Coordination of Indigenous and Campesino Organizations (CONIC). And other approach is the one that is more relevant here, rooted in what has become the traditional "popular" approach, which is the approach of CUC and its current indigenous umbrella organization, Majawil Q'ij.[94]

Those who have adopted the indigenista approach believe that Maya are in error when they ally themselves with non-Maya, and that ladino leftists have manipulated Maya into participating in a sort of confrontational politics which is not really "the Maya way."[95] According to Carol Smith the Maya nationalists emphasize the following three points with regard to the guerrilla struggle in which large numbers of Maya have participated:

(1) ladino leaders were so consumed by class (as opposed to ethnic) issues that they did not even know the most likely areas and issues for Maya recruitment;

(2) the ladino leadership was unable to take seriously any cultural issues of importance to Maya, like Maya women's clothing; and

(3) Maya take tremendous risks if they follow non-Maya leadership in any political venture, evident in the terrible costs paid by Maya "innocents" in the latest round of state repression [second-cycle reactionary assault].[96]

The Maya nationalists believe that the Maya who were victims of the genocidal campaign of the late 1970s were manipulated by both the armed forces and the ladino leaders of the guerrilla struggle. They claim that Maya do not want to participate in this type of armed conflict if given a choice. The COMG is concerned with political issues as they relate to the ethnic integrity and ethnic autonomy of the Maya people. They are interested in preserving native languages and dress, community forms, and Maya cosmology as legitimate forms of expression in Guatemala. They claim that ladinos, of both the left and the right, have belittled these important cultural expressions. On a general level they claim that the traditional left and the popular movement has been unable to understand the real significance and pervasiveness of racism in Guatemala.[97]

Most Maya nationalists are "literate, self-proclaimed Maya" according to Smith and other critics of the movement.[98] Critics argue that this is a description that fits few of the most exploited Maya, and that their economic status could explain their avoidance of a strictly class-based analysis. Ricardo Cajas Mejía, an important leader in the Maya nationalist movement explained their approach well:

If we allow our interests to be misrepresented by people who are not even Maya, we will lose one of the few chances we have to be heard [during the debate which surrounds the quincentenary]. And our agenda will be confused with those pursuing a program of direct and violent confrontation with the state, which will put us all in danger.[99]

The popular approach of CUC is also interested in eliminating racism, and it is devoted to addressing ethnic issues that are specific to indigenous people—but CUC members also see themselves in an alliance with other poor and exploited nonindigenous people. According to Rigoberta Menchú, CUC is inclusive because there are ladino campesinos who, through no fault of their own, have lost their ethnic identity.[100] Beyond this there is a recognition of a certain commonality of interests among *all* poor and exploited Guatemalans, particularly campesinos. To affirm this does not have to imply the denial of ethnicity. For indigenous people to ally their interests with nonindigenous people behind a popular political banner does not have to imply that the Maya in the alliance are being "used" or "manipulated."[101]

## Conclusion

Popular organizations were highly innovative in the 1970s. By the end of the cycle, these organizations had been molded by the violent atmosphere in which they had operated for more than two decades. This period, the height of the second cycle of violence, produced the most significant changes in popular organization in modern Guatemalan history. Contemporary organizations no longer find it necessary to go back to 1954 for lessons and inspiration. The lessons of the 1970s are bitter but they lend themselves to a contemporary approach to organization that is both more pragmatic and radical. Popular organizations today are decidedly more democratic and less vertical in their organizational structure. They are more innovative and creative in their mobilization strategy. They are more political, and more ideologically creative and less dogmatic as well. The lessons learned during the worst periods of political violence uniquely qualify these organizations, these representatives of Guatemalan civil society, to take a leading role in the democratization process.

The history of rural popular organizations in Guatemala provided here (chapters 5 and 6) illustrates the effects of political violence on the development of popular organizations. These effects will be discussed more explicitly in chapter 7.

# Chapter Seven

## *The Effects of Violence on Popular Organizations*

VIOLENCE HAS BEEN the most important variable to shape the evolution of popular organizations in the postrevolutionary period. The evolution of popular organizations has followed a regular course through two cycles of violence. In both the first cycle of the late 1950s, 1960s, and early '70s, and the second cycle of the 1970s and early '80s, what had been thriving, broad-based campesino organizations found themselves under an attack that would decimate their memberships and radically alter their goals. As each cycle progressed from turmoil to coordinated counterattack, the organizations did enliven and fortify their responses by adapting their ideologies, structures, and mobilization strategies. But as the cycles moved toward internal war and ultimately reactionary terror, the organizations submerged. Nevertheless, due to the changes they underwent, the popular organizations which emerged after each cycle were more appropriate to the hostile environment than the organizations of the previous cycles. The modifications of ideology and tactics, structure, and mobilization strategy which occurred at regular intervals within each cycle ironically conveyed a new strength.

Many questions remain concerning the role these popular organizations should have in the construction of a newly democratic Guatemala. However, it is clear that *without* popular organizations—without civil society, as the popular movement came to be called by the 1990s[1]—Guatemala will be vulnerable to repeated cycles of violence. These organizations and their descendants are the only political actors which have real experience with democratization, and they have demonstrated their sophisticated understanding and ability to respond to violence. This chapter highlights the modifications which salient campesino organizations made to ideology and tactics, internal structure, and mobilization strategy in response to the violence of 1954–85.

## *The Evolution of Organizations within the Cycles of Violence*

Popular organizations constitute themselves during the first stage of a cycle—turmoil. In fact, the organizations become the political manifestations of popular turmoil. In both cycles we have examined, the initial stage of turmoil led to a coordinated guerrilla response (the second stage). The presence of a guerrilla insurgency launched the violence in both cycles into the third stage—internal war. During this stage some popular organizations began to shift ideologically—this tactical and ideological shifting caused internal ruptures of the popular movements of both cycles. When the violence changed into reactionary terror (the fourth and final stage), personalistic leaders were targeted and removed (assassinated). Traditionally organized popular organizations found themselves very vulnerable to "decapitation," as power and organizational legitimacy were concentrated in the hands of a small number of vulnerable leaders, and the internal structures of the organizations were both rigid and well-understood by governmental authorities. As the reactionary terror became more generalized the organizations were easily dismantled.

Experience in postrevolutionary Guatemala suggests that organizations require a full cycle to pass before they appropriately adapt their ideologies, organizational structures, and mobilization strategies to the existing environment. Although some changes were made to all these variables within the first cycle, the shape of the organizations' learning curves with regard to these variables is determined by a number of factors. Some of these factors are unique to the Guatemalan case and others are inherent characteristics of the dependent variables—ideologies, internal structures, and mobilization strategies.

The Guatemalan case is unique in that the relationship between the popular sectors and the state changed dramatically between 1954 and 1962 (when campesino trade unions first reemerged). Prior to 1954, the popular sectors had been at least partially co-opted by the revolutionary governments of Juan José Arévalo and Jacobo Arbenz (1944–54). During this period, campesinos were organized—for the first time in Guatemalan history—into sophisticated political blocs. Thus the first organizational experience for Guatemalan campesinos was carefully orchestrated by a sympathetic government. The state invited workers and campesinos to participate in the defining of policy. The government actively took the side of workers in labor disputes, and actively organized campesinos into agrarian committees. This created both a corporate constituency and a vehicle for agrarian reform and economic development.

When the revolutionary government was overthrown in 1954, the state and its military apparatus underwent a six- to eight-year transition. The military-controlled state that emerged in the mid-1960s was staunchly anticommunist and fearful of an organized popular sector, particularly organized campesinos. Because this environment was new, popular organizations were unable to properly gauge their situation vis-à-vis the state. It was not until they suffered great losses and structural breakdown during the very end of the first cycle of violence that they were able to reevaluate their ideologies and internal structures. In other words, the extent of state hostility toward popular sectors was unanticipated and difficult to react to during the first cycle.

On a general level, ideology and internal structure are more difficult variables to change than is mobilization strategy. Ideology is defined by Juan Luis Segundo as the system of means that are used to achieve certain prioritized goals. The nature of ideology is such that changing it implies a dramatic restructuring of priorities and tactics. Ideology, unlike faith, is tied to one's perception of reality and thus subject to change when material circumstances change; however, ideology is contingent upon a clear and broad understanding of the nature of material circumstances. This broad understanding of the nature of the relationship between material circumstances and the political environment in Guatemala could not be achieved until a late point in the cycle of violence, and was much easier to perceive after the cycle had run its course.

A mechanistic organizational structure[2] can only be changed within existing organizations through a deliberate, complex, and somewhat lengthy plan of action. This plan of action involves a shifting power distribution and changes in political and organizational culture. In the case of Guatemala, popular organizations had neither the expertise nor the time to make a proper diagnosis and change the internal organizational structure of groups that were already collapsing in the late 1960s.

Despite these difficulties, popular leaders who initiated the new wave of popular organizations in the mid-1970s were able to perceive how the rigidity of popular organizations contributed to their collapse during the first cycle. Thus the successful leaders intuitively chose more organic[3] organizational structures—this type of structure represented a significant break from political tradition in Guatemala.

Despite the nontraditional nature of organic organizational structure, in the business world it is a structure better suited to a rapidly changing environment, and in the political world—as has been demonstrated here—an organic structure is better suited to a violent environment.

Mobilization strategy is a simpler variable than either of the other two. It involves decisions about where potential membership lies and the methods used to encourage potential members to participate. Changing mobilization strategy does not require a complete understanding of the changing situation or dramatic changes in power distribution. To some degree, the organizations were born in response to popular turmoil; thus violence was both the initiating spark and an obvious tool for mobilization, although mobilization of campesinos was particularly challenging during the 1960s. However, as authoritative violence escalated, it ironically became a tool for popular organizations, particularly in the mid-1970s. At the point where violence became an immediate physical threat to members of popular organizations (at the reactionary terror stage), mobilization strategy had to be altered immediately if the organizations were to survive. The necessity of this change was immediately obvious.

### THE FIRST CYCLE

Popular movements during the 1960s (the first cycle) were relatively scarce, due to the legal constraints placed on organizing activity, particularly in rural areas. Despite this quietude, there was a minor resurgence of the labor movement in the campo in 1962. The most important national labor organizations in rural Guatemala during this period were the Campesino Federation of Guatemala (FCG), the Autonomous Labor Federation of Guatemala (FASGUA), and the Confederation of Guatemalan Workers (CONTRAGUA). Local cooperatives, trade unions (sindicatos), and campesino leagues (which closely resembled sindicatos) made up the base of these national labor organizations.

Relatively speaking, the cooperative movement was much more influential in the 1960s than was *sindicalismo* (trade unionism). This is reflected in levels of participation. However, even though some local cooperatives belonged to national trade union organizations, the cooperative movement was not as organized on the national level as were trade unions. There was, however, one important national cooperative organization—the National Federation of Savings and Credit Cooperatives (FENACOAC).

Two important "professional organizations" also played a role in the popular struggle of the 1960s—the Institute for the Economic and Social Development of Central America (IDESAC), and the National Squatters Movement (MONAP). These two organizations, both associated with the Christian Democrats, supervised much of the organization taking place in rural areas and marginal urban areas.

Guerrilla organizations also emerged during the 1960s after the unsuccessful 1960 military coup attempt against Ydígoras Fuentes. The disgruntled military officers, who called themselves the 13th of November Revolutionary Movement (MR-13), eventually found themselves allied with the illegal communist party (PGT). Their alliance was called the Rebel Armed Forces (FAR). The MR-13, the FAR, and the Edgar Ibarra Guerrilla Front (FGEI)—which came out of the MR-13—suffered from internal divisions and therefore had a tenuous alliance at best. Nevertheless, they were the dominant guerrilla organizations during the first cycle.

*The Effect on Ideologies and Tactics.* As demonstrated in chapter 4, the national labor federations and cooperative federations of the 1960s had a tendency to gravitate toward international "lines" or doctrines. The FCG had always been associated with the (then Conservative) Social Christians and Catholic Action, and later, through IDESAC, the FCG was heavily influenced by the Christian Democrats. FASGUA began as a Social Christian alternative to communist-inspired unions, and it was influenced by European doctrine. Later FASGUA moved to the left and allied itself with the Marxist-oriented FSM. CONTRAGUA was affiliated, albeit indirectly, with the U.S.-backed ORIT and was officially favored by USAID. The cooperative federations likewise became inextricably linked to the rabidly anticommunist ideology of both the Christian Democrats and USAID.

The guerrilla organizations were also influenced by international lines, such as Soviet-line Marxism, Trotskyism, and Guevara's *foquismo*. Ideological debate became an elite exercise with disastrous effects on the guerrilla effort.

These international affiliations signified a certain ideological loyalty to European doctrines. The international affiliations could sometimes absorb organizational energies and inhibit efforts to clarify strategies. This weakened the organizations, especially during times of violence. Many leaders within these organizations were "radicalized" because of the violence, and consequently came to object to the moderate path advocated by the international organizations that pertained to AIFLD as well as the Social Christian and Christian Democratic ideologies. Many campesino organizations began to dissolve over ideological disputes precisely when the violence had escalated into reactionary terror.

The ideological debate often centered around questions of tactics and priorities. Disagreement arose over the question of balancing and prioritizing long-term political goals (the empowerment of the popular sector) versus short term fulfillment of the immediate needs in specific local communities. Some argued that if the poor could achieve political power, then material comforts would naturally follow, and to put resources into the satisfaction of immediate needs was a Band-Aid measure that would only divert energy and resources from the long-term goals. That is, they advocated a *national* strategy. Others argued that immediate needs had to be satisfied before a struggle for political power could take place. That is, they believed that questions of solidarity and long-term struggle could not be contemplated by people with empty bellies. They were advocating a *local* strategy. Although the former position was clearly the more radical of the two, campesinos clearly preferred the latter strategy during the first cycle since they received immediate benefit. Nevertheless, after those who benefited from the cooperative movement were abandoned by the Guatemalan government and USAID— and then targeted by the state security forces during the second cycle—priorities within the base shifted.

*The Effect on Internal Structures.* When labor and cooperative organizations began to organize campesinos again in the early 1960s, the internal structure of the national organizations was conditioned by the experiences of labor organizers during the Arévalo-Arbenz period. New national labor organizations had top-heavy, rigid hierarchical structures which resembled the earlier organizations. One of the labor centrals, FASGUA (the descendent of FAS), had a corporatist relationship with the Castillo Armas government. It did not emphasize the concept of labor unity because large, all-encompassing labor unions were viewed as communistically inclined. During the 1960s the organizations continued to petition the government for legal recognition ("juridical personality"). Since recognition was contingent upon an acceptable and explicitly described internal organization, a traditional rigid and hierarchical structure was the norm. As I have argued, both the imposed structure and the growing disenfranchisement caused increasing fragmentation. As the decade progressed there were fewer incentives for local organizations to join large national organizations. By the end of the cycle, many of the organizations had disintegrated, and overall membership in popular organizations was down. Thus the weaknesses of the traditional system and its vulnerability to reactionary terror became evident, but no alternative form of national organization emerged during this period.

Guerrilla organizational structures mirrored nonviolent organizations in many ways. Although clearly not corporatist, their bureaucratic arrangements were also hierarchical, and their leadership was powerful and disassociated from the rank and file. Fragmentation was also common in guerrilla organizations, and over time there was also an overall decline, and a decreased tendency toward national unity.

*The Effect on Mobilization Strategies.* Mobilization strategy of popular organizations during the 1960s was influenced by the legal definitions of the organizations and Catholic Action. During the revolutionary period, labor had a corporatistlike relationship with the government, and it took some experimentation during the 1960s in order to articulate a new more appropriate strategy for the hostile environment. The lack of clearly defined mobilization strategies was one of the weaknesses of the labor movement during the first cycle; this led to a discussion of new strategies by the late 1960s. Among these new strategies was the use of "radio schools" designed to forge links between rural communities and prepare campesinos for involvement in organizations (*educación sindical*).[4]

Despite the significant and penetrating discussion of the late 1960s, very few workers were mobilized during the first cycle. Because of the inability of these organization to mobilize potential members at the base, the labor organizations of the 1960s were top-heavy—there were too many leaders and not enough rank-and-file members.

Likewise, guerrilla organizations did not build an adequate popular base. They did not actively recruit popular sectors at all in the early 1960s. By the mid-1960s, they had modified their strategy and attempted to mobilize ladino campesinos (mostly small landholders) and students. But as shown in chapter 5, this effort proved to be too little, too late. The organizations had become so fragmented by this point that even innovative mobilization strategies were doomed to failure. Moreover, the organizations rarely recruited the popular sectors into their power structures, and had practically no mobilization strategy among highland Indians. Consequently, they had very weak popular support.

Through Catholic Action the cooperative movement imbued a greater number of people with a sense of dignity and political power. For the first time indigenous people began to participate in national politics. They found benefits from making demands on the system, and cooperatives increasingly offered political incentives (as opposed to strictly material incentives) as the decade progressed. Despite this labor and cooperative organizers often did not take into account the ethnic reality of the country.

THE SECOND CYCLE

During this latter period, the level of popular organization increased significantly. The mid-1970s was a much more active period for popular organizations. The earthquake of February 1976 was a major turning point, both for the political administration of Laugerud and for the search for a new mode of rural political organization. It sparked both new nonviolent popular organization and a wave of repression. The two most important new popular organizations of the mid-1970s were the National Trade Union Committee (CNUS) and the Campesino Unity Committee (CUC).

CNUS was the third attempt at labor unity since 1954, but one of the reasons it succeeded (unlike the other attempts) was that CNUS was not intended as a labor "central." It was a movement that came together because of the need created by violent repression, and it was organized like a political action organization (e.g., in commissions) rather than as a traditional labor federation.

CUC has its origins in the activities of Christian base communities during the early 1970s. These base communities created a level of political consciousness in rural communities that had not existed before. In addition, starting in the mid-1970s new indigenous organizations that promoted ethnic pride and political consciousness created the perception among many campesinos that it was time for a new autonomous campesino organization. Many previously isolated communities began forging crucial links during the earthquake reconstruction effort.

With the advent of CNUS, these campesinos came into contact with numerous labor organizers as CNUS was attempting to actively recruit campesinos to forge a strong worker-campesino alliance. Both FASGUA and the National Confederation of Workers (CNT)—which were both part of CNUS—began to focus on rural organization in 1976. This greatly increased the number of affiliated rural leagues and unions.

The end result of these influences was the founding of CUC in April 1978. It emerged from the grassroots at a time when the urban working class also desired a close bond to the rural proletariat, and indeed CUC allied itself with CNUS soon after its official formation. However, the importance of CUC was its new vision for rural organization as articulated by the rural, primarily indigenous rank and file—that is, a series of coordinating bodies.

New guerrilla organizations also emerged during this period, the most important being the Guerrilla Army of the Poor (EGP) and the revolutionary Organization of the People in Arms (ORPA). These two organizations emerged from the remnants of FAR, particularly the FGEI, which was the most indigenous of FAR factions. The new guerrilla organizations were composed of an indigenous majority.

*The Effect on Ideologies and Tactics.* Ideology became less rigid and dogmatic as a result of the experience acquired in the 1960s and during the early to mid-1970s. The dominant tactic was now clearly a strategy of national political power acquisition, rather than the satisfaction of immediate needs. This was largely a response to the violence. The violence itself became much more problematic than poverty, and being victimized by violence was much more directly associated with political weakness than was poverty. That is, there was no way to assure protection from violence on a strictly local, community-by-community level. Since the late 1970s, violence was recognized as a problem not easily solvable in the short term.

The violence radicalized elements within both CNUS and CUC, as evidenced by the alliance of CNUS with the FSM, and CUC's alliance with the Popular Front organization FP-31, which included guerrilla organizations. Nevertheless, the association with an international line (the path taken by the radical elements of CNUS) was more divisive than CUC's approach of allying with radical (and even violent) Guatemalan elements.

Even though CUC had similar ideological influences, it adapted more deftly to its radicalization process because of the fact that the leadership and the rank and file were and continue to be one and the same. They do not have leadership crises that revolve around the constituencies of a few personalistic men. Moreover, because the most important aspect of the ideology of CUC has been unity itself, it has maintained a great deal of organizational and ideological flexibility. This flexibility on the local level allows CUC to incorporate campesinos of many ethnic, religious, and ideological backgrounds. Imported ideologies played a very small role. CUC's ideology is more Maya than Marxist. This has proved to be key.

The guerrilla organizations were also clearly influenced by the ethnic concerns of the indigenous majority. The ideologies of both the EGP and the ORPA are distinctly Guatemalan. The ORPA went so far as to reject outright any association with a Soviet line.


*The Effect on Internal Structures.* Organizations during this period moved away from a rigid corporatist structure, toward a more participatory structure. Both CNUS (which refused to adopt the structure of a labor confederation) and CUC (with its coordinating bodies) replaced traditional structural models with more participatory ones. In addition CUC rejected the concept of legal recognition and instead chose to maintain a great deal of secrecy about its internal structure as a protective measure.

The participatory nature of both organizations is what truly distinguished them from previous labor organizations. CNUS had a coordinated organization that functioned through various "commissions." They utilized input from the rank and file through the Commission of Organization. CNUS also rejected the idea of a powerful leader (secretary general), and instead instituted a leadership cadre made up of the leaders from several different labor organizations.

In the beginning, the organization of CUC was internally hierarchical (although it clearly lacked a powerful leader), but this arrangement was dismantled after the second cycle. Since 1985 the internal structure of CUC has been more flexible, and is regularly adapted on the local level to meet the specific needs and comply with the unique traditions of local communities.[5] CUC representatives are working campesinos and not professional labor leaders.

Guerrilla organizations were also more flexible during the second cycle, especially in their relations with each other. There were four major guerrilla organizations which worked together within the umbrella organization of the URNG. The 1980 formation of this umbrella organization signaled a new tolerance for ideological difference. No organization within the URNG tried to impose its authority over another. The shifting alliances and fragmentation of the first cycle seem to have been remedied. Although guerrilla organizations did not alter their vertical hierarchies in the manner of other popular organizations, the new emphasis on unity mirrored the structural changes embodied in CNUS and CUC.

The second-cycle guerrilla organizations also recruited indigenous campesinos into the ranks of their local and regional leadership. And, although they maintained a traditional military hierarchy, the guerrilla organizations of the 1970s were still more democratic than the guerrilla organizations of the first cycle.

*The Effect on Mobilization Strategies.* Both CNUS and CUC used violence as a tool of mobilization at the beginning of cycle two. After widely publicized events such as Panzós massacre, the murders of the Coca-Cola workers, and the massacre at the Spanish embassy, there were upswings in popular organization. After a certain point, however, membership in an organization, or participation in any form of public protest, became a sure means of suicide. Thus, the organizations had to adopt new strategies in order to survive. The use of the caminata and the solidarity strike were the first of these strategies. These strategies afforded considerable press attention that in turn gave people a certain measure of protection, at least for a short period. As the rank and file of the movement came into contact with other poor people on the marches, they became much more directly involved in mobilizing other people, and in the educational (concientización) aspect of the process. CNUS also created "self-defense groups" within factories, and CUC adopted a "commission of self-defense," which sponsored smaller self-defense units on the local level. Both of these organizations were trying to adapt to the violence by providing safety to their members and potential members.[6]

CUC was clearly the most adept at concientización, as it was the only organization that survived after the second cycle. CUC spent much effort on concientización, and developed an extensive network of communication and education. CUC was particularly innovative in its use of migrant workers as educators and organizers. Many leaders became multilingual, and they urged campesinos to learn Spanish as a means of empowerment. One of the more innovative strategies was to train migrant workers to forge ties between relatively isolated communities and farms.

Guerrilla organizations also changed their mobilization strategies. The two most successful organizations, the EGP and the ORPA, chose to focus their efforts in the indigenous highlands. They steered clear of direct association with European internationals and emphasized racism as an important social problem in Guatemala. These changes represented an attempt to appeal to a broad indigenous base. They also spent years carefully developing a popular base before launching their attack. By the time they emerged publicly they had established well-developed infrastructures of campesino support.

## Conclusion

Piero Gleijeses calls Guatemalan political culture "a culture of fear," tracing this national psychological condition back to the Conquest.[7] This is both an accurate and limited characterization of Guatemala. In the short run, within a single cycle of violence, violence can have a disastrous effect on popular movements and the basic human struggle for dignity. Despite this vulnerability, popular organizations have reemerged after each violent cycle, and each time they are better adapted to the violence, and they have a more practical and paradoxically more radical long-term strategy of changing the political, social, and economic structure of Guatemala.

Nobel Peace Prize winner Rigoberta Menchú, a former member of the national directive board of CUC, said, "we have learned from our experiences." She explained how CUC emerged in 1985 with a greater degree of flexibility and strength than they had ever had ever had before.[8] "To survive all changes is your destiny. . . . men do not come to an end." Miguel Angel Asturias referred to this as "*sabiduría*

## Table 7.1
## The Effects of Violence on Popular Organizations

| | TURMOIL | COORDINATED COUNTERATTACK | INTERNAL WAR | REACTIONARY TERROR |
|---|---|---|---|---|
| Ideologies and Tactics (Cycle 1) | n.a. | n.a. | Ideological polarization | Ideological breakdown |
| Internal Structures (Cycle 1) | Popular orgs. created on existing models | Guerrilla orgs. created on existing models | n.a | Structural breakdown |
| Mobilization strategies (Cycle 1) | Turmoil used as a tool | Urban elements and some ladinized campesinos organized; political and economic incentives emphasized | Political incentives emphasized | Innovation |
| Ideologies and tactics (Cycle 2) | Popular orgs. adopt a modified ideology | "Indigenista" ideology adopted | n.a. | Some polarization and breakdown |
| Internal structures (Cycle 2) | Popular orgs. adapted to violent atmosphere | Guerrilla orgs. created on a modified mode | Structural flexibility shows strength | Some structural breakdown |
| Mobilization strategies (Cycle 2) | Turmoil used as a tool | Indigenous campesinos organized; political incentives emphasized | Campesinos receive more attention; political incentives emphasized | Mobilization strategies more innovative |

*indígena"* (indigenous wisdom). It is precisely this wisdom that has insured the ultimate survival of the modern popular struggle in Guatemala. And it is this popular struggle that will prove to be the key to the future of democratic Guatemala.

# Abbreviations in Notes and Bibliography

| | |
|---|---|
| ASIES | Asociación de Investigación y Estudios Sociales |
| CECADE | Centro de Capacitación para el Desarollo |
| CEDEP | Centro de Estudios Políticos |
| CIDE | Centro de Investigación y Docencia Económica |
| EDUCA | Editorial Universitaria Centroamericana |
| FLACSO | Facultad Latinoamericana de Ciencias Sociales |
| MARI | Middle American Research Institute |
| NACLA | North American Congress on Latin America |
| UNAM | Universidad Autónoma de México |
| USAC | Universidad de San Carlos |

# Notes

## Chapter 1

1. Juan Luís Segundo, *Faith and Ideologies* (Maryknoll, N.Y.: Orbis Books, 1984), 15–20.

2. Henry Landsberger, ed., *Latin American Peasant Movements* (Ithaca, N.Y.: Cornell University Press, 1969), 55–56.

3. The tactical decisions that an organization makes regarding mobilization are, almost by definition, conditioned by ideology.

4. See Piero Gleijeses, *Shattered Hope: The Guatemalan Revolution and the United States, 1944–1954* (Princeton, N.J.: Princeton University Press, 1992) and Suzanne Jonas, *The Battle for Guatemala: Rebels, Death Squads, and U.S. Power* (Boulder: Westview, 1991).

5. The Plan of Tegucigalpa was issued by Castillo Armas on 23 December 1953. It outlined the general goals of the *ejercito de liberación*.

6. Part of the process required for juridical personality was the registration of the leadership.

7. Decree 21 of the junta, 16 July 1954, in *Recopilación de las leyes de la Republica de Guatemala,* ed. Roberto Azurdia Alfaro (Guatemala City: Tipografía Nacional, 1960), vol. 73, p. 65; "Personería jurídica de 533 organizaciones laborales se cancela en el DAT," *El Imparcial,* 17 July 1954, p. 1.

8. Laws specifically outlawed certain organizations: the CGTG, CNCG, FSG, SAMF, STEG, the UFCO unions, the unions of the workers of Agrícola de Guatemala, the Young Democratic Alliance, the Guatemalan Women's Alliance, Grupo Saker-Ti, the Democratic University Front, PGT, PRG, PAR, PRN, and "all other political parties, groups or associations which were Arévalo-Arbenz-inspired or which figured into the service of the communist cause." Decree 48 of the junta, 10 August 1954, in

*Recopilación de la leyes,* vol. 73, p. 84; "Organizaciones obreras, partidos y entidades con afinidad roja," *El Imparcial,* 11 August 1954, p. 1; Mario López Larrave, *Breve historia del movimiento sindical guatemalteco* (Guatemala: Editorial Universitaria, 1979), 49; Brian Murphy, "Stunted Growth of Campesino Organizations," in *Crucifixion by Power,* ed. Richard Adams (Austin: University of Texas Press, 1970), 449. For the histories of these outlawed organizations, see López Larrave, *Movimiento sindical;* Jim Handy, "Revolution and Reaction: National Policy and Rural Politics in Guatemala, 1944–1954" (Ph.D. diss., University of Toronto, 1985); and Rachel A. May, "The Mobilization of Guatemalan Campesinos into National Labor Organizations, 1954–1984" (M.A. thesis, Tulane University, 1990).

9. Serafino Romualdi, "Report on Guatemala," *American Federationist* 61:9 (September 1954): 26.

10. *El Imparcial* referred to these individuals as *"campesinos agrarios,"* meaning that they supported or were part of Arbenz's agrarian committees or the implementation of the agrarian reform law.

11. "Diecisiete asesinados en un camión se entierran hoy en Tiquisate," *El Imparcial,* 2 July 1954, p. 1; "En Escuintla y en Antigua mantienese en el pie de órden," *El Imparcial,* 2 July 1954, p. 1; "Angustia en Malacatán a causa de merodear campesinos armados," *El Imparcial,* 10 July 1954, p. 1; "Estragos del comunismo en la finca 'El Maricón,'" 16 July 1954, p. 1; "Ataque bate el Ejercito de Liberación," *El Imparcial,* 20 August 1954, p. 1.

12. Stephen Schlesinger and Stephen Kinzer, *Bitter Fruit* (Garden City N.Y.: Anchor Books, 1983), 219.

13. López Larrave, *Movimiento sindical,* 50.

14. "Diecisiete asesinados en un camión se entierran hoy en Tiquisate," *El Imparcial,* 2 July 1954, p. 1.

15. John Gillin and Kalman Silvert, "Ambiguities in Guatemala," *Foreign Affairs* 34 (April 1956): 477.

16. Estimates from Stokes Newbold [Richard Newbold Adams], "Receptivity to Communist Fomented Agitation in Rural Guatemala," *Economic Development and Cultural Change* 5:4 (1954). The Department of State's Research and Intelligence Division sent Adams to Guatemala in 1954 to research the article. Adams's regular employer at that time, the World Health Organization, requested that he use the pseudonym.

17. Murphy, "Stunted Growth," 469.

18. Decree 23 of the junta, 19 July 1954, *Recopilación de las leyes,* vol. 73, p. 66; Thomas Melville and Marjorie Melville, *Guatemala: The Politics of Land Ownership* (New York: Free Press, 1971), 100.

19. Decree 59, 24 August 1954, "Ley Preventativa Penal Contra el Comunismo" (chap. 1, art. 1), *Recopilación de las leyes,* vol. 73, p. 91.

20. Ibid. (chap. 1, art. 3).

21. Decree 59, 24 August 1954, "Ley Preventativa Penal Contra el Comunismo" (chap. 1, art. 6b), *Recopilación de las leyes,* vol. 73, p. 92; (chap. 2, art. 8), p. 92; (chap. 3, arts. 10, 18), pp. 93–94; (chap. 5, art. 30), p. 94.

22. Edwin Bishop, "The Guatemalan Labor Movement, 1944–1959" (Ph.D. diss., University of Wisconsin, 1959), microfilm, 184.

23. This was Castillo-Armas's political party, rooted in his Liberation Army.

24. This rhetoric should not be characterized as conciliatory. By the mid-1960s "national reconciliation" and "an end to violence" were often the rhetorical justifications for eliminating (not reconciling with) communists. Peace has been the rhetorical goal of those in power, but the rhetoric has not been conciliatory.

25. The MDN candidate in the January election was Colonel José Luis Cruz Salazar.

26. The concept of "legal recognition" or "juridical personality" is particularly relevant to Latin America, where various leaders and organizational elements must be identified and defined in order to receive official legal status.

27. Corporatism is identified as a traditional political organizational structure in Latin America by many distinguished historians and political scientists. These scholars point out that the tradition of an organic-corporatist state comes out of medieval European Christianity and that it characterized fifteenth-century Spain. The tradition was then transferred to the Americas during the Conquest. Latin America's conservative colonial roots are thought to be more important in shaping political tradition in contemporary Latin America than political ideologies and structures that emanate from liberal enlightenment thought (i.e., the political traditions that shape North American political tradition). It is this conservative "corporatist" history of Spanish America that gave rise to what Howard Wiarda terms Latin America's "distinct political tradition." Corporatism is defined

by Wiarda as "a system based on a belief in or acceptance of a natural hierarchy of social or functional groups, each with its place in the social order and with its own rights and obligations; more specifically, corporatist systems are organized on a sectoral basis with restrictions usually placed on their autonomy and horizontal relations with other groups. . . . In the corporatist system it is the central state that usually licenses, directs, and controls these corporate-societal units, holding the power to grant and withhold official recognition (without which the group cannot function legitimately) but also controlling access to official funds and favors, without which the group is unlikely to succeed or survive." Howard Wiarda, "Conclusion: Toward a Model of Social Change and Political Development in Latin America," in *Politics and Social Change in Latin America: Still A Distinct Tradition?* ed. Howard Wiarda (Boulder: Westview, 1992), 324. Thus corporatist political tradition has implications for organizational structure on both the state level and on the level of the individual organization. It implies a rigid hierarchy, or a highly vertical type of organization with a limited ability for horizontal organization. Horizontal relationships both between and within groups are limited by corporatist tradition. It also implies a distinct relationship between political organizations and the state in which the state acts as the ultimate authority in the vertical chain of command. We can see this tendency manifest in many ways in Latin American political organizations, including Guatemalan organizations. In recent decades a conflict has arisen in Guatemala in the effort to reconcile a corporatist tradition with the reality of a hostile state.

28. Jaime Malamud-Goti describes the pitfalls of "post–Dirty War" transitions in his critique of the utility of war trials in Argentina. Malamud-Goti, *Game without End: State Terror and the Politics of Justice* (Norman: University of Oklahoma Press, 1996).

## Chapter 2

1. Revolution is usually understood in one of two ways: as the political manifestation of rebellion, or as the actual implementation of a popular "revolutionary" political or socioeconomic agenda in the form of a new gov-

ernment or political regime. Jack Goldstone categorized the vast literature on revolution into three generational categories in a landmark essay. Goldstone, "Theories of Revolution: The Third Generation," *World Politics* 32 (April 1980): 425–53. According to Goldstone the first generation of theorists (pre-1940) produced broadly descriptive works about the American, French, and Russian revolutions. The second generation of theorists (1940–1975) was interested in causality and the conditions (social, economic, and political) that produce "potentially revolutionary situations." The third generation has extended the analysis beyond the chain of events that prompts a potentially revolutionary situation to examine how these events affect different types of political regimes and societies.

2. And of course there is very large body of literature on the phenomenon of war, but as Hannah Arendt explains, this literature actually deals with "the implements of violence, not with violence as such." Arendt, *On Violence* (New York: Harcourt Brace, 1970), 8.

3. Gellner describes "civil society" as "that set of nongovernmental institutions which is strong enough to counterbalance the state and while not preventing the state from fulfilling its role of keeper of the peace and arbitrator between major interests, can nevertheless prevent it from dominating and atomizing the rest of society." Gellner, *Conditions of Liberty: Civil Society and Its Rivals* (New York: Penguin, 1996), 5.

4. Charles Bergquist, Ricardo Peñaranda, and Gonzalo Sánchez, eds., *Violence in Colombia: The Contemporary Crisis in Historical Perspective* (Wilmington Del.: Scholarly Resources, 1992); Ana Carrigan, *The Palace of Justice: A Colombian Tragedy* (New York: Four Walls, Eight Windows, 1993); Marc Chernick and Michael F. Jiménez, "Popular Liberalism, Radical Democracy, and Marxism: Leftist Politics in Contemporary Colombia, 1974–1991," in *The Latin American Left: From the Fall of Allende to Perestroika*, ed. Barry Carr and Steve Ellner (Boulder: Westview, 1993), 61–81.

5. Malamud-Goti, *Game without End.*

6. Edelberto Torres-Rivas and Gabriel Aguilera Peralta, *Del autoritarismo a la paz* (Guatemala City: FLACSO, 1998), 46–68.

7. Ibid., 48.

8. Ibid., 70–71.

9. The rise in so-called delinquent violence that has accompanied a

decrease in political violence in some countries may force us to reconsider the distinctions between these two categories. This is particularly true in light of the politically charged neoliberal economic strategies that seem to exacerbate the problem of criminality. Colombian historian Gonzalo Sánchez has proposed a replacement typology of "negotiable" and "non-negotiable" violence.

10. Gurr outlines several different classifications of political violence at the beginning of his seminal work *Why Men Rebel* before adopting a modified version of Rudolph Rummel's typology of twenty-five different types of domestic conflict. Rummel, "Dimensions of Conflict Behavior," *General Systems Yearbook* (Ann Arbor: Society for the Advancement of General Systems Theory, 1963) 8: 1–50; Ted Robert Gurr, *Why Men Rebel* (Princeton, N.J.: Princeton University Press, 1970), 10–11. Implicit in Gurr's typology is his more narrow definition of political violence, which is characteristic of all the revolution theorists. Gurr and his contemporaries defined political violence as a "non-authoritative" phenomenon. That is, political violence is assumed to be political because it is directed toward the state (by nonauthoritative political actors—"rebels"). It is important to recognize how important this analysis has been in shaping our understanding of political violence, despite the fact that more recent analyses and narrative accounts have focused more appropriately on state-sponsored violence and human rights (with the state as the most serious and egregious violator of these rights).

11. Commission for Historical Clarification in Guatemala, *Guatemala: Memory of Silence*. This document can be found at <http://hrdata.aaas.org/ceh/index.html>.

12. Oficina de Derechos Humanos del Arzobispado de Guatemala, *Guatemala, Nunca más: Impactos de la violencia,* 4 vols. (Guatemala City: ODHAG, 1998).

13. Gurr only implicitly defines authoritative and nonauthoritative violence. Gurr, *Why Men Rebel,* 7.

14. Intra-elite conflicts and military coups are examples of authoritative violence which is not directed at nonauthoritative groups. It will be necessary to clearly define what constitutes authoritative violence when official state-sponsored vehicles are not used to perpetrate the violent acts. That is, death squad activity is often "authorized" by the state, even though the per-

petrators do not wear police or military uniforms. Where it is not directly authorized by the state (such as the MLN's Mano Blanco in Guatemala during the 1960s), it will be authoritative only if those who authorize the violence have official roles in the political power structure, and they are authorizing such violence in retaliation for nonauthoritative violence, or as a means of preventing change to the status quo. Thus death squad activities in the 1960s and 1970s in Central America would for the most part be authoritative violence; however, in the case of Colombia, narco-terrorism aimed at popular sectors, or the killing of street children or homosexuals by right-wing paramilitary organizations, would not be examples of authoritative violence.

15. Goldstone defines this important "second generation" (1940-1975) as those scholars who were concerned with causality and preconditions for violent rebellion. Gurr is one of the psycho-social theorists who analyzed the political and social conditions from a behavioral standpoint. See Goldstone, "Theories of Revolution," 428. The second generation theorists include: Chalmers Johnson, *Revolutionary Change* (Boston: Little, Brown, 1966); Neil Smelser, *Theory of Collective Behavior* (New York: Free Press, 1963); Bob Jessop, *Social Order, Reform, and Revolution* (New York: Macmillan, 1972); Edward Tyrakian, "A Model of Societal Change and Its Lead Indicators," in *The Study of Total Societies*, ed. Samuel Z. Klausner (New York: Anchor Books, 1967), 69-97; Mark Hagopian, *The Phenomenon of Revolution* (New York: Dodd, Mead, 1974).

16. John Booth, "Socio-Economic and Political Roots of National Revolts in Central America," *Latin American Research Review* 26:1 (1991): 35.

17. Ibid.

18. See E. Bradford Burns, *The Poverty of Progress: Latin America in the Nineteenth Century* (Berkeley: University of California Press, 1980); Robert Williams, *Export Agriculture and the Crisis in Central America* (Chapel Hill: University of North Carolina Press, 1986); David McCreery, "Hegemony and Repression in Rural Guatemala, 1871-1940" *Peasant Studies* 17:3 (Spring 1990): 155-77; Booth, "Socio-Economic and Political Roots."

19. Williams, *Export Agriculture*.

20. Yvon Le Bot, *La guerra en tierras mayas: Comunidad, violencia y modernidad en Guatemala (1970-1992)* (Mexico City: Fondo de Cultura Económica, 1995), 39-72; Carol Smith, "Labor and International Capital in the Making of a Peripheral Social Formation: Economic Transformation of Guatemala, 1850-1980," Working Paper no. 138 (Washington D.C.: Wilson Center, 1983), 12.

21. At the same time urban middle-class discontent was also brewing. In El Salvador, Guatemala, Honduras, and Nicaragua, real wages consistently declined beginning in the early 1970s and continuing through the mid-1990s. At the same time the rate of unemployment increased in all four countries. Starting in the mid-1950s, trade unions, political parties, and other urban middle-class popular organizations became increasingly mobilized and radicalized as a result.

22. Donald Schultz, "Ten Theories in Search of the Central American Reality," in *Revolution and Counter-Revolution in Central America,* ed. Donald Schulz and Douglas Graham (Boulder: Westview, 1984).

23. Ibid., 28.

24. Ibid.

25. Beatriz Manz, *Refugees of a Hidden War: The Aftermath of Counterinsurgency in Guatemala* (Albany: State University of New York Press, 1988); Rigoberta Menchú, *I, Rigoberta Menchú: An Indian Woman in Guatemala,* ed. Elisabeth Burgos-Debray, trans. Ann Wright (New York: Verso, 1984); originally *Me llamo Rigoberta Menchú y así nació mi conciencia* (Barcelona: Editorial Argos Vergara, 1983); George Black, *Garrison Guatemala* (New York: Monthly Review Press, 1984); Jonathan L. Fried et. al., eds., *Guatemala in Rebellion: Unfinished History* (New York: Grove Press, 1985); Robert M. Carmack, ed., *Harvest of Violence: The Maya Indians and the Guatemalan Crisis* (Norman: University of Oklahoma Press, 1988). Also see published reports by Amnesty International, Americas Watch, Oxfam International, and other international human rights organizations.

26. Suzanne Jonas, *The Battle for Guatemala: Rebels, Death Squads, and U.S. Power* (Boulder: Westview, 1991), 63, 148-50.

27. Pierre van den Berghe, *State Violence and Ethnicity* (Niwot: University of Colorado Press, 1990), 2.

28. See Brook Larmer, "Army Steers Clear of Conflict with Rebels," *Christian Science Monitor,* 8 February 1990, p. 5.

29. Van den Berghe, *State Violence*, 13.

30. Jennifer Schirmer, *The Guatemalan Military Project: A Violence Called Democracy* (Philadelphia: University of Pennsylvania Press, 1998), 4, 264.

31. Ibid., 4.

32. Schirmer does not describe the "military project" in Guatemala in terms of cycles as I do; rather she describes in brilliant detail the evolution of military thinking from 1944 up through the period of negotiated peace (early 1990s). The analysis is an exceedingly useful and detailed explanation of state terror.

33. The Permanent Peoples' Tribunal was an "international public opinion tribunal" founded in 1979 as the successor to the Bertrand Russell Tribunal on Latin America to clarify and evaluate charges of man's inhumanity to man. See Suzanne Jonas et al, eds., *Guatemala: Tyranny on Trial* (San Francisco: Synthesis Publications, 1984), v-vii.

34. Ibid., 241-42.

35. The Convention on the Prevention and Punishment of the Crime of Genocide was adopted by the United Nations General Assembly on 9 December 1948 and ratified by the Guatemalan State by Decree 704 on 30 November 1949. Article II of this instrument defines the crime of genocide and its requirements in the following terms: " . . . genocide means any of the following acts committed with intent to destroy, in whole or in part, a national, ethnical, racial or religious group, as such: (a) Killing members of the group; (b) Causing serious bodily or mental harm to members of the group; (c) Deliberately inflicting on the group conditions of life calculated to bring about its physical destruction in whole or in part; (d) Imposing measures intended to prevent births within the group; (e) Forcibly transferring children of the group to another group." See Comisión para el Esclarecimiento Histórico, *Guatemala Memorias del Silencio* (Guatemala City: CEH, 1999). This document can be found at <http://hrdata.aaas.org/ceh/report/english/conc2.html>.

36. CEH, article II, 110-11 (p. 40, Spanish print version).

37. Schirmer, *Guatemalan Military Project*, 261.

# Chapter 3

1. This analysis does not consider the evolution of the pan-Maya movement and Maya cultural organizations which do not really emerge until after 1985. Precursors to the indigenous rights movement (the cofradía and other local associational forms) are not really comparable to the national political organizations that I am analyzing here. See Edward Fischer and R. McKenna Brown, *Maya Cultural Activism in Guatemala* (Austin: University of Texas Press, 1996); Kay Warren, *Indigenous Movements and Their Critics: Pan-Maya Activism in Guatemala* (Princeton, N.J.: Princeton University Press, 1998); Diane Nelson, *A Finger in the Wound: Body Politics in Quincentennial Guatemala* (Berkeley: University of California Press, 1999). Similarly, women's organizations were not present in Guatemala until after 1985. Many women were involved and even rose to prominence in some of the popular organizations considered here, and in 1988 a group of Guatemalan widows organized the National Coordination of Guatemalan Widows (CONAVIGUA), the first gender-specific human rights group in the country. But the proliferation of organizations committed to "women's issues" occurs after the period under study here. See Jane S. Jaquette, ed., *The Women's Movement in Latin America: Feminism and Transition to Democracy* (Boulder: Westview, 1991); Lynn Stephen, *Women and Social Movements in Latin America* (Austin: University of Texas Press, 1997); Elizabeth Dore, ed., *Gender Politics in Latin America: Debates in Theory and Practice* (New York: Monthly Review Press, 1997).

2. The idea of civil society is, as John Ehrenberg points out, "a very old idea," which has "long provided a fruitful vantage point from which to evaluate the central categories of political thought." Ehrenberg, *Civil Society: The Critical History of an Idea* (New York: New York University Press), x. The idea was resurrected by anticommunist dissidents in Eastern Europe during the early 1980s.

3. Ernest Gellner and others argue that "civil society is based upon the separation of the polity from economic and social life." Gellner, *Conditions of Liberty*, 212. But Latin America illustrates something different. Civil society is a necessary precondition for and component of democracy because it creates a space for the politically (and economically) marginalized to

influence the polity. Civil society (popular organizations) may choose to force the polity to address social and economic issues. The Mexican EZLN explicitly uses the notion of civil society in this way. They claim to be demanding an acceptance of "civil society," which they see as having a historical presence in Chiapas, and they see this as a way of allowing economically marginalized peoples to demand reforms in the political *and economic* realm.

4. Landsberger refers to organizations as "formally structured interest groups." Because I am excluding collective acts of defiance that do not emanate from a structured interest group, the many historical examples of peasant rebellions, which are normally part of the category of popular movements or peasant movements, are more properly grouped with the phenomenon of violence in this analysis. Simply stated, a rebellion constitutes an act, not an entity. An incident of nonauthoritative rebellion is an act of violence that often does not emanate from an organization with enduring structural characteristics. Henry Landsberger and Cynthia N. Hewitt, "Ten Sources of Weakness and Cleavage in Latin American Peasant Movements," in *Agrarian Problems and Peasant Movements in Latin America,* ed. Rodolfo Stavenhagen (New York: Anchor Books-Doubleday, 1970), 561.

5. The term popular organization is relatively new, and has only been widely used in the last twenty-five years. It is often used in conjunction with or interchangeably with the term *social* movement or organization. In this analysis *popular organization* is defined as a more specific type of social organization. Social organizations are defined by Daniel Camacho as organizations which intentionally set out to defend specific interests. See Daniel Camacho, introduction to *Los movimientos populares en América Latina,* ed. Daniel Camacho and Rafael Menjívar (Mexico City: Siglo Veintiuno Editores, 1989), 15. Camacho actually defines a social "movement" as a societal "dynamic . . . la cual se orienta intencionalmente a la defensa de intereses específicos" (dynamic . . . that specifically orients itself to defend particular interests). It can therefore be inferred that social "organizations" are "formally recognized interest groups" which do the same.

6. Camacho, introduction, 15–16.

7. Similar changes have also taken place in other underdeveloped regions, and in fact much of the literature about modernization and the politicization of "peasants" refers specifically to non–Latin American states.

8. Eric Wolf contributed to this new view of the campesino as an important actor in politics with *Peasant Wars in the Twentieth Century,* published in 1969. Wolf explicitly took issue with the idea that peasants must be led into an organized rebellion. Wolf concentrates on the legitimacy of the campesinos' grievances and the particular circumstances that have fueled the great peasant uprisings of the twentieth century. "There is no evidence for the view that if it were not for 'outside agitators,' the peasant would be at rest." Wolf goes on to describe the insecurity (and often the bloodshed) created by the radical nature of autonomous political activity of campesinos. He places the campesinos' tragedy at the center of societal progression and a positive kind of human evolution. "The peasants' role is thus essentially tragic: his efforts to undo a grievous present only usher in a vaster, more uncertain future. Yet if it is tragic, it is also full of hope. For the first time in millennia, human kind is moving toward a solution of the age-old problem of hunger and disease, and everywhere ancient monopolies of power and received wisdom are yielding to human effort to widen participation and knowledge. In such efforts—however uncertain, however beset with difficulties, however ill understood—there lies the prospect for increased life, for increased humanity" (pp. 301-2). Evidence borne out in contemporary Guatemala would seem to justify Wolf's conclusions about the optimistic side of tragedy. Guatemalan campesinos have been subjected to brutal terror, yet they emerge from this violence with more resolve and more skill—more genuine hope of change. Perhaps every kind of popular organization—from rural to urban, local to national, both the violent and the peaceful organizations—holds out the possibility of hope for a new and changed society, even in the face of violence, repression, and tragedy. Wolf, *Peasant Wars in the Twentieth Century* (New York: Harper and Row, 1969).

9. The Spanish term *campesino* is not adequately translatable. The usual translation, "peasant," has a more complex meaning (that includes associations with feudalism, primitive modes of production, etc.) that is not necessarily applicable to contemporary Latin American campesinos, who are the subject here. For the sake of precision, I will use the term *campesino,* except where I am referring to someone else's analysis or interpretation. A campesino is a rural worker, in some way tied to agricultural production, who is of a low socioeconomic status.

10. Landsberger and Hewitt, "Ten Sources," 561.

11. This was often interpreted as a particularly radical goal which is intimately associated with the idea of subversion.

12. ONG is an international term, and it often implies organizations which receive international funds.

13. These are the legal terms for nonprofit organizations in the respective countries named. They aren't limited to "community organizations," or even "popular" organizations. Their defining legal characteristic is that they are private and nonprofit. Many of them receive international funding. "Cooperatives" have a different juridical personality in both Guatemala and Mexico.

14. Timothy Wickham-Crowley, *Guerrillas and Revolution in Latin America* (Princeton, N.J.: Princeton University Press, 1992), 24–25.

15. Ibid., 53.

16. Charles Bergquist, *Labor in Latin America: Comparative Essays on Chile, Argentina, Venezuela, and Colombia* (Stanford, Calif.: Stanford University Press, 1986), 9.

17. Camacho, introduction, 15.

18. John Magill, *Labor Unions and Political Socialization: A Case Study of Bolivian Workers* (New York: Praeger, 1974), 12–13.

19. Landsberger, *Peasant Movements*, 55–56.

20. Ibid., 56.

21. See, for example, Maurice Duverger, *Political Parties: Their Organization and Activity in the Modern, State* 2d ed. (New York: Wiley, 1959).

22. Malamud-Goti, *Game without End*, 122–39.

23. See, for example, Camacho and Menjívar, *Movimientos populares en América Latina*; or López Larrave, *Movimiento sindical*.

24. *Unidad del CNUS* (CNUS newsletter) nos. 4–5, Año 1. Printed in Centro de Investigación y Educación Popular América Central, Equipo de Apoyo Sindical, doc. 5, *Experiencias del Auge de Masas* (1975–1981), n.d. CITGUA, doc. 203136.

25. Landsberger, *Peasant Movements*; Wolf, *Peasant Wars;* Rodolfo Stavenhagen, ed., *Agrarian Problems and Peasant Movements in Latin America* (Garden City, N.Y.: Doubleday, 1970); Henry A. Landsberger, ed., *Rural Protest: Peasant Movements and Social Change* (New York: Barnes and Noble, 1973); Gerrit Huizer, *Peasant Rebellion in Latin America* (Harmondsworth: Penguin, 1973); Richard Gott, *Rural Guerrillas in Latin*

*America* (Harmondsworth: Penguin Books, 1973); Jeffrey Paige, *Agrarian Revolution: Social Movements and Export Agriculture in the Underdeveloped World* (New York: Free Press, 1975); Howard Handelman, *Struggle in the Andes: Peasant Political Mobilization in Peru* (Austin: University of Texas Press, 1975); Cynthia McClintock, *Peasant Cooperatives and Political Change in Peru* (Princeton. N.J.: Princeton University Press, 1981); Héctor Bejar and Carlos Franco, *Organización campesina y restructuración del estado* (Lima: CEDEP, 1985); Charles Bergquist, *Coffee and Conflict in Colombia, 1886-1910* (Durham, N.C.: Duke University Press, 1986); Jeffrey Gould, *To Lead As Equals: Rural Protest and Political Consciousness in Cinandega, Nicaragua, 1912-1979* (Chapel Hill: University of North Carolina Press, 1990); See also sections of Susan Eckstein, ed., *Power and Popular Protest: Latin American Social Movements* (Berkeley: University of California Press, 1989); Camacho and Menjívar, *Movimientos populares en América Latina;* Camacho and Menjívar, eds., *Movimientos populares en Centroamérica* (Costa Rica, EDUCA, 1986).

26. I am looking at this within the context of Charles Anderson's power-contenders model; see Anderson, "Toward a Theory of Latin American Politics," in *Politics and Social Change in Latin America: The Distinct Tradition,* ed. Howard J. Wiarda (Amherst: University of Massachusetts Press, 1982).

27. See León Zamosc, *The Agrarian Question and the Peasant Movement in Colombia* (Cambridge: Cambridge University Press, 1986); Jan Black, "Ten Paradoxes of Rural Development: An Ecuadorian Case Study," *Journal of Developing Areas* 19:4 (July 1985): 527-55.

28. For example, Jorge Eliécer Gaitán and Gaitanismo in Colombia, or Abimael Guzmán and the Shining Path of Peru.

## Chapter 4

1. There are clearly historical antecedents for both phenomena. *Reparti-mientos* and *reducciones* were commonplace in the colonial period, as were forced migration and vagrancy laws (tied to the expansion of the coffee industry) in the Liberal period. See Julio Pinto Soria, *Estructura agraria y asen-*

*tamiento el la Capitanía General de Guatemala* (Guatemala City: Editorial Universitaria, Colección Monografía, vol. 13, 1981); William Sherman, *Forced Native Labor in Sixteenth-Century Central America* (Lincoln: University of Nebraska Press, 1979); David McCreery, *Development and the State in Reforma Guatemala* (Athens: Ohio University Center for International Studies, 1983); McCreery, "Hegemony and Repression"; John Swetnam, "What Else Did Indians Have to Do with Their Time? Alternatives to Labor Migration in Prerevolutionary Guatemala," *Economic Development and Cultural Change* 38:1 (1989): 89–112.

2. The most notable contemporary example of campesino displacement resulted from nickel mining by EXMIBAL (Exploraciones y Explotaciones Mineras de Izábal) in the Lake Izábal region of the northeastern highlands. The EXMIBAL case is detailed more fully below. The relocation of campesinos and accompanying violence associated with growth in the cotton and cattle industries is also common; it is documented by Williams, *Export Agriculture*.

3. Parts of this chapter appear in an abbreviated form in Andrew R. Morrison and Rachel A. May, "Escape from Terror: Violence and Migration in Post-Revolutionary Guatemala," *Latin American Research Review* 29:1 (January 1994): 111–32.

4. Some scholars would argue that the presidential administration of Julio César Méndez Montenegro (1966–1970), a civilian, was a respite in what was otherwise a period of military rule. It is argued here that Lic. Méndez did not himself wield enough authority to challenge the authority of the military. In other words, this administration in retrospect has been viewed as a puppet of the Guatemalan military, and in fact this was precisely the period in which military power became firmly entrenched.

5. Jim Handy, *Gift of the Devil* (Boston: South End Press, 1984), 152.

6. Gabriel Aguilera Peralta and Jorge Romero Imery, et al., *Dialéctica del terror en Guatemala* (Costa Rica: EDUCA, 1981), 87–88, 107.

7. "Desorden, trifulcas se arman," *El Imparcial,* 9 March 1962, p. 1; "Desorden aumenta," *El Imparcial,* 12 March 1962, p. 1; "Ministro de Gobernación dice que no tolera manifestaciones," and "Pedrea and lacrmógenas: heridos," *El Imparcial,* 13 March 1962, p. 1; "Muertos y heridos," and "Cincuenta cuatro heridos atiende La Cruz Roja," *El Imparcial,* 16 March 1962, p. 1.

8. "Choque con facciones: Ejercito los derrota," *El Imparcial*, 14 March 1962, p. 1; "Huelga declarada por los treneros," 14 March 1962, p. 1; "Solo tres los sindicatos que estan en huelga," *El Imparcial*, 19 March 1962, p. 1.

9. "Asociación Estudiantil Universitaria del Occidente," *El Imparcial*, 19 March 1962, p. 1; "Xelaju: INVO puso fin a la huelga," *El Imparcial*, 29 March 1962, p. 1.

10. "Contramanifestantes intentaron copar," *El Imparcial*, 11 March 1963, p. 1; "Gobierno no puede dar garantías par el Dr. Arévalo," *El Imparcial*, 14 March 1963, p. 1; "Arévalo hace incitación a la guerra civil esos es ponerse fuera de la ley: Flores A," *El Imparcial*, p. 1; "Apoyo masivas de todas clases sociales al nuevo gobierno," *El Imparcial*, p. 1.

11. Jonas, *Battle for Guatemala*, 60.

12. The words "outside the law" seem to be deliberately vague. "AEU preocupada por persecución a estudiantes," *El Imparcial*, 23 March 1963, p. 1; "No se persigue a estudiantes dirigentes dice," *El Imparcial*, 25 March 1963, p. 1; "Manifestación estudiantil en Quezaltenango," *El Imparcial*, 18 March 1963, p. 1.

13. "Estudiantes de derecho protestan," *El Imparcial*, 9 March 1963, p. 1.

14. "Frente a la Escuela Dolores Bedoy enfrentan la policia," *El Imparcial*, 15 March 1963, p. 1; "Profesor en libertad tras ser detenido," *El Imparcial*, 22 March 1963, p. 1; "Captura que es efectuó en el PRO," *El Imparcial*, 28 March 1963, p. 1.

15. "Captura que efectuó en el PRO," *El Imparcial*, 28 March 28 1963, p. 1; "Profesor en libertad tras ser detenido," *El Imparcial*, 22 March 1963, p. 1. Literally those accused were often charged with "soliviantar los ánimos," which ironically could be translated as "inciting courage, or thought."

16. "Huelga de hambre en Retalhuleu," *El Imparcial*, 27 March 1963, p. 1.

17. Arbenz was himself a colonel in the Guatemalan army, and there was a small base of support for the democratic ideals of the Revolution within the military, until the consolidation of the armed forces after the coup of 1963.

18. Aguilera Peralta and Romero Imery, *Dialéctica del terror*, 106.

19. Ibid., 107–8.

20. The organizational aspects of the FAR as a popular organization will be discussed in chapter 5.

21. Marco Antonio Yon Sosa, "Organizar y unir a las masas, desarollar la guerra revolucionaria del pueblo," reprinted in *Movimientos Revolu-*

*cionarios de America Latina* (Caracas: Información Documental de América Latina, 1972), 18.

22. Aguilera Peralta and Romero Imery, *Dialéctica del terror*, 89.

23. Gabriel Aguilera Peralta, "La militarización del estado guatemalteco," Polémica (Costa Rica) 1 (September-October 1981); René Poitevin, *El proceso de industrialización en Guatemala* (Costa Rica: EDUCA, 1977), 191–92.

24. Jonas, *Battle for Guatemala*, 61.

25. Guatemala became one of the main Third World sources of arms sales for the United States. David Tobis, "The Alliance for Progress: Development Program for the United States," *Monthly Review* (N.Y.), January 1968.

26. Handy, *Gift of the Devil*, 153–64.

27. The PR emerged from the October Revolution of 1944. In the mid-1960s they were led by the civilian politician Mario Méndez Montenegro. He appeared to be willing to ally himself and the PR with the military, and was therefore allowed to officially register the party for the 1966 elections. He died, an apparent suicide, before the elections, and his brother Julio César Méndez Montenegro ran as the PR candidate; he did *not* ally himself with the military during the campaign. Nevertheless, after winning the election, Julio César Méndez signed an agreement with the military, promising not to interfere in military affairs.

28. Aguilera Peralta, "Militarización."

29. See chapter 2 for a definition of terrorism, and for a definition of authoritative reactionary terror and genocide.

30. Aguilera Peralta and Romero Imery, *Dialéctica del terror*, 125.

31. See Aguilera Peralta and Romero Imery, *Dialéctica del terror* (entire book); Jonas, *Battle for Guatemala*, 57–74.

32. "Bandolerismo y acción subversiva en primer plano," *Inforpress centroamericano* 10 (3 October 1972): 1; Aguilera Peralta and Romero Imery, *Dialéctica del terror*, 130; Jonas, *Battle for Guatemala*, 63.

33. Aguilera Peralta and Romero Imery, *Dialéctica del terror*, 172.

34. Ibid., 125.

35. Ibid., 125–34; Schlesinger and Kinzer, *Bitter Fruit*, pp. 236–47; Handy, *Gift of the Devil*, 153–64; Lawrence Yates, "The United States Rural Insurgency," in *Central America: Historical Perspectives on the Contemporary Crisis*, ed. R. L. Woodward (New York: Greenwood Press, 1988), 59.

36. This dispute was considered to be one of the most important events of 1972 by the weekly periodical *Inforpress centroamericana*. "Conflicto en el SAMF por la venta del muelle de Puerto Barrios," *Inforpress centroamericana* 17 (21 November 1972): 13; "Conflicto por la venta del muelle de Puerto Barrios," *Inforpress centroamericana*, special ed. (3 January 1973): 4.

37. "Huelgistas de CIDASA siguen firmes," *Inforpress centroamericana* 13 (24 October 1972): 7–8.

38. "Trabajo," *Inforpress centroamericana* 19 (5 December 1972): 17–18.

39. Mario Solarzano, "El Movimiento maisterial," *Inforpress Centroamericana* 38 (25 April 1973): i–iii; "Desordenes y represión en conflicto magisterial," *Inforpress centroamericana* 52 (1 August 1973): v–vii; "Termina el conflicto magisterial," *Inforpress centroamericana* 53 (8 August 1973): iv–v.

40. "Recrudecimiento de la violencia," *Inforpress centroamericana* 21 (19 December 1972): 12.

41. For violence data for January, February, and March 1973, see "Hechos," in *Inforpress centroamericana* 28 (6 February 1973): 11, and 36 (4 April 1973): 11.

42. "'Alero' y la libertad de expresión," *Inforpress centroamericana* 30 (21 February 1973): 8; "'El Honorable,' una lucha ideológica," *Inforpress centroamericana* 34 (21 March 1973): 6–7.

43. "Vecinos de Chinautla se openen a su traslado," *Inforpress centroamericana* 55 (22 August 1973): 2.

44. "Sangriente enfrentamiento campesino," *Inforpress centroamericana* 43 (30 May 1973): 11–12.

45. See Williams, *Export Agriculture*.

46. Carol Smith, "Labor and Capital," 12.

47. See Luisa Frank and Philip Wheaton, *Indian Guatemala: Path to Liberation* (Washington, D.C.: EPICA Task Force, 1984), 41–43.

48. G. Asturias Montenegro and R. Gatica Trejo, *Earthquake S.O.S.: Guatemala '76* (Guatemala City: Girblan and Company, 1976), 39–41; Handy, *Gift of the Devil*, 173.

49. Montenegro and Gatica Trejo, *Earthquake S.O.S.*, 39–41; Handy, *Gift of the Devil*, 173.

50. José Manuel Fernández Fernández, *El Comité de Unidad Campesina: Origen y desarollo*, Cuaderno 3 (Guatemala City: CERCA, 1988): 7–8; inter-

view, Julio Celso de León, offices of ASIES, Guatemala City, 12 June 1989; interview, Helmer Melásquez, offices of IDESAC, Guatemala City, 21 June 1989.

51. A new death squad autonomous of the MLN and closely associated with Lucas himself emerged soon after the election. This Ejercito Secreto Anti-Comunista (ESA) was the most infamous death squad organization in Guatemalan history. Its activities were widespread and brutal. Little attempt was made to hide this activity, or to separate it from the activity of the military and the National Police.

52. For information about an excellent database of documented acts of rural state terror, see Paul Edward Yamauchi, "Patterns of Death: Descriptions of Geographic and Temporal Patterns of Rural State Terror in Guatemala 1978–1985," *Physicians for Social Responsibility* (PSR) *Quarterly* 3:2 (June 1993): 67–78.

53. The best source for these communiqués and Manifestos is *Noticias de Guatemala,* which began publication in 1978. They also published all recorded incidents of political "disappearances," tortures, and murders. The data are not particularly consistent, but this is a reflection of the availability of such information—even at the time the abuses were occurring.

54. EXMIBAL (Exploraciones y Explotaciones Mineras de Izábal) was one of many mineral exploration-exploitation projects in the northeastern highlands of Guatemala during the late 1970s.

55. Gabriel Aguilera Peralta, "The Massacre at Panzós and Capitalist Development in Guatemala," in *Revolution in Central America,* ed. Stanford Central America Action Network (Boulder: Westview, 1983); World of Information, *Latin America Annual Report* (1979), 155–56.

56. Ana Beatriz Mendízabal, "Estado y políticas de desarollo agrario: La masacre campesina de Panzós," *Política y sociedad* (Guatemala) 6:11 (July–December 1978): 71–74; "The Massacre at Panzós," doc. 33, ed. International Work Group for Indigenous Affairs (IWGIA), Copenhagen, 1978, 7.

57. "Panzós: Cien muertos; seiscientos huyen a la montaña," *La Tarde,* 31 May 1978, p. 1.

58. Latin American Bureau, "Peasant Massacre in Guatemala," 2 June 1978, reprinted in IWGIA, doc. no. 33, 9–10.

59. "Veinte tres organizaciones sindicales y estudiantiles denuncian

masacre de campesinos en Panzós," *La Tarde*, 31 May 1978, p. 3; "Más que cien muertos en Panzós," *La Nación*, 31 May 1978, p. 1; "Ambiente de cementerio persiste," *El Imparcial*, 2 June 1978, p. 1.

60. For documentation of the massacre at Finca San Francisco, see "Voices of Survivors: The Massacre at Finca San Francisco," a publication of Cultural Survival, and Anthropology Resource Center, no. 10 (September 1983); and Ricardo Falla, *Masacre de la finca San Francisco. Huehuetenengo, Guatemala* (Copenhagen: IWGIA, document no. 1, 1983).

61. See Oficina de Derechos Humanos, *Guatemala: Nunca más*; Historical Clarification Committee, *Memory of Silence*; Manz, *Refugees of a Hidden War*; Menchú, *I, Rigoberta Menchú*; testimonies reprinted in "Terror and Counter-Insurgency," in *Guatemala in Rebellion: Unfinished History*, ed. Jonathan Fried et. al. (New York: Grove Press, 1983); Jonas, *Tyranny on Trial*; testimonies reprinted in Frank and Wheaton, *Indian Guatemala*; G. Black, *Garrison Guatemala*; Bernice Kita, *What Prize Awaits Us: Letters from Guatemala* (Maryknoll, N.Y.: Orbis Books, 1988); Americas Watch, *Human Rights in Guatemala: No Neutrals Allowed* (New York: Americas Watch, 1982); Amnesty International, *Guatemala: A Government Program of Political Murder* (London: Amnesty International, 1981); "Death and Disorder in Guatemala," *Cultural Survival Quarterly* 7:1 (Spring 1983). See also other published reports by Amnesty International, Americas Watch, Oxfam International, Cultural Survival, Inc., and North American Congress on Latin America (NACLA).

62. Grahame Russell, Sarah Kee, and Ann Butwell, *Unearthing the Truth: Exhuming A Decade of Terror in Guatemala* (Washington, D.C.: EPICA, 1996).

## Chapter 5

1. As described in chapter 1, many active trade unionists and most union leaders were eliminated through self-imposed exile, incarceration, or execution under the Preventive Penal Law against Communism.

2. Schlesinger and Kinzer, *Bitter Fruit*, 219.

3. "Romualdi aclara razones de su llegada a nuestro pais," *El Imparcial*, 29 July 1954, p. 7.

4. Serafino Romualdi, *Presidents and Peons: Recollections of a Labor Ambassador in Latin America* (New York: Funk and Wagnalls, 1967), 244.

5. "Comité de reorganización sindical," *El Imparcial*, 22 July 1954, p. 1.

6. "Comité de reorganización sindical," *El Imparcial*, 22 July 1954, p. 1; "Normalización de sindicatos y no central obrera," *El Imparcial*, 22 July 1954, p. 1; Serafino Romualdi, "Report on Guatemala," *American Federationist* 61:9 (September 1954): 27.

7. López Larrave, *Movimiento sindical*, 55.

8. CITGUA, *El movimiento sindical en Guatemala (1975-1985): Formación y capacitación* 1:1 (Mexico City: CITGUA, January 1986): 25; López Larrave, *Movimiento sindical*, 54.

9. Edwin Bishop, "The Guatemalan Labor Movement, 1944-1959" (Ph.D. dissertation, University of Wisconsin, 1959), microfilm, 190-92.

10. "Movimiento sindical libre con orientación social-cristiana," *El Imparcial*, 19 July 1954, p. 1.

11. "Federación autónoma de sindicatos libres: Veinte cinco sindicatos ya escritos," *El Imparcial*, 21 July 1954, p. 1.

12. Bishop, "Guatemalan Labor Movement," 185.

13. The MDN was the political party associated with Castillo Armas's "liberation" movement.

14. Handy, *Gift of the Devil*, 227.

15. Ibid., 186.

16. Bishop, "Guatemalan Labor Movement," 186; "Federación autónoma de sindicatos libres: Veinte cinco sindicatos ya escritos," *El Imparcial*, 21 July 1954, p. 1.

17. Bishop, "Guatemalan Labor Movement," 187; "Esta noche elección en la FAS," *El Imparcial*, 9 February 1957, p. 1; Brian Murphy, "Stunted Growth," 457.

18. Asociación de Investigación y Estudios Sociales, *Más de cien años del Movimiento Obrero Urbano en Guatemala*, 4 vols. (Guatemala City: ASIES, 1991), 3:110-12.

19. The FSM is an international labor organization which adheres to a Marxist line; CITGUA, 1:1, 20.

20. ASIES, *Más de cien años*, 3:245-48, 299.

21. The obligation of the Church to exercise a "preferential option for the poor" was articulated at the 1968 conference of Latin American bishops

(CELAM) in Medellín, Colombia. The Medellín document is one of the cornerstones of liberation theology.

Of course there were many examples of priests and other Catholic political actors who had historically worked for the interests of the poor, most notably the sixteenth-century Dominican bishop Bartolomé de Las Casas. Nevertheless, as an institution, the Catholic Church clearly represented elite interests in the Americas from the very beginning of the Conquest. This institutional position changed radically and quickly after 1960.

22. Zacaerias Heren Andez Guillen (first secretary general of SETUFCO after 1958), notes from interview conducted by Henry Frundt.

23. The agrarian committees were set up by Jacobo Arbenz in 1952 to carry out the agrarian reform act of that year (Decree 900). Most members of the committees were local union representatives.

24. Bishop, "Guatemalan Labor Movement," 205–6.

25. Ibid., 202.

26. Romualdi, "Report," 219.

27. Constitution of 1956 (Title IV, chap. 4, arts. 114, 116), in *Recopilación de las leyes,* ed. Roberto Azurdia Alfaro (Guatemala City: Tipografía Nacional, 1965), vol. 74, pp. 25–26.

28. Ibid. (Title IV, chap. 5, art. 116) p. 26.

29. During the Revolution, the guarantees of the Constitution and the Labor Code were enforced through the trade unions and the system of labor inspectors.

30. Decree 217, 28 January 1956, *Recopilación de las leyes,* vol. 73, p. 203.

31. Decree 570 (arts. 28, 37), 28 February 1956, *Recopilación de las leyes,* vol. 74, p. 384.

32. The function of the labor inspectors was to seek out infractions of the labor code, and to provide a device for the settlement of dispute out of court; Adams, *Crucifixion by Power,* 194.

33. Adams, *Crucifixion by Power,* 194; Bishop, "Guatemalan Labor Movement," 164.

34. Romualdi, *Presidents and Peons,* 245.

35. Ibid.

36. Romualdi, *Presidents and Peons,* 246.

37. Ibid., 245–46.

38. Ibid., 246.

39. "Decision de que la ley caiga," *El Imparcial*, 12 July 1954, p. 5; "Fincas nacionales retornan al patrimonio del estado," *El Imparcial*, 23 August 1954, p. 1; "Retorno de las dadas a parcelarios," *El Imparcial*," 20 August 1954, p. 7.

40. Decree 57, 20 August 1954, *Recopilación de las leyes*, vol. 73, p. 89.

41. Melville and Melville, *Guatemala*, 86.

42. The AGA was the official interest group of traditional landed elites. It was the precursor of the contemporary organization UNAGRO.

43. This lack of representation stands in sharp contrast to the Triangle of Escuintla Congress held in 1945, where not only were campesinos represented, but their concerns were actively addressed; see Melville and Melville, Guatemala, 106.

44. Mary Felise Smith, "Agricultural Development in Guatemala: The Indian Cooperative Movement, 1965–1982" (M.A. thesis, Tulane University, 1991), 30–34.

45. Castillo Armas, as quoted in Astenogenes R. Batista, "Proyecta Castillo Armas," *Guatemala* 1:1 (September 1956): 55.

46. This was done mostly through the National Institute for Agrarian Transformation (INTA), and the Catholic Action Cooperative movement after the mid-1960s, and those who colonized these areas were in many cases the same ones who became victims of massacres like the one at Finca San Francisco (see chap. 3).

47. Decree 1551, 11 October 1962, Ley de Transformación Agraria (chap. 1, art. 1), *Recopilación de las leyes*, vol. 81, p. 39–40.

48. Dina Jiménez, "El movimiento campesino en Guatemala, 1969–1980," in *Movimientos populares en centroamérica*, ed. Daniel Camacho and Rafael Menjívar (Costa Rica: EDUCA, 1985), 304.

49. See Williams, *Export Agriculture*.

50. Marilyn Moors, "Indian Labor and the Guatemalan Crisis," in R. L. Woodward, ed., *Central America: Perspectives on the Contemporary Crisis* (New York: Greenwood Press, 1988). Her figure comes from the deaths which were actually reported to the Guatemalan Institute for Social Security (IGSS), which probably represents only a fraction of the actual number of work-related deaths.

51. The Independent Campesino Movement, or Movimiento Campesino Independiente (MCI), and the National Campesino Central, or Central Nacional Campesino (CNC). Both were outgrowths of the FCG.

52. The Institute for the Economic and Social Development of Central America (IDESAC), and the National Movement of *Pobladores* (MONAP).

53. FECETRAG started out as the FCTG—*Frente Cristiano de Trabajadores de Guatemala* in 1962. It received juridical recognition as FECETRAG in 1966.

54. Interview, Julio Celso de León, offices of ASIES, Guatemala City, 20 June 1989; ASIES, vol. 2 (1991), 252–53.

55. Interview, Celso de León; interview, José Pinzón, offices of the CGTG, Guatemala City, 10 July 1989.

56. Interview, Celso de León; CITGUA, 1:1, 14; Murphy, "Stunted Growth," 459.

57. ASIES, vol. 2 (1991), 260.

58. Miguel Angel Albizures, "El Movimiento Sindical y popular guatemalteco: Recomposición, auge y desarollo, resurgimiento y situación actual, 1960–1995," unpublished manuscript in possession of author.

59. Amaro, "Análisis preliminar del movimiento de promoción popular en Guatemala hasta 1968," in *El reto del desarollo en Guatemala,* ed. IDESAC (Guatemala City: IDESAC, 1970), 414–16; interview, Celso de León.

60. Interview, Celso de León.

61. Ibid. The 1961 Labor Code and subsequent amendments gave more freedom to organize rural workers.

62. Amaro, "Análisis preliminar," 413; interview, Celso de León.

63. Interview, Celso de León; CITGUA, 1:1, 20–22.

64. Interview, Celso de León; Murphy, "Stunted Growth," 460.

65. CONTRAGUA and CONSIGUA were unofficially cooperative before 1976.

66. López Larrave, *Movimiento sindical,* 55–57; Murphy, "Stunted Growth," 460.

67. Amaro, "Análisis preliminar," 413, 414; interview, Celso de León; interview, Pinzón.

68. Amaro, "Análisis preliminar," 414; interview, Celso de León.

69. "Surge Nueva Organización Campesina," *Inforpress centroameri-cana* 55 (22 August 1973): 10; Gerald Michael Greenfield and Sheldon L. Maram, eds., *Latin American Labor Organizations* (New York: Greenwood Press, 1987), 420; López Larrave, *Movimiento sindical,* 57.

70. Interview, Celso de León; López Larrave, *Movimiento sindical*, 55–58; Murphy, "Stunted Growth," 463.

71. Interview, Celso de León; Klaus Oehler, ed., *Minifundios en Guatemala, situación y perspectivas: Enfoque especial del indígena* (Guatemala City: IDESAC, Editorial Financiera, 1971), 371.

72. M. F. Smith, "Agricultural Development," 43.

73. Roland Ebel, *Political Modernization in Three Guatemalan Indian Communities* (New Orleans: Middle American Research Institute, 1969); Gonzalo Sichar Moreno, *Guatemala: Contrainsurgencia o contra el pueblo?* (Madrid: Hidalgo más Hidalgo, 1998), 35–37.

74. A centrist ideology which stresses humanitarian concerns and non-revolutionary tactics. This ideology had much in common with the international movements of Christian Democracy and Social Democracy; yet in Guatemala, groups which associated themselves with "Social Christianity" (e.g., FASGUA and IDESAC) tended to become more radical during the 1960s than did the Christian Democrats or the Social Democrats. *Social-cristiano* movements in other Latin American countries did not necessarily parallel the Guatemalan pattern.

75. The party is also referred to as simply the DC, *Democracia Cristiana*.

76. IDESAC, "Boletín semestral," no. 4, 25th Anniversary Issue (January–June 1989): 1; Otto Rivera, "MONAP y su relación campo-ciudad," Guatemala City, 1988, unpublished paper in possession of author.

77. *Pobladores* are settlers, or squatters. Many urban squatters were displaced campesinos. MONAP eventually extended some of its activities outside Guatemala City.

78. Interview, Carlos Enríque Aguirre R., offices of MONAP, Guatemala City, August 1, 1989; Rivera, "MONAP."

79. Amaro, "Análisis preliminar," 412–14; Oehler, Minifundios, 371.

80. Philip Berryman, *The Religious Roots of Rebellion: Christians in Central American Revolutions* (Maryknoll, N.Y.: Orbis Books, 1984).

81. M. F. Smith, "Agricultural Development," 51.

82. As opposed to grassroots organizations, which are initiated and organized by the rank and file themselves.

83. "Credit unions" were by far the most successful of the three types of cooperatives which had juridical personality. See Amaro, "Análisis preliminar," 395.

84. M. F. Smith, "Agricultural Development," 80–81.

85. Rivera, "MONAP."

86. The introduction of fertilizer into subsistence farming in Guatemala is now considered to be a classic example of misguided development strategy. Although the subsidized use of fertilizers increased yields and consumption in the short run, the continual use of fertilizer was neither economically nor environmentally feasible. When campesinos could no longer afford expensive chemical inputs, they found that the soil was no longer suitable for subsistence farming without them. Many smallholders and subsistence farmers were unable to return their land to the condition it had been in prior to the introduction of fertilizers and pesticides, and overall yields fell in the long run, forcing some smallholders to abandon subsistence farming. This is sometimes referred to as the fertilizer debacle.

87. M. F. Smith, "Agricultural Development," 84–85; Handy, *Gift of the Devil*, 240.

88. *"El concepto de autonomia relativa"*—Interview, Arnoldo Noriega, offices of IPES, Guatemala City, 16 August 1999.

89. Gott, 64.

90. Adolfo Gilly, "Part Two: The Guerrilla Movement in Guatemala," *Monthly Review* (June 1965), 28–29.

91. Gott, *Guerrilla Movements in Latin America* (Garden City, N.Y.: Doubleday, 1971), 54; Aguilera Peralta and Romero Imery, *Dialéctica del terror* 107–8.

92. These students were the same ones who had been involved in the turmoil that broke out in March and April 1962. See chapter 4.

93. Gott, *Guerrilla Movements,* 62; Gilly, 16.

94. Sichar Moreno, *Guatemala*, 32–33.

95. Edgar Albert Marroquín, *Turcios Lima: Éste sí era comandante* (Jalapa, Guatemala: Imprenta Vasquez, 1998).

96. Gott, *Guerrilla Movements,* 45–53; Aguilera Peralta and Romero Imery, *Dialéctica del terror*, 106–7.

97. Morrison and May, "Escape from Terror."

98. Between 1957 and 1962 (the Ydígoras administration), the labor movement as a whole (which was predominantly *urban*) was fairly stagnant. Mario López Larrave attributed this sluggishness to corruption rather than repres-

sion. In 1962 a wave of new national organizations and alliances began with the National Christian Workers' Front, which later became the Central Federation of Guatemalan Workers (FECETRAG). In 1963, SAMF (the railroad workers' union) and some smaller unions joined together to form the Confederation of Guatemalan Workers (CONTRAGUA), and in 1964 the Union Federation of Guatemala (CONSIGUA) was formed through an agreement of the UFCO union, SETUFCO, and the union of the Social Security Administration, STIGSS. Also in 1964 the FTG was reorganized on a small scale, mostly as a federation of the public service sector unions. In 1965 the National Federation of Transport Workers (FENOT), founded by the "Social Christians" or Christian Democrats, was officially recognized, as were the other two Social Christian coalitions, FECETRAG (in 1966) and the FCG (in 1967). In 1968 the three Social Christian Federations came together as the National Workers Confederation (CNT). In 1969 a federation of bank workers was recognized as the Federation of Bank Employees of Guatemala (FESEB). Between 1970 and 1973, divisions within the FCG sparked the formation of national campesino union, the Movement of Independent Campesinos (MCI) and two National Campesino Federations, the National Federation of Campesino Organizations (FENOCAM), and the National Federation of Agricultural and Indigenous Communities (FEN-CAIG). Also during this period CONTRAGUA and CONSIGUA joined together to form the Central of Federated Workers (CTF), which subsequently joined with FASGUA, CNT, FTG, and FESEB to form the National Council of Union Consultation (CNCS). This union was created in response to the labor repression of the late 1960s. The sheer amount of organizational activity during this period is startling, but it can be misleading if used as a gauge of actual participation. López Larrave, *Movimiento sindical*, 55–58; Jiménez, "Movimiento campesino," 308.

99. López Larrave, *Movimiento sindical*, 56–57; World Bank, *World Economic Tables, 1976* (Baltimore: Johns Hopkins University Press, 1976), 412–14 and 420–22; Shelton Davis, "Social Roots of Political Violence in Guatemala," *Cultural Survival* 7 (Spring 1983): 8.

## Chapter 6

1. Albizures, "Movimiento sindical."

2. The CTF was the organization created in 1970 when CONTRAGUA and CONSIGUA joined forces. As mentioned in chapter 4, CONTRAGUA and the MCI (and thus the CNC) had unfriendly relations with one another. See López Larrave, *Movimiento sindical*, 57.

3. Albizures, "Movimiento sindical."

4. López Larrave, *Movimiento sindical*, 58.

5. The first CNUS came together in 1946—it was the first modern attempt at *unión sindical* in Guatemala. See López Larrave, *Movimiento sindical*, 33-34.

6. The first two attempts were the FNS in 1968, and the CNCS in 1974.

7. Henry Frundt, *Refreshing Pauses: Coca-Cola and Human Rights in Guatemala* (New York: Praeger, 1987), 15. See also Miguel Angel Albizures, *Tiempo de sudor y lucha* (Mexico City: Praxis gráfica editorial, 1987).

8. CITGUA, *Movimiento sindical* (1975-1985), 39.

9. Interview, José Pinzón, offices of the CTCG, Guatemala City, 10 July 1989; interview, Julio Celso de León, offices of ASIES, Guatemala City, 12 June 1989.

10. CITGUA, 1:1, 81.

11. Ibid., 42-44.

12. There were commissions of advertising and the press, finances, legal matters, etc.

13. CITGUA, 1:1, 42.

14. Albizures, "Movimiento sindical."

15. Miguel Angel Albizures, "Struggles and Experiences of the Guatemalan Trade Union Movement, 1976-June 1978," *Latin American Perspectives* 25-26 (Spring and Summer 1980): 151.

16. Ibid., 153.

17. "Resuelto hoy el conflicto de los mineros," *El Imparcial*, 17 November 1977, p. 1.

18. Albizures, "Movimiento sindical"; interview, Miguel Angel Albizures, office of FAMDEGUA, Guatemala City, 10 August 1999.

19. Albizures, "Struggles," 153-54; Concerned Guatemala Scholars,

*Guatemala: Dare to Struggle, Dare to Win,* rev. ed. (Brooklyn: CGS, 1982), 30; "Marcha sindical llega," *El Imparcial,* 19 November 1977, p. 1.

20. CNT reaction to Panzós, printed in *Alero* (Guatemala USAC) no. 30, Tercera Época (June 1978): 170–202.

21. "La clase obrera en la revolución centromericana," *Cuadernos de CIDANO* (Mexico City: Centro de Información, Documentación y Análisis sobre el Movimiento Obrero Latinoamericano, 1980)—CITGUA document no. 203220, 37.

22. CUC marched for the first time in the May Day demonstration one month before this rally, but they were not marching as part of CNUS.

23. The Committee for Labor Unity (CNUS) in exile submitted a letter in the early 1980s to the Committee for Labor Freedom of the ILO at their annual meeting in Geneva, which lists the names of dozens of labor leaders who were known to have been murdered by state security forces in the early 1980s, as well as other incidents of egregious acts of repression and violence directed at organized labor. Albizures, "Movimiento sindical," anexo, no. 2.

24. See Hank Frundt, "AIFLD in Guatemala: End or Beginning of a New Regional Strategy," *Social and Economic Studies* 44:2–3 (1995): 287–319.

25. CITGUA, 1: Año 6, 97–100; Frundt "AIFLD in Guatemala," 297.

26. Frundt, "AIFLD in Guatemala," 297.

27. The organization of UNSITRAGUA was preceded by a short-lived attempt at reorganization called the Coordinator of National Trade Union Unity (CONUS). See Hank Frundt, "To Buy the World a Coke: Implications of Trade Union Redevelopment in Guatemala," *Latin American Perspectives* 54:14:3 (Summer 1987): 381–416.

28. Ibid., 106–12.

29. Frank and Wheaton, *Indian Guatemala*, 38–39.

30. M. F. Smith, "Agricultural Development," 66.

31. Luís Gurriarán (testimony), in Frank and Wheaton, *Indian Guatemala*, 33.

32. Amaro, "Análisis preliminar," 413. Savings and loan cooperatives provided access to loans for agricultural inputs. Consumer and agricultural cooperatives had a broader range of functions. They made bulk purchases of consumer goods and agricultural inputs and they provided technical assistance.

33. M. F. Smith, "Agricultural Development," 87.

34. Frank and Wheaton, *Indian Guatemala*, 34.

35. Luis Gurriarán, in Frank and Wheaton, *Indian Guatemala*, 33.

36. M. F. Smith, "Agricultural Development," 128.

37. Jonas, *Battle for Guatemala*, 135–36; "Los fundamentos teóricos de la Fuerzas Armadas Rebeldes," document produced by FAR Dirección Nacional Ejecutiva, Guatemala City, March 1973. CITGUA archives, Mexico City.

38. Jonas, *Battle for Guatemala*, 136.

39. Concerned Guatemala Scholars, *Dare to Struggle*, 19–21; Longman Group, *Latin American Political Movements* (London: Longman, 1985), 145.

40. Jonas, *Battle for Guatemala*, 138.

41. Ibid.

42. Wickham-Crowley, *Guerrillas and Revolution*, 224; Jonas, *Battle for Guatemala*, 136–37; Tom Barry and Deb Preusch, *The Central American Fact Book* (New York: Grove Press, 1986), 232–33.

43. Jonas, *Battle for Guatemala*, 137; Mario Payeras, *Days of the Jungle: The Testimony of a Guatemalan Guerrillero* (New York: Monthly Review Press, 1983), 71–77.

44. For a discussion of the Indian question by the EGP leadership see *Articles from* Compañero: *The International Magazine of Guatemala's Guerrilla Army of the Poor* (San Francisco: Solidarity Publications, 1982), 17–26.

45. Concerned Guatemala Scholars, *Dare to Struggle*, 19–21; Longman, *Political Movements*, 45.

46. Wickham-Crowley, *Guerrillas and Revolution*, 217, 289; Jonas, *Battle for Guatemala*, 138; Concerned Guatemala Scholars, *Dare to Struggle*, 19–21; Longman, *Political Movements*, 145.

47. Interview, Arnoldo Noriega, office of IPES, Guatemala City, August 16, 1999.

48. Wickham-Crowley, *Guerrillas and Revolution*, 224; Barry and Preusch, *Fact Book*, 233; Jonas, *Battle for Guatemala*, 138.

49. Interview, Molina; interview, Noriega.

50. Albizures, "Movimiento sindical."

51. Interview, Noriega; interview, Ing. Raul Molina, Guatemala City, 14 August 1999.

52. Jonas, *Battle for Guatemala*, 137.

53. For a discussion of the changing nature of the campesinado, see Ricardo Falla, *Quiché rebelde* (Guatemala City: USAC, 1978); José Luis Chea, *Guatemala: La cruz fragmentada* (Costa Rica: FLACSO, 1988); Fernández, *Comité de Unidad Campesina*, notebook 2; Carlos Figueroa Ibarra, *El proletariado rural en el agro guatemalteco* (Guatemala: Editorial Universitaria, 1980); and Frank and Wheaton, *Indian Guatemala*.

54. Wickham-Crowley, *Guerrillas and Revolution*, 217–18.

55. Interview, Noriega.

56. Interview, Molina.

57. Barry and Preusch, *Fact Book*, 233; interview, Molina.

58. Wickham-Crowley, *Guerrillas and Revolution*, 217; Jonas, *Battle*, 138.

59. Wickham-Crowley, *Guerrillas and Revolution*, 289–90.

60. Fernández, *Comité de Unidad Campesina*, 6.

61. CUC, interview by CITGUA, 22 August 1985, CITGUA doc. 300744; Arturo Arias, "El movimiento indígena en Guatemala: 1970–1983," in *Movimientos populares en centroamérica*, ed. Daniel Camacho and Rafael Menjívar (San José, Costa Rica: EDUCA, 1985), 76–81.

62. CUC, interview by CITGUA.

63. Press release submitted by CUC concerning the third meeting of the National Assembly of CUC, published in *Noticias de Guatemala* 1:15 (23 April 1979): 199–201. (Emphasis in original.)

64. Ibid., 1:15.

65. Fernández, *Comité de Unidad Campesina*, 35–36, 41.

66. Menchú, *I, Rigoberta Menchú*, 186.

67. Fernández, *Comité de Unidad Campesina*, 24.

68. "Declaración de los pueblos indígenas reunidas in Iximche," reprinted in Fernández, *Comité de Unidad Campesina*, 57.

69. Pablo Ceto, one of the founders of CUC, quoted in Arias, "Movimiento indígena," 85 (emphasis mine).

70. CUC preferred to call itself a secret organization rather than a clandestine organization, as the latter term is thought to imply subversion. CUC was secret in the sense that it was not legally recognized by the Guatemalan government and it did not provide access to the organization by noncampesinos; however, for most of its years CUC was "public" as well as secret.

It was public in the sense that it issued public statements, it was involved in organizing labor strikes, making demands on the government institutions, and openly participating in public demonstrations. CUC openly acknowledged its own existence and maintained an office in Mexico City prior to the signing of the peace accords. Now it maintains an office in Guatemala City. During the period in which CUC went underground, they ceased these public activities.

71. CUC, interview by CITGUA.

72. Young men were often taken from their villages against their will, placing great hardship on their families.

73. Interview, anonymous leader of CUC, Guatemala City, 3 August 1989.

74. CUC statement printed in Carlos Felipe Castro Torres, "Crecimiento de las luchas campesinas en Guatemala," *Estudios centroamericanos* (El Salvador) 33: 356–57 (June–July 1978): 466–74.

75. For example, they were already publishing a multilingual newsletter, *De Sol a sol* (From sun to sun).

76. Pablo Ceto, quoted in Frank and Wheaton, *Indian Guatemala,* 54.

77. Fernández, *Comité de Unidad Campesina,* 21. "Patria chica" is the cultural phenomenon of strong local or regional identification.

78. Interview, Rigoberta Menchú, offices of CUC, Mexico City, 16 January 1992.

79. Menchú, *I, Rigoberta Menchú.*

80. Fernández, *Comité de Unidad Campesina,* 35, 37–40.

81. By 1980 more than half a million highland peasants migrated to the coast to work for part of the year as wage laborers on large plantations in order to supplement their incomes.

82. CUC, interview by CITGUA; "La clase obrera en la revolución," 37.

83. Fernández, *Comité de Unidad Campesina,* 40, 42.

84. Noticias de Guatemala, no. 33:8 (January 1980): 490–91.

85. *De sol a sol,* in Fried, et al., 206; Fernández, *Comité de Unidad Campesina,* 43–44.

86. *De sol a sol,* in Fried et al., 206–8; Fernández, *Comité de Unidad Campesina,* 44.

87. *De sol a sol,* in Fried et al., 208, 209; Fernández, *Comité de Unidad Campesina,* 45.

88. Albizures, "Movimiento sindical."

89. *De sol a sol*, in Fried et al., 209.

90. Fernández, *Comité de Unidad Campesina*, 45, 47–48.

91. Ibid., 32.

92. Ibid., 32, 48–50.

93. Interview, Menchú.

94. The *Majawil Q'ij* represents, in addition to CUC, the Mutual Support Group (GAM, or Grupo de Apoyo Mutuo) which documents the cases of the disappeared and pushed for human rights reforms in Guatemala, the National Council of Guatemalan Widows (CONAVIGUA, or the *Comité Nacional de Viudas de Guatemala*), the Council of Ethnic Communities "All Equal" (CERJ, or the Consejo de Comunidades Etnicas "Runujel Junam"), the National Committee for the Displaced of Guatemala (CONDEG, or the Comité Nacional de los Desplazados de Guatemala), and the Campesino Committee of the Altiplano (CCDA, or the Comité Campesino del Altiplano). These organizations are predominantly—but not exclusively—indigenous. They include ladino members and define their goals in broader political terms that do not exclude the concerns of poor and exploited campesinos; see Carol Smith, "Maya Nationalism," *NACLA Report on the Americas*, 25:3 (December 1991): 29–33; Carol Smith, "The Second 'Encuentro Continental,'" *Guatemala Scholars Network News* (April 1992): 1.

95. Carol Smith uses David McCreery's recent research on the history of Maya passive resistance as the basis for defining what *is* the Maya way.

96. Carol Smith, "Maya Nationalism," 32–33.

97. See Ted Fischer and Robert McKenna Brown, eds., *Mayan Cultural Activism in Guatemala* (Austin: University of Texas Press, 1996); Warren, *Indigenous Movements;* and Nelson, *Finger in the Wound*.

98. Carol Smith, "Maya Nationalism," 30.

99. Carol Smith, "Second Ecuentro," 3.

100. Interview. Menchú.

101. Carol Smith, "Maya Nationalism"; interview, Menchú.

## Chapter 7

1. I am using the term civil society to refer to the popular movement during the period under consideration here (1954–1985), even though the term is not widely used in Guatemala before the 1990s. The popular organizations of this earlier period are the precursors to the Assembly of Civil Society (ASC), which serves as the official representative body of civil society in the implementation of the peace accords and the democratization process. It is the appropriate term because I am making an explicit connection between the evolution of the popular movement (between 1954 and 1985) and the contemporary process of democratization. See chapter 2.

2. A mechanistic organizational structure is defined by management specialists James Bowditch and Anthony Buono as one in which there is "(1) a clear definition of jobs, (2) senior administrators [professional labor organizers] have more knowledge of problems facing an organization than those at a lower level, (3) standardized policies or procedures [which in the case of Guatemala were legally defined by the state] govern organizational decision-making, and (4) rewards are determined by adherence to instructions from supervisors." Elsewhere these authors characterize a mechanistic structure as "rigid" and "hierarchical." See James Bowditch and Anthony Buono, *A Primer on Organizational Behavior*, 2d ed. (New York: Wiley, 1990), 221.

3. Organic structures are defined by Bowditch and Buono as those organizations in which "(1) there is a de-emphasis on formal job descriptions and specializations . . . ; (2) there is no assumption that people in higher positions are better informed than those lower in the organization (many times the reverse is true); (3) horizontal relationships are equal or more important than vertical, chain of command relationships . . . ; (4) organizational atmosphere is more collegial (strict superior-subordinate relationships are de-emphasized); and (5) the formal structure of the organization is fluid and changeable." Bowditch and Buono, *Organizational Behavior*, 221.

4. Amaro, "Análisis preliminar," 412.

5. Interview, Menchú.

6. "La Clase obrera en la revolución centroamericana," *Cuadernos de CIDANO* (Mexico City: Centro de Información, Documentación y Análisis

sobre el Movimiento Obrero Latinoamericano, 1980)—CITGUA doc. 203220, 37; CUC, interview by CITGUA.

7. Piero Gleijeses, "Politics and Culture in Guatemala" (Ann Arbor: Center for Political Studies, Institute for Social Research at the University of Michigan, 1988), 4.

8. Interview, Menchú.

# Bibliography

## Newspapers and Periodicals

*Alero* (Guatemala)

*Christian Science Monitor* (U.S.)

*El Gráfico* (Guatemala)

*Estudios centroamericanos* (El Salvador)

*Guatemala* (Guatemala)

*El Imparcial* (Guatemala)

*Inforpress centroamericana* (Guatemala)

*La Nación* (Guatemala)

*Noticias de Guatemala* (Guatemala, Costa Rica, and Mexico)

*Política y sociedad* (Guatemala)

*Prensa libre* (Guatemala)

*La Tarde* (Guatemala)

## Interviews

Lic. Carlos Enrique Aguirre R., office of MONAP, Guatemala City, 1 August 1989.

Lic. Miguel Angel Albizures, office of FAMDEGUA, Guatemala City, 10 August 1999.

Campesinos from Suchitepéquez, 18 July 1989.

Lic. Julio Celso de León, offices of ASIES, Guatemala City, 12 June 1989.

Comité de Unidad Campesina, anonymous leader, Guatemala City, 3 August 1989.

Pdr. Andres Girón de León, Nueva Concepción, Escuintla, 12 August 1988.

Lic. Helmer Melásquez, offices of IDESAC, Guatemala City, 21 June 1989.

Rigoberta Menchú, offices of the CUC, Mexico City, 16 January 1992.

Ing. Raul Molina, Guatemala City, 14 August 1999.

Arnoldo Noriega, URNG, offices of IPES, Guatemala City, 16 August 1999.

José Pinzón, offices of the CTCG, Guatemala City, 10 July 1989.

Rolando Rodríguez, offices of IGEFOS, Guatemala City, 18 July 1989.

## Other Primary Sources

Albizures, Miguel Angel. "El Movimiento sindical y popular guatemalteco: Recomposición, auge y desarollo, resurgimiento y situación actual, 1960–1995." Unpublished manuscript in possession of author.

———. "Struggles and Experiences of the Guatemalan Trade Union Movement, 1976–June 1978." *Latin American Perspectives* 7 *(Spring and Summer* 1980): 145.

———. *Tiempo de sudor y lucha.* Mexico City: Praxis gráfica editorial, 1987.

Amaro, Nelson. "Análisis preliminar del movimiento de promoción popular en Guatemala hasta 1968." In *El reto del desarollo en Guatemala*, ed. IDESAC. Guatemala City: IDESAC, 1970.

Americas Watch. *Human Rights in Guatemala: No Neutrals Allowed.* New York: Americas Watch, 1982.

Amnesty International. *Guatemala: A Government Program of Political Murder.* London: Amnesty International, 1981.

Azurdia Alfaro, Roberto, ed. *Recopilación de las leyes de la Republica de Guatemala.* Guatemala City: Tipografía Nacional, 1944–1984.

Batista, Astenogenes R. "Proyecto Castillo Armas." *Guatemala* No. 1, Año 1 (September 1956): 54–55.

CIDANO. *Cuadernos de CIDANO.* Mexico City: Centro de Información, Documentación y Análisis sobre el Movimiento Obrero Latinoamericano.

CITGUA. *El movimiento sindical en Guatemala* (1975–1985): *Formación y capacitación.* Vol. 1, Año 6 (January 1989). Mexico City: CITGUA, 1989.

———. *El movimiento sindical en Guatemala* (1986–1988): *Formación y capacitación Parte* 1. Vol. 2, Año 6 (February 1990). Mexico City: CITGUA, 1990.

———. *Transcribed interview with CUC.* CITGUA archives, doc. 30074.

CNUS. Unidad del CNUS (CNUS newsletter) Año 1. Printed in Centro de Investigación y Educación Popular America Central, Equipo de Apoyo Sindical, doc. 5: Experiencias del Auge de Masas (1975–1981), n.d. CITGUA archives, doc. 203136.

Comisión para Esclarecimiento Histórico [CEH]. *Guatemala: Memoria del Silencio Tz'inil Na'tab'al.* Guatemala City: CEH, 1999.

Comité Interamericano de Desarollo Agrícola. *Tenencia de la tierra y desarollo socio-economico del sector agrícola: Guatemala.* Washington D.C.: Pan-American Union, OAS, 1965.

Cultural Survival, Inc. *Voices of the Survivors: The Massacre at Finca San Francisco.* Cambridge, Mass.: Anthropology Resource Center, 1983.

———. "Death and Disorder in Guatemala." *Cultural Survival Quarterly* 7:1 (Spring 1983).

EGP. *Articles from* Compañero: *The International Magazine of Guatemala's Guerrilla Army of the Poor.* San Francisco: Solidarity Publications, 1982.

FAR. "Los fundamentos teóricos de la fuerzas armadas rebeldes." *Guatemala,* March 1973. CITGUA archives.

Historical Clarification Committee for Guatemala. *Guatemala: Memory of Silence.* This document can be found at <http://hrdata.aaas.org/ceh/report/english/index.html>.

Instituto para el Desarrollo Económico Social de América Central [IDESAC]. "Boletin Semestral," no. 4, 25th Anniversary Issue. (January–June 1989).

Información Documental de América Latina. *Movimientos revolucionarios de América Latina.* Caracas: Información Documental de América Latina, 1972.

International Work Group for Indigenous Affairs [IWGIA]. *Guatemala 1978: The Massacre at Panzós.* Copenhagen: IWGIA, 1978.

INTA. INTA Memorias. Guatemala City: INTA, 1970–1983.

Jonas, Suzanne, et al., eds. *Guatemala: Tyranny on Trial.* San Francisco: Synthesis Publications, 1984.

Kita, Bernice. *What Prize Awaits Us: Letters from Guatemala.* Maryknoll, N.Y.: Orbis Books, 1988.

Macías, Julio César. *La Guerrilla fue mi camino.* Guatemala City: Editorial Piedra Santa, 1999.

Menchú, Rigoberta. *I, Rigoberta Menchú: An Indian Woman in Guatemala.* Edited by Elisabeth Burgos-Debray. Trans. by Ann Wright. London: Verso Editions, 1984.

Ministerio de Agricultura, Ganadería, y Alimentación. "Bases para sostener la política agraria del país." Guatemala, Ministerio de Agricultura, 1986. Photocopy.

Montejo, Victor. *Testimony: Death of a Guatemalan Village.* Willimantic, Conn.: Curbstone Press, 1987.

Oehler, Klaus, ed. *Los minifundios en Guatemala, situación y perspectivas: Enfoque especial del indígena.* Guatemala City: IDESAC, Editorial Financiera, 1971.

Oficina de Derechos Humanos del Arzobispado de Guatemala [ODHAG]—Proyecto Interdiocesano de Recuperación de la Memoria Histórica [REMHI]. *Guatemala, Nunca más: Impactos de la violencia.* 4 vols. Guatemala City: ODHAG, 1998.

Organization of American States and the Inter-American Development Bank. *Tax Systems of Latin America.* Washington, DC: OAS, 1966.

Pan-American Union. *Tenencia de la tierra y desarrollo socio-economico del sector agrícola.* Washington D.C.: Pan American Union, 1965.

Payeras, Mario. *Days of the Jungle: The Testimony of a Guatemalan Guerrillero.* New York: Monthly Review Press, 1983.

Reed, Thomas F., and Karen Brandow, eds. *The Sky Never Changes: Testimonies from the Guatemalan Labor Movement.* Ithaca, N.Y.: ILR Press, Cornell University Press, 1996.

Romualdi, Serafino. *Presidents and Peons: Recollections of a Labor Ambassador in Latin America.* New York: Funk and Wagnalls, 1967.

———. "Report on Guatemala." *American Federationist* 61:9 (September 1954): 26–27, 31.

World of Information. *Latin America Annual Report.* 1979.

## Secondary Sources

Adams, Richard Newbold. *Crucifixion by Power: Essays on Guatemalan National Social Structure, 1944–1966.* Austin: University of Texas Press, 1970.

Adams, Richard Newbold, Roland H. Ebel, et al. *Community Culture and National Change.* New Orleans: MARI, Tulane University, 1972.

Aguilera Peralta, Gabriel. "The Massacre at Panzós and Capitalist Development in Latin America." In *Revolution in Central America,* ed. Stanford Central America Action Network. Boulder: Westview, 1983.

———. "La militarización del estado guatemalteco." *Polémica* (Costa Rica) 1 (September–October 1981).

Aguilera Peralta, Gabriel, Jorge Romero Imery, et al. *Dialéctica del terror en Guatemala.* Costa Rica: EDUCA, 1981.

Alba, Victor. *Politics and the Labor Movement in Latin America.* Stanford, Calif.: Stanford University Press, 1968.

American Anthropological Association. Abstracts of the 87th Annual Meeting of the American Anthropological Association, Phoenix, November 1988.

Amman, Peter. "Revolution: A Redefinition." *Political Science Quarterly* 77 (March 1962): 36–53.

Anderson, Charles. "Toward a Theory of Latin American Politics." In *Politics and Social Change in Latin America: The Distinct Tradition,* ed. Howard J. Wiarda. Amherst: University of Massachusetts Press, 1982.

Arendt, Hannah. *On Violence.* New York: Harcourt Brace, 1970.

Arias, Arturo. "El movimiento indígena en Guatemala: 1970–1983." In *Movimientos populares en Centroamérica,* ed. Daniel Camacho and Rafael Menjívar. San José, Costa Rica: EDUCA, 1985.

Asociación de Investigación y Estudios Sociales [ASIES]. *Más de cien años del movimiento obrero urbano en Guatemala.* 4 vols. Guatemala City: ASIES, 1991.

Asturias Montenegro, G., and R. Gatica Trejo. *Earthquake S.O.S.: Guatemala 76.* Trans. Noel Thomas. Guatemala City: Girblan and Company, 1976.

Aya, Rod. "Theories of Revolution Reconsidered." *Theory and Society* 8 (July 1979): 33–99.

Barry, Tom, and Deb Preusch. *The Central American Fact Book.* New York: Grove Press, 1986.

Bejar, Héctor, and Carlos Franco. *Organización campesina y restructuración del estado.* Lima: CEDEP, 1985.

Bergquist, Charles. *Coffee and Conflict in Colombia, 1886–1910.* Durham, N.C.: Duke University Press, 1986.

———. *Labor in Latin America: Comparative Essays on Chile, Argentina, Venezuela, and Colombia.* Stanford, Calif.: Stanford University Press, 1986.

Bergquist, Charles, Ricardo Peñaranda, and Gonzalo Sánchez, eds. *Violence in Colombia: The Contemporary Crisis in Historical Perspective.* Wilmington, Del.: Scholarly Resources, 1992.

Bishop, Edwin. "The Guatemalan Labor Movement, 1944–1959." Ph.D. diss., University of Wisconsin, 1959. Microfilm.

Black, George. *Garrison Guatemala.* New York: Monthly Review Press, 1984.

Black, Jan. "Participation and Political Process." In *Latin America: Its Problems and Its Promise,* ed. Jan Black. Boulder: Westview, 1984.

———. "Ten Paradoxes of Rural Development: An Ecuadorian Case Study." *Journal of Developing Areas* 19:4 (July 1985): 527–55.

Booth, John. "Socio-Economic and Political Roots of National Revolts in Central America." *Latin American Research Review* 26:1 (1991): 33–74.

Bowditch, James, and Anthony Buono. *A Primer on Organizational Behavior*. 2d ed. New York: Wiley, 1990.

Brinton, Crane. *The Anatomy of Revolution*. Englewood Cliffs, N.J.: Prentice Hall, 1938. Reprint, New York: Random House, 1965.

Bulmer-Thomas, Victor. *The Political Economy of Central America since 1920*. New York: Cambridge, 1987.

Burns, E. Bradford. *Elites, Masses, and Modernization in Latin America, 1850–1930*. Austin: University of Texas Press, 1979.

———. *The Poverty of Progress: Latin America in the Nineteenth Century*. Berkeley: University of California Press, 1980.

Bush, Archer C. "Organized Labor in Guatemala, 1944–1949." M.A. thesis, Colgate University, 1950.

Camacho, Daniel, and Rafael Menjívar, eds. *Movimientos populares en América Latina*. Mexico City: Siglo Veintiuno Editores, 1989.

———, eds. *Movimientos populares en Centroamérica*. San José, Costa Rica: EDUCA, 1985.

Cambranes, J. C. *Agrarismo en Guatemala*, Monograph 1, CERCA. Guatemala City: Serviprensa Centroamericana, 1987.

———. *Coffee and Peasants*. Stockholm: Institute of Latin American Studies, 1985.

———. *Democratización y movimientos campesinos pro-tierras en Guatemala*. CERCA, Cuaderno 3. Guatemala City: CERCA, 1988.

———. "Origins of the Crisis of the Established Order in Guatemala." In *Central America: Crisis and Adaptation*, ed. Steve C. Ropp and James A. Morrison. Albuquerque: University of New Mexico Press, 1984.

———. *Sobre los empresarios agrarios y el estado en Guatemala*. CERCA, Cuaderno 1. Guatemala City: CERCA, 1988.

Cancian, Frank. "Political and Religious Organization." In *Handbook of Middle American Indians*, 16 vols., 6:283–98. Austin: University of Texas Press, 1967.

Carmack, Robert M., ed. *Harvest of Violence: The Maya Indians and the Guatemalan Crisis*. Norman: University of Oklahoma Press, 1988.

Carr, Barry, and Steve Ellner, eds. *The Latin American Left: From the Fall of Allende to Perestroika.* Boulder: Westview, 1993.

Carrière, Jean, Nigel Haworth, and Jacqueline Roddick, eds. *The State, Industrial Relations and the Labour Movement in Latin America.* New York: St. Martin's Press, 1989.

Carrigan, Ana. *The Palace of Justice: A Colombian Tragedy.* New York: Four Walls, Eight Windows, 1993.

Castrillo Zeledón, Mario. *Aspectos jurídico-laborales de la actividad agropecuraria.* Monograph 3, Facultad de Economía (USAC), Instituto de Investigaciones Económicas y Sociales, Guatemala City, October 1961.

Castro Torres, Carlos Felipe. "Crecimiento de las luchas campesinas en Guatemala." *Estudios centroamericanos* (El Salvador) 33 (January–July 1978): 462–77.

Chea, José Luis. *Guatemala: La cruz fragmentada.* Costa Rica: FLACSO, 1988.

Chorley, Katharine. *Armies and the Art of Revolution.* London: Faber and Faber, 1943.

Cohan, A. S. *Theories of Revolution: An Introduction.* New York: Halsted Press/Wiley, 1975.

Cohen, Youssef. *The Manipulation of Consent: The State and Working-Class Consciousness in Brazil.* Pittsburgh: University of Pittsburgh Press, 1989.

Colby, Benjamin N., and Lore M. Colby, eds. *The Daykeeper: The Life and Discourse of an Ixil Diviner.* Cambridge, Mass: Harvard University Press, 1981.

Collier, Ruth Berins, and David Collier. *Shaping the Political Arena: Critical Junctures, the Labor Movement, and Regime Dynamics in Latin America.* Princeton, N.J.: Princeton University Press, 1991.

Concerned Guatemala Scholars. *Guatemala: Dare to Struggle, Dare to Win.* Rev. ed. Brooklyn: CGS, 1982.

Davies, James. "Toward a Theory of Revolution." *American Sociological Review* 27 (February 1962): 5–19.

Davis, Shelton. "Social Roots of Political Violence in Guatemala." *Cultural Survival* 7 (Spring 1983).

Dix, Robert H. "Varieties of Revolution." *Comparative Politics* 15 (April 1983): 281–94.

Dunkerley, James. *Power in the Isthmus*. New York: Verso, 1988.

Duverger, Maurice. *Political Parties: Their Organization and Activity in the Modern State*. Trans. Barbara North and Robert North. 2d ed. New York: Wiley, 1959.

Ebel, Roland H. "The Development and the Decline of the Central American City-State." In *Rift and Revolution: The Central American Imbroglio,* ed. Howard J. Wiarda. Washington, D.C.: American Enterprise Institute for Public Policy Research, 1984.

Eckstein, Harry. "On the Etiology of Internal Wars." *History and Theory* 4 (1965): 133–65.

Edwards, Lyford P. *The Natural History of Revolution*. Chicago: University of Chicago Press, 1927.

Eisenstadt, S. N. *Revolution and Transformation of Societies: A Comparative Study of Civilizations*. New York: Free Press, 1978.

Ehrenberg, John. *Civil Society: The Critical History of an Idea*. New York: NYU Press, 1999.

Ellwood, Charles. "A Psychological Theory of Revolutions." *American Journal of Sociology* 11 (July 1905): 49–59.

Falla, Ricardo. *Masacre de la finca San Francisco, Huehuetenango, Guatemala*. Copenhagen : International Work Group for Indigenous Affairs, 1983.

———. *Quiché rebelde*. Guatemala City: USAC, 1978.

Feierabend, Ivo K., and Rosalind L. Feierabend. "Systematic Conditions of Political Aggression: An Application of Frustration-Aggression Theory." In *Anger, Violence, and Politics: Theories and Research,* ed. I. K. Feierabend, R. L. Feierabend, and Ted Robert Gurr, 136–83. Englewood Cliffs, N.J.: Prentice Hall, 1972.

Feierabend, Ivo K., Rosalind L. Feierabend, and Betty Nesvold. "Social Change and Political Violence: Cross-National Patterns." In *Violence in America,* ed. Hugh D. Graham and Ted Robert Gurr, 606–88. New York: Signet, 1969.

Fernández Fernández, José Manuel. *El Comité de Unidad Campesina: Origen y desarollo*. CERCA, Cuaderno 2. Guatemala City: CERCA, 1988.

Figueroa Ibarra, Carlos. *El proletariado rural en el agro guatemalteco.* Guatemala: Editorial Universitaria, 1980.

Flores Alvarado, Humberto. *Proletarización del campesino de Guatemala.* Guatemala City: Editorial Piedra Santa, 1977.

Floridi, Alexis U., and Annette E. Stiefbold. *The Uncertain Alliance: The Catholic Church and Labor in Latin America.* Miami: University of Miami Center for Advanced International Studies, 1973.

Frank, Luisa, and Philip Wheaton. *Indian Guatemala: Path to Liberation.* Washington D.C.: EPICA Task Force, 1984.

Fried, Jonathan, Marvin Gettleman, Deborah Levenson, and Nancy Packenham, eds. *Guatemala in Rebellion: Unfinished History.* New York: Grove Press, 1985.

Frundt, Henry J. "AIFLD in Guatemala: End or Beginning of a New Regional Strategy?" *Social and Economic Studies* 44:2–3 (1995): 287–319.

———. *Refreshing Pauses: Coca-Cola and Human Rights in Guatemala.* New York: Praeger, 1987.

———. "To Buy the World a Coke: Implications of Trade Union Redevelopment in Guatemala." *Latin American Perspectives* Issue 54, vol. 14, no. 3 (Summer 1987): 381–416.

Galeano, Eduardo. *Guatemala: País ocupado.* Mexico City: Editorial Nuestro Tiempo, 1967.

García Añoveras, Jesús. "La reforma agraria de Arbenz en Guatemala." Ph.D. diss., Instituto de Cooperación Iberoamericano, Departamento de Historia de América de la Facultad de Geografía e Historia, Universidad de Complutense de Madrid, 1982.

Gellner, Ernest. *Conditions of Liberty: Civil Society and Its Rivals.* New York: Penguin, 1996.

———. "La universidad y el campesinado." *Alero* 3:28 (1978): 133–234.

Geschwender, James. "Explorations in the Theory of Social Movements and Revolution." *Social Forces* 47 (December 1968): 127–35.

Gillin, John, and Kalman Silvert. "Ambiguities in Guatemala." *Foreign Affairs* 34 (April 1956): 469–82.

Gilly, Adolfo. "Part Two: The Guerrilla Movement in Guatemala." *Monthly Review* (June 1965): 7–41.

Gleijeses, Piero. "Politics and Culture in Guatemala." Center for Political Studies, Institute for Social Research, University of Michigan, 1988.

———. *Shattered Hope: The Guatemalan Revolution and the United States, 1944–1954.* Princeton, N.J.: Princeton University Press, 1992.

Goldstone, Jack A. "Theories of Revolution: The Third Generation." *World Politics* 32 (April 1980): 425–53.

Gott, Richard. *Guerrilla Movements in Latin America.* Garden City, NY.: Doubleday, 1971.

———. *Rural Guerrillas in Latin America.* England: Penguin Books, 1973.

Gould, Jeffrey. *To Lead as Equals: Rural Protest and Political Consciousness in Cinandega, Nicaragua, 1912–1979.* Chapel Hill: University of North Carolina Press, 1990.

Greenfield, Gerald Michael, and Sheldon L. Maram. *Latin American Labor Organizations.* New York: Greenwood Press, 1987.

Guerra Borges, Alfredo. "La cuestión agraria, cuestión clave de la crisis social en Guatemala." *Perspectiva*, n.s. 4 (August 1984).

Guevara, Ernesto [Che]. *Guerrilla Warfare.* New York: Monthly Review Press, 1961.

———. *Che: Selected Works of Ernesto Guevara*, ed. Rolando E. Bonacheu and Nelson Valdés. Cambridge, Mass: MIT Press, 1969.

Guinea, Gerardo. *Evolución agraria en Guatemala.* Guatemala City: La Nueva Editorial (government), 1958.

Gurr, Ted Robert. "A Causal Model of Civil Strife: A Comparative Analysis Using New Indices." *American Political Science Review* 62 (December 1968): 1104–24.

———. *Why Men Rebel.* Princeton, N.J.: Princeton University Press, 1970.

Hagopian, Mark. *The Phenomenon of Revolution.* New York: Dodd, Mead, 1974.

Handelman, Howard. *Struggle in the Andes: Peasant Political Mobilization in Peru.* Austin: University of Texas Press, 1975.

Handy, Jim. *Gift of the Devil.* Boston: South End Press, 1984.

————. "Revolution and Reaction: National Policy and Rural Politics in Guatemala, 1944–1954." Ph.D. diss., University of Toronto, 1985.

————. *Revolution in the Countryside: Rural Conflict and Agrarian Reform in Guatemala, 1944–1954.* Chapel Hill: University of North Carolina Press, 1994.

Hart, Mark. *The Dynamics of Revolution.* Stockholm: Rotobeckman, 1971.

Herrera, Francisco. *Agrarismo guatemalteco: Sinopsis histórica.* Guatemala City: Editorial Landívar, 1966.

Huizer, Gerrit. *Peasant Rebellion in Latin America.* Harmondsworth, Middlesex: Penguin, 1973.

Huntington, Samuel P. *Political Order in Changing Societies.* New Haven: Yale University Press, 1968.

Immerman, Richard H. *The CIA in Guatemala: The Foreign Policy of Intervention.* Austin: University of Texas Press, 1982.

Jessop, Bob. *Social Order, Reform, and Revolution.* New York: Macmillan, 1972.

Jiménez, Dina. "El movimiento campesino en Guatemala: 1969–1980." In *Movimientos populares en Centroamérica,* ed. Daniel Camacho and Rafael Menjívar. San José, Costa Rica: EDUCA, 1985.

Johnson, Chalmers. *Revolutionary Change.* Boston: Little, Brown, 1966.

Jonas, Suzanne. *The Battle for Guatemala: Rebels, Death Squads, and U.S. Power.* Boulder: Westview, 1991.

————. *Of Centaurs and Doves: Guatemala's Peace Process.* Boulder: Westview, 2000.

Jonas, Suzanne, and David Tobis, eds. *Guatemala.* New York: North American Congress on Latin America, 1974.

Keane, John. *Reflections on Violence.* New York: Verso, 1996.

Krammick, Isaac. "Reflections on Revolution: Definition and Explanation in Recent Scholarship." *History and Theory* 11 (1972): 26–63.

Landsberger, Henry A. "Role of Peasant Movements and Revolts in Development." In *Latin American Peasant Movements,* ed. H. A. Landsberger. Ithaca, N.Y.: Cornell University Press, 1969.

————, ed. *Latin American Peasant Movements.* Ithaca, N.Y.: Cornell University Press, 1969.

————, ed. *Rural Protest: Peasant Movements and Social Change.* New York: Barnes and Noble, 1973.

Landsberger, Henry, and Cynthia N. Hewitt. "Ten Sources of Weakness and Cleavage in Latin American Peasant Movements." In *Agrarian Problems and Peasant Movements in Latin America,* ed. Rodolfo Stavenhagen. New York: Anchor Books/Doubleday, 1970.

Laswell, Harold, and Abraham Kaplan. *Power and Society: A Framework for Political Inquiry.* New Haven: Yale University Press, 1950.

Le Bon, Gustave. *The Psychology of Revolution.* New York: Ernest Benn, 1913.

Lederer, Emil. "On Revolutions." *Social Research* 3 (February 1936): 1–18

Levenson-Estrada, Deborah. *Trade Unionists against Terror: Guatemala City, 1954–1985.* Chapel Hill: University of North Carolina Press, 1994.

Longman Group. *Latin American Political Movements.* London: Longman, 1985.

López Larrave, Mario. *Breve historia del movimiento sindical guatemalteco.* Guatemala: Editorial Universitaria (San Carlos), 1979.

López Porras, Roberto. *Formas de tenencia de la tierra y algunos otros aspectos de la actividad agropecuraria.* Monograph 1. Guatemala: Facultad de Economia (USAC), Instituto de Investigaciones Económicas y Sociales, October 1961.

Magill, John. *Labor Unions and Political Socialization: A Case Study of Bolivian Workers.* New York: Praeger, 1974.

Malamud-Goti, Jaime. *Game without End: State Terror and the Politics of Justice.* Norman: University of Oklahoma Press, 1996.

Manz, Beatriz. *Refugees of a Hidden War: The Aftermath of Counter-insurgency in Guatemala.* Albany: State University of New York Press, 1988.

Marroquín, Edgar Alberto. *Turcios Lima: Éste sí era comandante.* Jalapa, Guatemala: Imprenta Vasquez, 1998.

Marshall, Neville Buck, Jr. "Patterns of Revolution Reconsidered: The Central American Laboratory." Ph.D. diss., Tulane University, 1992.

May, Rachel. "The Mobilization of Guatemalan Campesinos into National Labor Organizations, 1954–1984." M.A. thesis, Tulane University, 1990.

McClintock, Cynthia. *Peasant Cooperatives and Political Change in Peru.* Princeton, N.J.: Princeton University Press, 1981.

———. "Peru's Sendero Luminoso Rebellion: Origins and Trajectory." In *Power and Popular Protest: Latin American Social Movements,* ed. Susan Eckstein, 61–101. Berkeley: University of California Press, 1989.

McClintock, Michael. *The American Connection.* Vol. 2, *State Terror and Popular Resistance in Guatemala.* London: Zed Books, 1985.

McCreery, David. *Development and the State in Reforma Guatemala.* Athens: Ohio University Center for International Studies, 1983.

———. "Hegemony and Repression in Rural Guatemala, 1871–1940." *Peasant Studies* 17:3 (Spring 1990): 157–77.

———. "An Odious Feudalism: Mandamientos and Commercial Agriculture in Guatemala, 1861–1920." *Latin American Perspectives* (Winter 1986): 99–117.

Melville, Thomas, and Marjorie Melville. *Guatemala: The Politics of Land Ownership.* New York: Free Press, 1971.

Mendízabal, Ana Beatriz. "Estado y políticas de desarollo agrario: La masacre campesina de Panzós." *Política y sociedad* 11: Epoca, no. 16 (July–December 1978).

Menjívar, Rafael. *Reforma agraria: Guatemala, Bolivia, Cuba.* San Salvador: Editorial Universitaria de El Salvador, 1969.

Migdal, Joel. *Peasants, Politics, and Revolution.* Princeton, N.J.: Princeton University Press, 1974.

Monteforte Toledo, Mario. *Centroamérica: Subdesarollo y dependencia.* 2 vols. Mexico City: Universidad Nacional Autónoma de México, 1972.

———. *Guatemala: Monografía sociológica.* Mexico City: UNAM, 1965.

———. *Mirada sobre latinoamérica.* Costa Rica: EDUCA, 1975.

———. "Reforma agraria en Guatemala." *Trimestre económico* 14:3 (July–September 1952).

Moore, Barrington. *Social Origins of Dictatorship and Democracy.* Boston: Beacon Press, 1966.

Moors, Marilyn. "Indian Labor and the Guatemalan Crisis." In *Central America: Historical Perspectives on the Contemporary Crisis,* ed. R. L. Woodward. New York: Greenwood Press, 1988.

Morrison, Andrew, and Rachel May. "Escape from Terror: Violence and Migration in Post-Revolutionary Guatemala." *Latin American Research Review* 29:1 (January 1994): 111–32.

Morrison, Denton E. "Some Notes towards a Theory on Relative Deprivation, Social Movements, and Social Change." *American Behavioral Scientist* 14 (May–June 1971): 675–90.

Murphy, Brian. "Stunted Growth of Campesino Organizations." In *Crucifixion by Power,* ed. Richard Adams. Austin: University of Texas Press, 1970.

Nash, June. *We Eat the Mines and the Mines Eat Us.* New York: Columbia University Press, 1979.

Navas Alvarez, María Guadalupe. *El movimiento sindical como manifestación de la lucha de clases.* Guatemala: Editorial Universitaria (San Carlos), 1979.

Nelson, Diane. *A Finger in the Wound: Body Politics in Quincentennial Guatemala.* Berkeley: University of California Press, 1999.

Noval, Joaquin. "Guatemala, the Indian, and the Land." *Americas* (March 1954).

Paige, Jeffrey M. *Agrarian Revolution: Social Movements and Export Agriculture in the Underdeveloped World.* New York: Free Press, 1975.

Painter, James. *Guatemala: False Hope, False Freedom.* London: Latin American Bureau, 1987.

Palacios, J. Antonio. "Formas de redistribución del ingreso en Guatemala." *Trimestre económico* 14:3 (July–September 1952).

Paredes Moreira, José Luis. *Reforma agraria: Una experiencia en Guatemala.* Guatemala: Imprenta Universitaria (San Carlos), 1963.

———. *Estudios sobre reforma agraria en Guatemala: Aplicación del decreto 900.* Guatemala: Facultad de Ciencias Económicas, San Carlos, 1964.

———. *Tierras y colonización.* Monograph 2. Guatemala: Facultad de Economía, San Carlos, Instituto de Investigaciones Económicas y Sociales, October 1961.

Pearson, Neale J. "The Confederación Nacional Campesina de Guatemala (CNCG) and Peasant Unionism in Guatemala." M.A. thesis, Georgetown University, 1964.

Petras, James. "The Anatomy of State Terror." *Science and Society* 51 (Fall 1987): 314–38.

———. "State Terror and Social Movements in Latin America." *International Journal of Politics, Culture and Society* 3 (Winter 1989): 179–212.

Pettee, George S. *The Process of Revolution.* New York: Harper, 1938.

Pinto Soria, Julio. *Estructura agraria y asentamiento en la Capitanía General de Guatemala.* Guatemala: Editorial Universitaria (USAC), 1981.

Plant, Roger. *Guatemala: Unnatural Disaster.* London: Latin American Bureau, 1978.

Poitevin, René. *El proceso de industrialización en Guatemala.* Costa Rica: EDUCA, 1977.

Popkin, Samuel. *The Rational Peasant.* Berkeley: University of California Press, 1979.

Ramos de Schmoock, Maria Eugenia. "El movimiento sindical en Guatemala, 1949–1954." *Alero* 3 a epoca, no. 30 (1978): 83–102.

Recios García, Maria Elena. "El movimiento obrero en Guatemala, 1900–1954." B.A. thesis, Facultad de Historia, Universidad de San Carlos, Guatemala, 1977.

Rivera, Otto. "MONAP y su relación campo-ciudad." Guatemala, 1988, unpublished paper in possession of author.

Rodríguez, Mario. *Central America.* Englewood Cliffs, N.J.: Prentice Hall, 1965.

Rodríguez Chang, Carlos Juan Antonio. "Las cooperativas como instrumento de desarrollo rural." B.A. thesis, Facultad de Ciencias Económicas, Universidad de San Carlos, Guatemala, 1976.

Rosada Granados, Hector. *Indios y ladinos: Un estudio antropológico-sociológico.* Guatemala: Editorial Universitaria, San Carlos, 1987.

Ruano Andrade, Sergio Rolando. "El cooperativismo en Guatemala: Un instrumento de desarollo?" B.A. thesis, Facultad de Historia, Universidad de San Carlos, 1977.

Rummel, Rudolph J. "Dimensions of Conflict Behavior." *General Systems Yearbook* (Ann Arbor: Society for the Advancement of General Systems Theory, 1963) 8: 1–50.

Russell, D. E. H. *Rebellion, Revolution and Armed Force: A Comparative Study of Fifteen Countries with Special Emphasis on Cuba and South Africa.* New York: Academic Press, 1974.

Russell, Grahame, Sarah Kee, and Ann Butwell. *Unearthing the Truth: Exhuming Decade of Terror in Guatemala.*Washington, D.C.: EPICA, 1996.

Sabine, George. "The Two Democratic Traditions." *Philosophical Review* 61 (1952): 451–74.

Sandoval, Leopoldo V. "Dos tipos de finca cooperativa como alternativas para reforma agraria de Guatemala." B.A. thesis, Facultad de Agronomía, Universidad de San Carlos, Guatemala, 1963.

———. *Estructura agraria y nuevo regimen constitucional en 1986.* Guatemala City: ASIES, 1986.

Schirmer, Jennifer. *The Guatemalan Military Project: A Violence Called Democracy.* Philadelphia: University of Pennsylvania Press, 1998.

Schlesinger, Stephen, and Stephen Kinzer. *Bitter Fruit.* Garden City, N.Y.: Anchor Books, 1979.

Schneider, Ronald. *Communism in Guatemala: 1944–1954.* New York: Octagon Books, 1979.

Schulz, Donald. "Ten Theories in Search of the Central American Reality." In *Revolution and Counter-Revolution in Central America and the Caribbean,* D. Schulz and Douglas Graham, ed. Boulder: Westview, 1984.

Schwartz, David. "Political Alienation: The Psychology of Revolution's First Stage." In *Anger, Violence, and Politics: Theories and Research,* ed. I. K. Feierabend, R. L. Feierabend, and Ted Robert Gurr, 58–66. Engelwood Cliffs, N.J.: Prentice Hall, 1972.

Scott, James. *The Moral Economy of the Peasant.* New Haven: Yale University Press, 1976.

————. *Weapons of the Weak: Everyday Forms of Peasant Resistance*. New Haven: Yale University Press, 1986.

Segundo, Juan Luís. *Faith and Ideologies*. Maryknoll, N.Y.: Orbis Books, 1984.

Sherman, William. *Forced Native Labor in Sixteenth-Century Central America*. Lincoln: University of Nebraska Press, 1979.

Shugart, Matthew Soberg. "Patterns of Revolution." *Theory and Society* 18 (1989): 249–71.

Sichar Moreno, Gonzalo. *Guatemala: Contrainsurgencia o contra el pueblo?* Madrid: Hidalgo más Hidalgo, 1998.

Skidmore, Thomas. "Workers and Soldiers: Urban Labor Movements and Elite Responses in Twentieth-Century Latin America." In *Elites, Masses, and Modernization in Latin America, 1850–1930*, ed. Virginia Bernhard. Austin: University of Texas Press, 1979.

Skocpol, Theda. *States and Social Revolutions: A Comparative Analysis of France, Russia, and China*. Cambridge: Cambridge University Press, 1979.

Smelser, Neil. *Theory of Collective Behavior*. New York: Free Press, 1963.

Smith, Carol, ed. *Guatemalan Indians and the State*. Austin: University of Texas Press, 1990.

————. "Labor and International Capital in the Making of a Peripheral Social Formation: Economic Transformations of Guatemala, 1850–1980." Paper presented for the Seventh Annual Political Economies of the World System Conference, Working Paper no. 138, Wilson Center, Washington D.C., 1983.

————. "Maya Nationalism." *NACLA Report on the Americas* 25:3 (December 1991): 29–33.

————. "The Second Ecuentro Continental." *Guatemala Scholars Network News* (April 1992): 1.

Smith, Mary Felise. "Agricultural Development in Guatemala: The Indian Cooperative Movement, 1965–1982." M.A. thesis, Tulane University, 1991.

Sorokin, Pitirim A. *The Sociology of Revolution*. Philadelphia: Lippincott, 1925.

Spalding, Hobart. *Organized Labor in Latin America: Historical Case Studies of Workers in Dependent Societies.* New York: Harper and Row, 1977.

Stavenhagen, Rodolfo, ed. *Agrarian Problems and Peasant Movements in Latin America.* Garden City, N.Y.: Doubleday, 1970.

Stinchcombe, Arthur. "Stratification among Organizations and the Sociology of Revolution." In *Handbook of Organizations,* ed. James March, 169–80. Chicago: Rand McNally, 1965.

Stone, Lawrence. "Theories of Revolution." *World Politics* 18 (January 1966): 159–76.

Suslow, Leo A. "Aspects of Social Reforms in Guatemala, 1944–1949." M.A. thesis, Colgate University, 1949.

Swetnam, John. "What Else Did Indians Have to Do with Their Time? Alternatives to Labor Migration in Prerevolutionary Guatemala." *Economic Development and Cultural Change* 38:1 (1989): 89–112.

Taylor, Stan. *Social Science and Revolutions.* London: Halsted Press, 1975.

Tilly, Charles. "Revolutions and Collective Violence." In *Handbook of Political Science,* ed. Fred Greenstein and Nelson Polsby. Vol. 3, *Macropolitical Theory.* Reading, Mass: Addison-Wesley, 1975.

Torres-Rivas, Edelberto. *Interpretación del desarollo social centroamericano.* Costa Rica: EDUCA, 1981.

———. "Notas para comprender la crisis política centroamericana." In *Centroamérica: Crisis política internacional,* ed. Jaime Labastida et al., 33–69. 3d ed. Mexico City: Siglo Veintiuno, 1985.

Torres-Rivas, Edelberto, and Gabriel Aguilera Peralta. *Del autoritarismo a la paz.* Guatemala City: FLACSO, 1998.

Trimberger, Kay Ellen. *Revolution from Above: Military Bureaucrats and Development in Japan, Turkey, Egypt, and Peru.* New Brunswick, N.J.: Transaction Books, 1978.

Tyrakian, Edward. "A Model of Societal Change and Its Lead Indicators." In *The Study of Total Societies,* ed. Samuel Z. Klausner, 69–97. New York: Anchor Books, 1967.

van den Berghe, Pierre. *State Violence and Ethnicity.* Niwot: University of Colorado Press, 1990.

Vries, Hent de, and Samuel Weber, eds. *Violence, Identity, and Self-Determination.* Stanford, Calif.: Stanford University Press, 1997.

Warren, Kay. *Indigenous Movements and Their Critics: Pan-Maya Activism in Guatemala.* Princeton, N.J.: Princeton University Press, 1998.

Wasserstrom, Robert. "Revolution in Guatemala: Peasants and Politics under the Arbenz Government." *Comparative Studies in Society and History* 17 (October 1975).

Wiarda, Howard J., ed. *Politics and Social Change in Latin America: Still a Distinct Tradition?* Boulder: Westview, 1992.

Wickham-Crowley, Timothy. *Guerrillas and Revolution in Latin America.* Princeton, N.J.: Princeton University Press, 1992.

———. "Terror and Guerrilla Warfare in Latin America. 1956–1970." *Comparative Studies of Society and History* 32:2 (April 1990): 201–37.

Williams, Robert G. *Export Agriculture and the Crisis in Central America.* Chapel Hill: University of North Carolina Press, 1986.

Wolf, Eric. "Peasant Rebellion and Revolution." In *National Liberation: Revolution in the Third World,* ed. Norman Miller and Roderick Aya. New York: Free Press, 1971.

———. *Peasant Wars of the Twentieth Century.* New York: Harper and Row, 1969.

———. "The Vicissitudes of Closed Corporate Communities." *American Ethnologist* 13: 325–29.

Woodward, R. L., Jr. *Central America: A Nation Divided.* 2d ed. New York: Oxford University Press, 1985.

———. "Communist Infiltration of the Guatemalan Urban Labor Movement, 1920–1954." M.A. thesis, Tulane, 1959.

———, ed. *Central America: Historical Perspectives on the Contemporary Crisis.* New York: Greenwood Press, 1988.

Yamauchi, Paul Edward. "Patterns of Death: Descriptions of Geographic and Temporal Patterns of Rural State Terror in Guatemala, 1978–1985." In *Physicians for Social Responsibility [PSR] Quarterly* 3:2 (June 1993): 67–78.

Yates, Lawrence. "The United States' Rural Insurgency." In *Central*

*America: Historical Perspectives,* ed. R. L. Woodward. New York: Greenwood Press, 1988.

Zamosc, León. *The Agrarian Question and the Peasant Movement in Colombia.* Cambridge: Cambridge University Press, 1986.

Zimmermann, Ekkart. *Political Violence, Crises and Revolutions: Theories and Research.* Boston: G. K. Hall, 1983.

# Index

absolutism, 49
Adams, Richard Newbold, 168 n.16
AEU. *See* Association of University Students (AEU)
AFL. *See* American Federation of Labor T(AFL)
AGA. *See* Association of Landowners (AGA)
agrarian campesinos, 5, 168 n. 10
agrarian policy, 81–84
agrarian reform, 82–83, 104, 139, 188 n. 23
Agrarian Reform Act (Decree 900), 81
agricultural cooperatives, 89, 122–23
agriculture: cattle industry growth, 64–65; chemical fertilizer introduction, 100–101, 192 n. 86; manipulation of labor force, 180–81 n. 1; modernization of, 24–25; shift away from subsistence production, 60–61
Aguilera Peralta, Gabriel, 54–55, 57, 58
AIFLD. *See* American Institute for Free Labor Development (AIFLD)
Albizures, Miguel Angel, 115, 117, 129, 132
Amado Granado, Francisco, 105
Amaro, Nelson, 86–87
American Federation of Labor (AFL), 72–73
American Institute for Free Labor Development (AIFLD), 91, 120, 153
anticommunist labor movement, 73
anticommunist sentiment, 56, 83–84, 149
Arana Osorio, Carlos, 58, 61, 62–63, 68*t*, 69*t*, 112–13
Arbenz, Jacobo, 4, 6, 54, 89, 182 n. 17, 188 n. 23
Arbenz government, 71, 149, 154
Archdiocesan Project for the Recuperation of Historical Memory (REHMI), 13, 19, 67
Arenas Barrera, Luís, 127
Arendt, Hannah, 15, 171 n. 2
Arévalo, Juan José, 4, 53, 78, 149, 154
Argentina, transition from violence, 16
armed forces: abuses by, 54, 182 n. 15; assassinations by, 64; assertion of dominance, 58–59, 61; demonstrations against excesses of, 119; land acquisition by, 66; strength of, 56

arms sales, to Guatemala, 56, 183 n. 25
ASC. *See* Association of Civil Sectors (ASC)
*asociaciones de desarollo integra*, 40
assassinations: of Arenas Barrera, 127; of Castillo Armas, 7, 76, 80, 84; of de León, 102; of López Larrave, 116; targeted, by armed forces, 64
Association for Maya-Quiché Culture, 131, 142
Association of Civil Sectors (ASC), 34–35
Association of Initiators of Quiché Ideals, 131, 142
Association of Landowners (AGA), 81, 189 n. 42
Association of University Students (AEU), 116
Asturias, Miguel Angel, 161, 163
Augusto César Sandino Front, 62, 126
authoritative violence: defining, 172–73 n. 14; relationship with turmoil, 25; theories of, 26–30; typology of, 19–21
Autonomous Federation of Labor Unions (FAS), 74–76, 80, 83
Autonomous Labor Federation of Guatemala (FASGUA): campesino assistance, 65; in first cycle of violence, 151, 152–53, 154; foundation, 85; internal structure, 88, 89–90; legal status, 76; mobilization strategy, 92; on Panzós massacre, 118; reorganization attempt, 119; rural labor organization, 86, 132; in second cycle of violence, 157; solidarity, 113

Balcarcel, Luís Felipe, 75
BANDESA (Bank of Agricultural Development), 133–34, 136
Benedict, David, 73
Bergquist, Charles, 43
Bishop, Edwin, 75
Booth, John, 23–24
broad-front organizations, 44–45, 131–42
bureaucracy, 49

Cajas Mejía, Ricardo, 144
Camacho, Daniel, 36, 41, 43, 177 n. 5

# Index

Committee for Defense against Communism, 6–7
Committee for the National Reorganization of Trade Unions (CNRS), 72–75
Committee of Campesino Unity (CUC): about, 131–32, 156–57; as broad-front organization, 44; *concientización*, 160; continued evolution, 141–42; in demonstrations, 119; foundation, 112; ideology, 158; ideology and tactics, 132–34; importance, 156; indigenous rank and file, 135–36; internal structure, 135–37, 159; and Maya nationalism, 142, 144; in May Day rally, 135–36, 195 n. 22; mobilization strategy, 137–39; mobilizing internal support, 134; nucleus, 130; participatory structure, 159; radicalization, 158; as secret organization, 135, 159, 197–98 n. 70; in sugar strike, 139–41; violence as tool of mobilization, 160
communism: anticommunist sentiment, 56, 83–84, 149; collapse of Soviet, 33; and labor unions, 75
Communist Party of Guatemala. *See* Guatemalan Workers' Party (PGT)
communists: ouster from labor organizations, 5, 73; repression of, 6–7; rhetorical justifications for eliminating, 169 n. 24
CONAVIGUA. *See* National Council of Guatemalan Widows (CONAVIGUA)
*concientización*, 98, 124, 160
CONDEG. *See* National Committee for the Displaced of Guatemala (CONDEG)
Confederation of Cuban Workers (CTC), 73
Confederation of Guatemalan Trade Unions (CUSG), 119–20
Confederation of Guatemalan Workers (CONTRAGUA): consolidation with other leagues, 93, 194 n. 2; and cooperatives, 86, 88; in first cycle of violence, 151, 153; foundation, 85, 90–91, 193 n. 98
Congress of Industrial Organizations (CIO), 73
CONIC. *See* National Coordination of Indigenous and Campesino Organizations (CONIC)
consciousness-raising programs, 98, 124
CONSIGUA. *See* National Trade Union Confederation (CONSIGUA)
Constitution of 1956, 78–79, 188 n. 29
CONTRAGUA. *See* Confederation of Guatemalan Workers (CONTRAGUA)
CONUS. *See* Coordinator of National Trade Union Unity (CONUS)

cooperatives: about, 95; agricultural, 89, 122–23; destruction of movement, 124–25; FCG avoided by, 87; in first cycle of violence, 102, 151–52; ideology, 95–98, 121–22; internal structure, 98–100, 122–23; legal status, 40; mobilization strategy, 100–102, 123–24; as officially preferred rural organization, 82; in second cycle of violence, 120–25; tactics, 95–98, 121–22
coordinated attack, 20*t*, 21
coordinated counterattack: in cycles of violence, 32*t*; in first cycle of violence, 54–55, 68*t*; in second cycle of violence, 61–63, 69*t*
Coordination of Organizations of the Maya People of Guatemala (COPMAGUA), 143
Coordinator of National Trade Union Unity (CONUS), 195 n. 27
COPMAGUA. *See* Coordination of Organizations of the Maya People of Guatemala (COPMAGUA)
corporate interests, of U.S., 17
corporatism: defining, 169–70 n. 27; in labor organizations, 43, 44, 154, 155; in Latin American states, 48; moving away from, 158–59; in rural community organizations, 40
Council of Ethnic Communities (CERJ), 199 n. 94
counterinsurgency: defining, 22*t*; military's logic of, 28; in second cycle of violence, 130–31
counterinsurgent violence, 18
coups: of 1954, 4–7, 17; military coups, 172–73 n. 14; of Peralta Azurdia, 53, 56; against Ydígoras government, 54, 102, 104
credit cooperatives, 99, 101, 122–23, 152, 195–96 n. 32
Cruz Martínez, Rogelia, 58
Cruz Salazar, José Luis, 169 n. 25
CSG. *See* Labor Union Council of Guatemala (CSG)
CTC. *See* Confederation of Cuban Workers (CTC)
CTF. *See* Federated Workers' Central (CTF)
Cuba, guerrilla organizations, 41
Cuban Revolution, 55
CUC. *See* Committee of Campesino Unity (CUC)
CUCO. *See* Committee for Campesino/Worker Unity (CUCO)
CUSG. *See* Confederation of Guatemalan Trade Unions (CUSG)

227

# Index

General Confederation of Guatemalan Workers (CGTC), 72, 76, 120, 132
General Department of Agrarian Affairs (DGAA), 81
genocide: about, 28–30; defining, 175 n. 35; Maya as victims, 143; as reactionary terror, 21; in second cycle of violence, 67; state-sponsored, 14, 58
Gerardi, José Juan, 67
Gilly, Adolfo, 106
Gleijeses, Pierro, 161
Goldstone, Jack, 23, 171 n. 1, 173 n. 15
Gott, Richard, 104–5
government: as first organizational experience for campesinos, 149; relationship with popular sectors, 149; terrorism sponsored by, 57; transition to civilian, 118
growth-oriented goals, 87
*Guatemala* magazine, 82
Guatemalan Council of Maya Organizations (COMG), 143–44
Guatemalan National Revolutionary Unity (URNG), 126, 128–29, 131, 159
Guatemalan Workers' Party (PGT): alliances, 152; criticism of, 109; guerrilla organizations, 102, 125–26; ideology and tactics, 127; internal structure, 105–6, 107t, 108; mobilization strategy, 130; outlawed, 54–55
Guerrilla Army of the Poor (EGP), 62, 66, 125–27, 129–30, 157–58, 161
guerrilla organizations: about, 102–3; in first cycle of violence, 152; ideology, 103–5, 126–28; internal structure, 105–8, 128–29; international influences, 153; military responses to, 56–57; mobilization strategy, 108–9, 130; national structure, 107t; Rebel Armed Forces (FAR) formation, 54–55; rural guerrilla organizations, 41–42; in second cycle of violence, 61–62, 125–31; tactics, 103–5, 126–28
Guevara, Ernesto "Che," 41, 42
Gurr, Ted, 19–21, 172 n. 10, 173 n. 15
Gutierrez, Victor Manuel, 76

Handy, Jim, 63, 75
Hernández Ixcoy, Domingo, 137
Ho Chi Minh, 127
Ho Chi Minh Front, 62, 125–26
horizontal organizational structures, 3, 9–10, 45–46, 99, 137

ideology: of broad-front organizations, 45;

changing, 150; of Committee of Campesino Unity (CUC), 132–34, 158; of cooperatives, 95–98, 121–22; defining, 2; effects of violence, 152–54, 157–58, 162t; of guerrilla organizations, 42, 103–5, 126–28; influence of international doctrines, 49; of labor organizations, 86–88, 114–15; Marxist influence, 62; mobilization strategy as outcome, 3; radicalization, 8–9; shift in Catholic social philosophy, 77
IDESAC. *See* Institute for the Economic and Social Development of Central America (IDESAC)
INACOP. *See* National Institute for Cooperatives (INACOP)
Indian question, 127, 128
indigenous culture: community organizations, 89; cooperatives, 121; development of, 128; political organization of, 130
indigenous rights movements, 176 n. 1
Institute for the Economic and Social Development of Central America (IDESAC), 86, 96, 99–100, 101, 152
Institutional Democratic Party (PID), 56
INTA. *See* National Institute of Agrarian Transformation (INTA)
internal structure: changing, 150–51; of Committee of Campesino Unity (CUC), 135–37, 159; of cooperatives, 98–100, 122–23; defining, 3; effects of violence, 9, 154, 158–60, 162t; of guerrilla organizations, 105–8, 128–29; of labor organizations, 88–91, 115–16
internal war: about, 21; in Central America, theories of, 23–26; in cycles of violence, 32t; defining, 20t, 22t; in first cycle of violence, 55–57, 68t; in second cycle of violence, 61–63, 69t
intra-elite conflicts, 172–73 n. 14
Israel, political violence in, 16–17

January's Popular Front (FP-31), 141, 158
JOC. *See* Young Christian Workers Association (JOC)
Jonas, Suzanne, 125, 126
juridical personality, 4, 76, 154, 167 n. 6, 169 n. 26

Keane, John, 15
Kekchi Indians, 65

Labor Code, 79–81, 140, 188 n. 29
labor contractor system, 52, 123

# Index

labor disputes, 59, 65

labor federations, breakup of, 92-94

labor inspector system, 79-80, 188 n. 32

labor organizations: about, 42-44, 85-86; of campesinos, 74-75, 77-78, 85-94; death and rebirth, 119-20; historical context, 4-7; ideology, 114-15; internal structure, 115-16; mass mobilization, 52; mobilization strategy, 43-44, 91-92, 116-19; most important in first cycle of violence, 151-52; outlawed in State of Emergency, 119; in second cycle of violence, 112-20; tactics, 114-15; top heaviness, 155

labor policy, of Castillo Armas, 78-81

labor reorganization process, 72-84

Labor Union Council of Guatemala (CSG), 74, 78, 80

labor unions. *See* unions

land: and agrarian reform, 82-83; disputes over, 60, 65-66; loss of, 136

Landsberger, Henry, 3, 36, 38, 45-46, 177 n. 4

*latifundismo*, 82

Latin America: popular organizations, 48-49; wave of revolutionary activity, 41-42

Latin American Confederation of Workers (CLAT), 114, 120

*Latin American Peasant Movements* (Landsberger), 38

Laugerud García, Kjell, 61, 62-63, 69t, 111, 156

Law of Agrarian Transformation, 83

leadership: of Committee of Campesino Unity (CUC), 137; of guerrilla organizations, 41; patriarchal, 48-49; personalistic, 48-49, 100, 125; in popular organizations, 37

legal popular struggle, 129

literature: about modernization, 177 n. 7; peasant studies genre, 37; of political violence, 14; of revolution, 23, 171 n. 1, 173 n. 15; of war, 171 n. 2

lockouts, 77-78

López Larrave, Mario, 6, 64, 112, 115, 116-17, 132, 193 n. 98

Lucas García, Romeo, 63, 124

Magill, John, 43-44

*Majawil Q'ij*, 143, 199 n. 94

Malamud-Goti, Jaime, 47

Mano Blanca, 57

Mao Tse Tung, 127

Marxism, 104, 127-28, 153

Marxist insurgencies, 42

massacres: Finca San Francisco, 65-66, 67; Panzós, 64-65, 67, 118-19; Spanish embassy occupation, 134, 140

Maya nationalism, 127, 128, 142-44

Maya renaissance, 121-22

MCI. *See* Movement of Independent Campesinos (MCI)

MDN. *See* National Democratic Movement (MDN)

mechanistic organizational structure, 150, 200 n. 2

Melville, Marjorie, 81

Melville, Thomas, 81

Menchú, Rigoberta, 134, 137, 144, 161

Menchú, Victor, 137

Méndez Montenegro, Julio César, 57, 68t, 90-91, 181 n. 4, 183 n. 27

Méndez Montenegro, Mario, 183 n. 27

migrant workers, 138, 198 n. 81

Mijangos, Adolfo, 58

military. *See* armed forces

military coups, 172-73 n. 14

military regimes: fearful of popular sector, 149-50; justification of control, 27-28; legitimacy crisis, 67

MLN. *See* National Liberation Movement (MLN)

mobilization strategy: in campesino organizations, 39-40; changing, 151; of Committee of Campesino Unity (CUC), 137-39; conditioned by ideology, 167 n. 3; in cooperatives, 100-102, 123-24; defining, 3; effects of violence, 10, 155-56, 160-61, 162t; in guerrilla organizations, 108-9, 130; with horizontal structure, 46; in labor organizations, 43-44, 91-92, 116-19; in rural community organizations, 40; thwarted by disarticulating power, 47

modernization, 24-25, 37, 38-39, 177 n. 7

Molina, Raul, 130

MONAP. *See* National Movement of Pobladores (MONAP)

Mothers of the Disappeared, 16

Movement of Independent Campesinos (MCI), 93, 112-13, 190 n. 51, 193 n. 98

movements, *vs.* popular organizations, 36-37

MR-13. *See* Revolutionary Movement 13th of November (MR-13)

murders: government-sponsored terrorism, 58; of labor leaders, 195 n. 23

Mutual Support Group (GAM), 199 n. 94

# Index

# Index

excluded from national power structure, 83–84; factioning, 49; group mobility, 39; growth of modern, 25; labeling, 46; in Latin America, 48–49; vs. movements, 36–37; nonviolent popular organizations, 63; organizational levels, 45–46; outlawed, 167–68n. 5; radicalization of ideologies, 8–9; in second cycle of violence, 111–12; state responses to, 46–47, 48–49; student-led protests, 52–54; terminology, 35, 177n. 5

postrevolutionary agrarian policy, 81–84

power: acquisition of political, 87–88, 157–58; concentration of, 49; disarticulating power, 47; seizure of, 71; of states, 47, 48; violence as extension of, 15

PR. *See* Revolutionary Party (PR)

Preventive Penal Law against Communism, 6–7, 79, 186n. 1

production cooperatives, 89

professional organizations, 85, 96, 99–100, 152

racism, 17–18, 126, 127, 128, 130

radicalization: of guerrilla organizations, 103–4, 153; of ideologies, 8–9; of popular organizations, 158

radio schools, 155

rape, 66

RDN. *See* National Democratic Reconciliation Party (RDN)

reactionary terror: against Autonomous Labor Federation of Guatemala (FASGUA), 90; against cooperatives, 102, 124–25; defining, 22*t*, 32*t*; in first cycle of violence, 57–58, 68*t*; against indigenous cooperatives, 121; in second cycle of violence, 63–67, 69*t*; theories of authoritative violence, 26–30

Rebel Armed Forces (FAR): alliances, 152; dissolution of MR-13, 57; factions, 62, 107*t*, 126, 157; failure, 125; formation, 54–55, 105–6; ideology and tactics, 127; mobilization strategy, 108, 130

rebellion, typology of, 20*t*, 21

rebellious violence, 19. *See also* nonauthoritative violence

Redemption (Redención), 7. *See also* National Democratic Reconciliation Party (RDN)

Regional Inter-American Organization of Workers (ORIT), 74, 78, 80, 90–91, 113, 153

REHMI. *See* Archdiocesan Project for the Recuperation of Historical Memory (REHMI)

Report of the UN Mission in Guatemala, 13

revolution: defining, 25; dialectic of, 26*t*; literature of, 23, 171n. 1, 173n. 15; understanding of, 170–71n. 1

Revolution, overthrow of, 4–5

Revolutionary Movement 13th of November (MR-13), 54–55, 57, 102–5, 105–6, 107*t*, 108–9, 152

Revolutionary Organization of the People in Arms (ORPA), 126–30, 157, 158, 161

revolutionary organizations, 103

Revolutionary Party (PR), 113, 183 n. 27

revolutionary scholarship, 14

revolutionary theory: about, 22–23; authoritative violence, 26–30; internal war in Central America, 23–26

Ríos Montt, Efraín, 61, 69*t*, 119–20, 124, 130–31

Romero, Jorge, 55, 57

Romualdi, Serafino, 5, 72–73, 74, 80

Rosales, Efraín, 137

Rummel, Rudolph, 172 n. 10

rural community organizations, 40–41

rural guerrilla organizations, 41–42

rural labor organizations, 42–44

rural military commissioners, 56–57

rural organizations: cooperatives as officially preferred type, 82; discouragement of, 73; dismantling of, 8; historical context, 5–7

rural trade unions, 89

SAMF (Sindicato de Acción y Mejoramiento de los Ferrocarriles), 90–91, 193 n. 98

Sánchez, Camilo, 106

Sánchez, Gonzalo, 172 n. 9

Sandino, Augusto, 104

Schirmer, Jennifer, 28

Schulz, Donald, 25–27, 30

Segundo, Juan Luís, 2, 150

self-defense groups, 119, 139, 160

self-education, 10

SETUFCO (Sindicato de Empresa de Trabajadores de la United Fruit Company), 77, 193 n. 98

Shining Path, 42

Smith, Carol, 61, 142, 143

Social Christian ideology, 75, 76, 84, 191 n. 74

Social Christians, 96, 121, 152–53

social class, and guerrilla leadership, 41

Social Democrats, 121

socially conscious ideologies, 96

social organizations, 177 n. 5

# Index

violence. *See also* political violence: Central
American violence, and theories of revolution, 22–30; and civil society, 15–18; cycles of,
30–31, 32*t*; defining, 19; as education for
organized campesinos, 94; effect on ideologies and tactics, 152–54, 157–58, 162*t*; effect
on internal structures, 9, 154–55, 158–60,
162*t*; effect on mobilization strategy, 10, 155,
160–61, 162*t*; effect on popular organizations,
9–10, 162*t*; evolution of popular organizations within cycles of, 148–51; as extension of
power, 15; first cycle of, 52–58, 68*t*, 88,
151–56; inertia of, 13–14; as reactionary terror,
27; second cycle of, 59–67, 69*t*, 156–61; terminology of, 19–22; as tool of mobilization,
160
violent conflict, 19

wage issues, 139–40, 141
war, literature of, 171 n. 2
wealth, unequal distribution of, 23–24
Wiarda, Howard J., 50, 169–70 n. 27

Wickham-Crowley, Timothy, 22*t*
Williams, Robert, 24
Wolf, Eric, 37, 178 n. 8
women's organizations, 176 n. 1
worker-campesino alliance, 43, 76
Workers' Labor Unity Organization of
Guatemala (UNSITRAGUA), 120, 195 n. 27
working conditions, 80–81
work-related deaths, 83, 189–90 n. 50
World Labor Federation (FSM), 76, 90, 114, 153,
158, 187 n. 19

Ydígoras Fuentes, Miguel, 7–8, 52–53, 56, 68*t*,
77, 152
Ydígoras regime, 74, 82–83, 102, 104
Yon Sosa, Marco Antonio, 54, 55, 102, 106, 108
Yos, Juan José, 140
Young Christian Workers Association (JOC),
86–86

Zamora, Ernesto, 80
Zapata, Emiliano, 41

234

Printed and bound by CPI Group (UK) Ltd, Croydon, CR0 4YY

09/06/2025